# DO ELECTIONS MATTER?

# DO ELECTIONS MATTER?

## Benjamin Ginsberg and Alan Stone Editors

**M. E. SHARPE, INC.**
ARMONK, NEW YORK
LONDON, ENGLAND

Copyright © 1986 by M. E. Sharpe, Inc.
80 Business Park Drive, Armonk, New York 10504

Available in the United Kingdom and Europe from M. E. Sharpe,
Publishers, 3 Henrietta Street, London WC2E 8LU.

**Library of Congress Cataloging in Publication Data**

Do elections matter?
    1. Elections 2. Voting. 3. Political parties.
    4. Public policy (Law) I. Ginsberg, Benjamin
II. Stone, Alan, 1931—   .
JF1001.D6    1986    324    86-3911
ISBN 0-87332-378-5
ISBN 0-87332-379-3 (pbk.)

Printed in the United States of America

*For
Anna and Herman Ginsberg
and Roberta Stone*

# Contents

# DO ELECTIONS MATTER?

# Preface

In June 1985 the attention of the American people was riveted on the fate of the American passengers aboard TWA Flight 847, who had been taken captive by Shiite terrorists, and on the Reagan Administration's efforts to secure their release. Most of the public—even the attentive public—was unaware that in that same month the Administration threatened to restrict the importation of pasta products from the European Economic Community (EEC) in retaliation for the EEC's refusal to revise its preferential trade agreements with the Mediterranean nations (which in effect restricted the import of citrus fruits from the United States). Notwithstanding the many differences between these two events, the central question of this book can be applied equally to both of them: Do elections matter? Was the election of 1984—the reelection of President Ronald Reagan—the main determinant of U.S. policy on hostage-taking or foreign trade in June 1985?

Even to raise such a question, and to do so in this way, may seem odd, or at least awkward. But the question bears reflection, and it is central not only to this book but also to the study of politics. Political scientists affirm that one of the fundamental differences between Western and Communist political systems is the presence of free elections in the former and their absence in the latter. Americans correctly argue that Soviet elections, in which the Communist candidates receive virtually 100 percent of the vote, are a sham. Critics of the American system countercharge that our two political parties are as alike as Tweedledum and Tweedledee, and that the American people's right to choose between them every four years is essentially meaningless. Perhaps the fact that the issue of whether elections matter is so deeply rooted in ideology, in the realm of unexamined beliefs, partially accounts for the fact that the issue is rarely raised. What is surprising is that political scientists—the professionals supposedly devoted to analyzing this sort of question—rarely do.

The agenda for contemporary electoral research in the United States was set by the great voting studies of the 1950s, in particular the Campbell, Converse, Miller, and Stokes study of *The American Voter* and Berelson, Lazersfeld, and McPhee's *Voting*. These two volumes, and the literally thousands of articles and books that followed in their wake, were mainly concerned with how voters made their decisions. The authors of *The American Voter* sought to "account for variation in whether a given individual voter is going to vote and which candidate he will choose.'' Similarly, the authors of *Voting* aimed to determine ''how people come to vote as they do.'' Both groups acknowledged that their primary focus on *how* voters decided rested on the assumption that *what* voters decided was important. In the three decades since the publication of these seminal works, election analysts have continued to show considerably more interest in the behavior of voters than in the effects, implications, and significance of elections. At the same time, scholars concerned with political institutions and public policies have primarily focused on questions of process or the evaluation of particular policies or institutions. Few studies have bridged the gap, yet the problem is important and challenging.

What are the linkages between voting, parties, and elections, on the one hand, and policy outputs, whether in the form of legislation, administrative action, or judicial decisions, on the other? It is when one joins these topics that one essentially asks: Do elections matter? Clearly, one cannot answer the question with a simple yes or no, but posing it in this way allows us to consider many topics of great concern—the growth of the administrative state, the increasing activism of the judiciary, and the seemingly unmanageable problem of the federal budget (which contains many items, such as pensions, about which elected officials can do little).

The essays in this volume address these issues. Some probe the principal question of the significance of elections generally, while others focus upon particular problems that illuminate the major question. The authors examine such particulars as the role of social forces, bureaucratic behavior, the distribution of benefits and entitlements, campaign contributions, the role of elites, and much more. They do not reach a single or a simple conclusion about elections, nor did the editors expect that they would. Rather, it was our intention to assemble a challenging volume that would stimulate thought and debate about an important question.

The essays are grouped into four sections. The first looks at the subject of elections generally. The essays in the second section examine the mechanism of elections, especially campaigns. The third section is focused on connections between elections and government policy outputs, and in the final section we take an in-depth look at the 1984 election.

What unites the essays is the view that the underlying question—Do elections matter?—is a vitally important one. It is our hope that the book will make a valuable and instructive contribution to the readers' thinking about politics.

\* \* \*

We would like to express our thanks to our editor, Patricia A. Kolb, copy editor Anita M. O'Brien, and all the staff of M. E. Sharpe, Inc. Their contribution to the successful completion of this book was invaluable and working with them was always a pleasure.

# 1. DO ELECTIONS MATTER?

Elections are generally considered to be the principal means through which citizens can influence their leaders. Certainly this applies to democratic elections, which permit citizens to select and depose public officials routinely. But this electoral santion, however effective it may be, is hardly the only way citizens can reward or punish officials for their actions. Spontaneous or privately organized forms of political activity, or even the threat of their occurrence, can also induce those in power to heed their subjects' wishes; even the most rigid autocrats can be influenced by the possibility that their actions may provoke popular disobedience, clandestine movements, or riot and insurrection. To be sure, the likelihood that an autocrat will be removed from power is generally less than the chance that an elected official will suffer defeat at the polls. Elections differ from other mechanisms of popular influence over officials' conduct in at least four respects.

1. Elections formalize, and thus fundamentally alter, the character of popular influence over government actions. The advent of democratic elections means that citizens' capacity to influence their rulers' conduct has become at least partially independent of rulers' military and administrative power. Even if rulers have the capacity to compel obedience, popular influence is not necessarily effaced.

2. Elections help to equalize citizens' capacities to influence rulers' conduct. In the absence of such an institutional mechanism, popular influence can be derived only from private activities and personal resources whose distribution in any population is certain to be unequal. The capacity to influence officials' actions will therefore vary—with wealth, social position, or even the propensity to riot. Elections, by introducing a formal, public means of influencing official conduct, can compensate for private inequalities in political resources.

3. Although they formalize and equalize the possibility of popular influence, elections, by institutionalizing popular influence, also create new and subtle means for its manipulation. Consider, for example, the mechanism of electoral rules and procedures, which specify how individual choices, or votes,

will be translated into collective decisions. These "rules of the game" are everywhere subject to definition and redefinition and can be adjusted, for example, to diminish or even preclude the possibility of electoral influence. Examples of authoritarian elections without choice are, of course, numerous, but even where competition and choice are built into the system, election laws can play an important role in preserving an established distribution of power.

4. Elections substitute participation in leadership selection for what might otherwise amount to direct popular intervention in, or resistance to, public policymaking and implementation. Whereas rioters may literally force a government to adopt or abandon a policy, voters are usually limited to the occasional selection of a certain number of public officials—and the link between leadership selection and policy selection may be tenuous at best.

In sum, while elections may institutionalize mass political influence, the implications of this are not simple and straightforward. Elections formalize and equalize mass influence, but they can at the same time constrain and delimit the effects of mass intervention into political life.

Those who assert that even free, competitive elections are of relatively limited consequence make four basic arguments which, for the sake of brevity, we will label (1) the administrative argument, (2) the elite argument, (3) the interest-group argument, and (4) the state management argument. Each of the arguments makes a different point, but all four share a common referent—the growth of the state. It is against the background of the state's sheer size and vast array of activities that we must examine the arguments urging that free elections are of limited consequence.

1. *The administrative argument.* How can elections matter if most public decisions are made by unelected officials—that is, administrators, bureaucrats, and judges? Isn't it the courts that have largely shaped civil rights policy and education policy? Isn't it true that in the famous A.T.&T. breakup decision, a single judge, together with professional administrators in the Justice Department, largely transformed the structure of the telecommunications industry? In one area after another—consumer affairs, monetary policy, environmental regulation, agriculture, natural resources, transportation and communication—the vital decisions are made by administrators. (It should not be surprising that in a poll of European businessmen the chairman of the Federal Reserve Board, and *not* an elected official, was named the second most important American political figure after the President.) Moreover, the complexity of the subjects with which courts and administrators deal requires that the statutes that administrators are appointed to enforce and that judges have to interpret must be broad and discretionary, allowing considerable latitude for application and interpretation.

In principle, of course, administrative agencies are empowered only to implement the laws promulgated by Congress, and courts are expected only to determine exactly what the lawmakers meant. In practice, however, administrative agencies make important policy decisions every day, and judges, in the face of legislative ambiguity, are relatively free to choose from among a variety of statutory interpretations. Public administration by bureaucrats and judges has become, in effect, the permanent government, substantially independent of members of Congress and presidents who come and go. Congress, of course, has the ultimate authority to change the law and to create, restructure, and destroy agencies; and the President, as chief of state, commands the bureaucracy. But in practice, the vast number of public decisions and the size of government preclude close supervision. Both Congress and the President lack the information, time, and expertise to oversee the daily operations of the bureaucracy and the judiciary.

In summary, those who make the administrative argument assert that the day-to-day management of national affairs is now principally in the hands of a number of semi-autonomous administrative agencies and judges, who operate with only sporadic interference from their elected overseers.

2. *The elite argument.* How can elections matter if candidates for public office are beholden to powerful groups, whether because the latter make large campaign contributions or because they command positions of great social and economic influence? Won't the preferences of such groups outweigh those of voters when it comes time for the elected official to make policy decisions? Some identify the elites who "pull the strings" as big Wall Street bankers, oil companies, or other narrow and powerful cliques intent on serving their selfish interests through government; in its more vicious forms this view takes on a paranoid cast, with assertions that international bankers, agents of Moscow, Jews, or the Vatican, etc., etc. secretly direct government officials. The belief that some sort of elite is in control is not unique to any part of the American political spectrum, and although the alleged culprits vary enormously, the view of the dynamic of politics is essentially the same: Candidates for office make private, surreptitious commitments to powerful groups—commitments that are not acknowledged during an election campaign; indeed, election rhetoric is mainly intended to assure popular commitment to the electoral process and continuing loyalty to the system. But once the successful candidate assumes office, his or her *primary* (though not necessarily exclusive) loyalties are to the needs of the special interests.

While one must reject the paranoid version of this perspective on politics (on the simple ground that it has no empirical support), the more moderate version certainly raises important issues, some of which are considered in the essays in this collection. There is plenty of evidence that campaign contributions can exert backstage influence on public officials, but this does not necessarily make them puppets. After all, it was not the rich and powerful who championed the many environmental, workplace safety, and consumer protection statutes that have been enacted by Congress and signed into law by the President. In the end, even if one were to concede that many aspects of the electoral process lie beneath the surface, that the influence of some is greater than that of others, and that much (most?) campaign rhetoric is hogwash, would it mean that elections do not matter?

3. *The interest-group argument.* How can elections matter if it is not the mass of voters, but rather intensely concerned and well-organized special interests, who influence the specific policy decisions that public officials make? Isn't there only a very tenuous link between the election-year rhetoric and the day-to-day actions of any elected official?

Public policymaking, of course, goes on continuously during and between election years. It is often a relatively quiet and informal activity that transpires in legislative, executive, and administrative offices, and at other times a formal activity that occurs in hearings, rule-making proceedings, and judicial and adminstrative trials. It involves lobbying, bargaining, the presentation of evidence, and a host of other techniques that come under the heading of interest-group activity. On a typical day in Washington a congressional committee may be holding a hearing on new banking legislation; the International Trade Commission may be considering the complaints of domestic producers that foreign competitors are engaging in unfair import practices; the Food and Drug Administration may be determining whether an important new drug can be marketed. Bankers, steel company executives, and pharmaceutical firm representatives will certainly be on hand to press their views.

The advocates of the interest-group perspective argue that neither the mass of voters nor political parties have much influence on the stand that elected officials take on many policies; the economy of a district or state, the demographic composition and ideological configuration of a legislator's constituency, and a host of other factors count for much more. A representative from eastern Texas, for example, will almost necessarily adopt a protective attitude toward domestic oil producers, regardless of his party's attitudes or voters' views on the price of gasoline and heating oil.

4. *The state-management argument.* How can elections matter if the vital decisions of the day are—and should and must be—left to experts, whether military, economic, or scientific, and not to politicians? For example, since Congress passed the Employment Act of 1946, the federal government has been responsible for pursuing policies that moderate economic fluctuations, maintain a high level of employment, stabilize prices, and encourage economic growth. The principal techniques that are used are monetary and fiscal policies, and professional economists are recruited into government to serve as advisers or actually to make economic policy decisions. The electorate, largely uninformed and certainly unskilled in the use of macroeconomic tools, cannot expect to play a role in the selection and application of these policy techniques.

Of course, experts may differ, but (and here is the critical point in this argument) these differences are based upon scientific judgments and not political or value judgments. Policy experts, in other words, disagree just as surgeons or astrophysicists may disagree. This does not mean that their decisions—when to increase the money supply, when to operate, when to launch a satellite—should be left to the voting public. In the same way, policy matters are best left in the hands of experts—state managers.

In the first three decades after World War II the United States seemed to be quite successful in achieving macroeconomic goals, as were other Western democracies that applied the policy prescriptions of economists. Not surprisingly, the cult of expertise spread to other policy areas as well. Trained experts on education, social welfare, defense, industrial structure, and virtually every other conceivable subject of potential concern to government began to staff the appropriate agencies, confident that they could solve the critical questions. Thus, the growth of administration has proceeded apace with the burgeoning of expertise, which, in any event, leaves little room for the policy preferences of an inexpert electorate.

Thus far we have examined and summarized both the changes wrought by the advent of elections and the arguments of those who say that elections do not matter much now, if they ever did. It is time to see what our authors have to say. First, Benjamin Ginsberg argues that free elections, although they are not an ironclad guarantee, play an important role in preserving civil liberties. In a word, because we can "throw the rascals out," the likelihood of an authoritarian dictatorship becoming established in the United States is relatively low. For Ginsberg, the value of free elections in preserving individual liberty is their most important (if sometimes taken for granted) aspect.

The other three essays in this section enter the realm of public policy, where, as we have seen, many consider elections to play little or no positive role. These authors, however, find important, albeit subtle, connections. David Brady and Joseph Stewart argue that in some elections—critical elections—the impact of elections on public policy can be substantial, while at other times the links between elections and public policy are weak. Similarly, Richard Barke and Alan Stone develop a hypothesis in the area of regulatory policy. They show when party differences are important in determining legislative voting behavior on regulation and when other factors are more important. Elections, then, are a way that the electorate, by supporting one or another party, can signal its general preferences with respect to *groups* of issues. Finally, as Elizabeth Sanders and Richard Bensel show, the very fact of participation in elections may have important policy consequences. Not until effective black enfranchisement, they argue, did government direct significant resources to black communities in the South.

Elections, then, do matter, but in ways far more complicated than many of us originally thought.

## 1.1

# Elections, Liberty, and the Consequences of Consent

## Benjamin Ginsberg

Electoral institutions are among the most important instruments of governance available to the modern state. Elections delimit mass political activity, popular influence, and access to power. Elections transform the potentially disruptive energy of the masses into a principal source of national power and authority. Governments rule through electoral institutions even when they are sometimes ruled by them.

But even though they may function as instruments of governance, when all is said and done, democratic electoral mechanisms do have one notable virtue. This virtue is simply that, relative to the known alternatives, democratic modes of governance appear to be most compatible with the existence of some measure of individual freedom. Though abuses occur in every nation, ganerally speaking, the same nations that possess democratic electoral and political institutions are also most likely to respect basic civil liberties. For example, in one 1979 survey that sought to rank all nominally independent nations on a 1 (most free) to 7 (least free) scale on the basis of citizens' civil rights and liberties, all eighteen nations in the "most free" group were also democracies. No nations with competitive electoral processes ranked below the second scale position on civil liberties.[1] In another recent study, freedom of the press was found to be "complete" in thirty-three of forty nations with competitive electoral systems, while only six of thirty-six electorally uncompetitive nations could boast a completely free press.[2]

Adapted from Benjamin Ginsberg, *The Consequences of Consent: Elections, Citizen Control and Popular Acquiescence* (New York: Random House, 1982). Reprinted with permission.

Benjamin Ginsberg teaches at Cornell University.

Such associations, however, do not necessarily indicate that it is democracy that serves as the basis for liberty. Indeed, the history of the relationship between liberty and democratic practices suggests that democratic institutions are often consequences rather than antecedents of freedom. In some respects, the citizens of the democracies are not free because they participate. Rather, they participate because they are—or once were—free. First, a measure of liberty is a necessary condition for the functioning of democratic processes. Beyond some minimal point, governmental interference with speech, assembly, association, the press, and so on precludes an open and competitive politics.[3]

But more fundamentally, democratic institutions are most likely to emerge where the public already possesses—or threatens to acquire—a modicum of freedom from governmental control. Indeed, democratic elections are typically introduced where governments are unable to compel popular acquiescence. In a sense, elections are inaugurated in order to persuade a resistant populace to surrender at least some of its freedom and allow itself to be governed. On occasion, the opportunity to participate is accompanied by guarantees of some civil liberties. But essentially, citizens are offered the opportunity to participate only when they are already free. Participation is offered to citizens as a substitute for freedom.

In the United States, for example, the introduction of democratic institutions as well as the adoption of formal constitutional guarantees of civil liberties were prompted by the fact that the citizenry was free—born free, as Tocqueville observed—and had the capacity to remain so. Even several of the framers of the Constitution who were somewhat antipathetic to the principle nevertheless urged the adoption of democratic governmental forms on the ground that the populace would otherwise refuse to accept the new government. John Dickinson, for example, asserted that limited monarchy was likely superior to any republican form of government. Unfortunately, however, limited monarchy was out of the question because of the "spirit of the times."[4] Similarly, George Mason concluded that, "notwithstanding the oppressions and injustice experienced among us from democracy, the genius of the people is in favor of it, and the genius of the people must be consulted."[5] Subsequently, the Constitution's proponents agreed to add the formal guarantees of civil liberties embodied in the Bill of Rights only when it appeared that the Constitution might otherwise not be ratified.[6] In effect, the public had to be persuaded to permit itself to be governed because it was, in fact, free to choose otherwise. Given especially the absence of national military forces and the virtually universal distribution of firearms and training in their use, the populace could not easily have been compelled to accept a government it did not desire. One aspect of their "genius" was, after all, that the people were heavily armed.

In general, democratic political practices are most likely to emerge and develop in "free societies"—societies in which politically relevant resources, including the capacity to employ armed force or violence, are relatively widely distributed outside the control of the central government. The importance of the distribution of military force is clear. Where at some critical historical juncture rulers lacked a preponderance of force, they tended to become much more concerned with the acquisition of voluntary compliance through participatory and representative mechanisms. In Britain and Switzerland, for example, as in the United States, the development of democratic institutions was greatly facilitated by the central government's lack of a monopoly of military force during important historical epochs. In Switzerland the military consisted of a citizen militia. In Britain the standing army was typically small, and control of police forces was in the hands of the local gentry.[7]

But simple military force is by no means the only important factor. Where other politically relevant resources and skills—wealth, education, communications, organization—are relatively widely diffused and at least partially outside the state's control, the potential for resistance or opposition to governmental authority and thus rulers' interest in their subjects' voluntary acquiescence are greatly increased. An active private press coupled with a modicum of popular literacy, as students of American history may recall, can obviously stimulate resistance to those in power.[8] Broadly distributed reservoirs of private financial resources can expedite the formation of opposition. And, of course, the potentially countervailing role of private associations and organizations needs no elaboration. When sizable segments of the public possess financial, organizational, educational, and other resources that can be used to foment and support opposition, those in power are more likely to see the merits of seeking to persuade rather than attempting to force their subjects to accept governance.

It is in part for this very reason that economic development, as Lipset and others have attempted to demonstrate, was historically conducive to the emergence of democratic institutions.[9] Industrialization and urbanization, especially under capitalist auspices, entailed the creation and dissemination of private wealth, organizational expertise, communications, literacy, and a host of other resources that facilitated political action and increased citizens' capacities for opposition and resistance.[10] Somewhat revised and updated, Lipset's original analysis is still quite suggestive on this score. First, the societies in which the availability and dissemination of wealth, access to communications, literacy, and exposure to privately controlled media are greatest are also most likely to have developed democratic governments. According to data from the *World Handbook*, for example, seventeen of the twenty nations with the highest per capita gross national products also have competitive electoral processes, as do sixteen of the nineteen nations that rank highest in literacy, nineteen of the twenty nations with the largest number of telephones per capita, eighteen of the twenty nations with the highest per capita newspaper, radio, and television use, and eighteen of the highest twenty nations in terms of percentage of labor force in professional and technical occupations.[11] On these as well as a variety of other indicators, citizens' possession of economic, technical, and educational resources seems at

Table 1

**Availability of political resources and democratic politics in Latin America**

| Country | Number of years of competitive or quasi-competitive elections from 1945 to 1980 | Per capita GNP rank | Literacy rank | Media avail-ability rank | % of population in technical or professional occupations rank |
|---|---|---|---|---|---|
| Uruguay | 35 | 3 | 2 | 1 | 5 |
| Mexico | 35 | 6 | 12 | 4 | 9 |
| Chile | 28 | 4 | 3 | 9 | 4 |
| Costa Rica | 27 | 7 | 4 | 10 | 8 |
| Columbia | 23 | 10 | 10 | 12 | 1 |
| Venezuela | 22 | 1 | 5 | 6 | 7 |
| Argentina | 20 | 2 | 1 | 3 | NA |
| Brazil | 19 | 12 | 13 | 13 | 3 |
| Ecuador | 15 | 16 | 9 | 14 | 12 |
| Bolivia | 15 | 19 | 19 | 7 | NA |
| Peru | 12 | 14 | 14 | 8 | NA |
| Guatemala | 11 | 11 | 18 | 17 | 10 |
| Panama | 11 | 5 | 7 | 2 | 6 |
| Cuba | 5 | 8 | 6 | 5 | 2 |
| Honduras | 3 | 17 | 17 | 18 | 13 |
| Dominican Republic | 1 | 13 | 11 | 19 | 6 |
| El Salvador | 0 | 15 | 16 | 11 | 15 |
| Paraguay | 0 | 18 | 8 | 15 | 11 |
| Nicaragua | 0 | 9 | 15 | 16 | 14 |
| Haiti | 0 | 20 | 20 | 20 | NA |

least to be associated with the existence of a democratic politics.

Second, consider the correlates of democratic government in Latin America. Few Latin American nations can boast a history of stable democracy. In most cases, democratic regimes have sooner or later been superseded by autocratic or military rule. Often, when more or less free elections have taken place, the results have been monitored by the military, which was willing to permit some outcomes but not others. Nevertheless, what is interesting is that the Latin American nations that have experienced the longest democratic or at least quasi-democratic interludes—even if this meant only that the generals found it expedient to step back for a time—are on the whole also those in which the availability of wealth, literacy, communications, and so on are greatest (see Table 1).[12] It is, in a sense, where citizens have the means with which to maintain or acquire a measure of freedom from governmental authority that they must occasionally be governed through democratic formulas. And it is in this sense that freedom is a historical antecedent of democracy.

Whatever their origins, where they do develop, democratic institutions can undoubtedly help to protect citizens from governmental encroachments upon their rights and liberties. Democratic elections may make those in power more sensitive to their subjects' rights. Few white elected officials in the southern United States, for example, now openly support a return to racial segregation. Democratic elections can presumably offer citizens an opportunity to reject candidates whose programs might appear to threaten basic rights and to support candidates in whose hands they believe their liberties to be more secure.

Of course, long before the advent of democratic elections, citizens possessed means of defending what they conceived to be their rights and liberties. More than one rebellion was prompted by rulers' efforts to abrogate some privilege that their subjects held dear. Indeed, where citizens were utterly unable to protect their rights without the suffrage, they also never came to acquire the suffrage. Once introduced, however, democratic electoral mechanisms at least give the public some means of safeguarding its freedom without violence, even when, for one reason or another, violent or disorderly opposition to governmental transgressions might no longer have much chance of success.

## Elections, Freedom, and Government

While elections may offer some measure of protection for civil liberties, the public is seldom satisfied to view democratic processes only as safeguards. The availability of democratic electoral institutions tends to persuade citizens that government is simply their servant. As a result, the public comes to wish to benefit from the state's power rather than merely to be protected from it. While elections can serve as safeguards against governmental excesses and encroachments, the availability of democratic controls tends eventually to persuade citizens that they may enjoy the benefits of the state's power without risk to their freedom. Why, after all, should it be necessary to limit a servant's capacity to serve?

Unfortunately, however, despite democratic controls, freedom and government inevitably conflict. This conflict does not necessarily entail deliberate and overt governmental efforts to abridge liberties. Typically, the erosion of citizens' liberties in the democracies is a more subtle, insidious, and often unforeseen result of routine administrative processes. Federal agencies such as the Interstate Commerce Commission, the Civil Aeronautics Board, and the Federal Trade Commission, to take the most mundane examples, have considerable control over who may enter the occupations and businesses that they regulate. The Food and Drug Administration has a good deal to say about what may be eaten. The Federal Communications Commission has a measure of influence over what Americans see and hear over the air waves. The Internal Revenue Service, in the course of collecting taxes, makes decisions about what is and is not a religion, whether given forms of education are or are not socially desirable, what types of philanthropy serve the public interest, and, of course, what sorts of information to acquire about every citizen. Congressional tax legislation and IRS regulations can have a critical effect upon every individual's business decisions, marital plans, child-bearing and child-rearing decisions, vacation plans, and medical care.[13] Though the administration of tax policy is among the most intrusive activities of the federal government, housing policies, educational policies, welfare programs, and so on, often directed by agencies given broad, discretionary mandates by Congress, affect the most minute details of citizens' lives.[14] For the citizens of the modern state, freedom has come to mean little more than a modicum of choice about the manner in which they will accommodate themselves to the state's directives.

Despite the availability of democratic institutions, the citizens of democracies cannot expect to use the state's power without surrendering at least some of their freedom. Their failure to realize that a choice is involved simply guarantees that the state will more rapidly transform itself from servant to master. The availability of democratic electoral controls, however, tends to obscure this threat. Because of the availability of electoral controls, the public believes that big government can be perfectly compatible with personal freedom. After all, how can a government controlled by its citizens represent a threat to the rights of those citizens? The twentieth-century public believes almost as a matter of course that democratic processes somehow guarantee its liberty.[15] Indeed, as Wollheim observes, democracy has come to be seen as a form of government in which "no limit" need be placed on the governing body.[16]

This notion that democratic processes somehow reconcile personal freedom and expanded governmental authority has even crept into twentieth-century democratic theory. Eighteenth- and nineteenth-century liberal theorists, such as Jeremy Bentham and James Mill, took the relatively modest position that electoral participation could help to protect citizens' interests against tyrannical actions by their rulers.[17] Similarly, the authors of the *Federalist* acknowledged that elections might function to protect citizens' liberties but emphasized the importance of collateral institutional and constitutional barriers against the "unlimited government" that might result despite or even from democratic processes.[18] Many twentieth-century theorists, however, appear to see a more intimate relationship between democratic practices and liberty. Harold Laski, for example, declares that "without democracy there cannot be liberty."[19] H. B. Mayo, anticipating a point of view recently endorsed by the United States Supreme Court, avers that "democracy has a marked tendency to extend the freedoms from the political to other spheres."[20] Indeed, from the perspective of some twentieth-century writers there is no necessary contradiction between individual liberty and the most unmitigated forms of governmental authority. Karl Mannheim, for example, argues that in the ideal centrally planned society, freedom does not require antiquated institutional or constitutional restrictions on the power of the "planning authority." Instead, "democratic control" should be sufficient to compel those in power to permit a measure of personal freedom. According to Mannheim:

> At the highest stage freedom can only exist when it is secured by planning. It cannot consist in restricting the powers of the planner, but in a conception of planning which guarantees the existence of essential forms of freedom through the plan itself. For every restriction imposed by limited authorities would destroy the unity of the plan, so that society would regress to the former stage of competition and mutual control. As we have said, at the stage of planning freedom can only be guaranteed if the planning authority incorporates it in the plan itself. Whether the sovereign authority be an individual or a group or a popular assembly, it must be compelled by democratic control to allow full scope for freedom in its plan. Once all instruments of influencing human behavior have been co-ordinated, planning for freedom is the only logical form of freedom which remains.[21]

Logical or not, democratic institutions encourage citizens to believe that they may have both freedom and government, thus increasing the certainty that the public will choose to have government. The final irony of democratic electoral politics is that democratic institutions, the archetypes of public choice, help to mask this most fundamental of choices. The critical question is whether the public will become aware of the nature of the decision it has made. Perhaps, despite the indications to the contrary, the public's mood during the 1980 elections reflected at least the beginnings of such an awareness. The more likely eventuality, though, as Tocqueville foresaw long ago, is that citizens will simply continue to take pride in their firm grips on what, more and more, constitute only the ends of their own chains.

## Notes

1. Raymond O. Gastil, ed., *Freedom in the World: Political Rights and Civil Liberties* (New York: Freedom House, 1979).
2. Arthur S. Banks and Robert B. Textor, *A Cross-Policy Survey* (Cambridge: MIT Press, 1963).
3. Still the most powerful discussion of the requisites for a democratic politics is Madison's in *The Federalist*, no. 10. E. M. Earle, ed., *The Federalist* (New York: Modern Library, 1937). See also Carl Cohen, *Democracy* (Athens: University of Georgia Press, 1971), ch. 10.
4. Max Farrand, ed., *The Records of the Federal Convention of 1787*, vol. 1 (New Haven: Yale University Press, 1966), p. 86.
5. Ibid., p. 101.
6. See, for example, Forest McDonald, *The Formation of the American Republic*

(Baltimore: Penguin, 1965), ch. 8.

7. See Robert A. Dahl, ed., *Political Oppositions in Western Democracies* (New Haven: Yale University Press, 1966), p. xv.

8. See Richard Hofstadter, *The Idea of a Party System* (Berkeley: University of California Press, 1969), ch. 3.

9. Seymour Martin Lipset, *Political Man* (Garden City, N.Y.: Doubleday, Anchor Books, 1963), ch. 2. See also Phillips Cutright, "National Political Development: Measurement and Analysis," in *Empirical Democratic Theory*, ed. Charles F. Cnudde and Dean Neubauer (Chicago: Markham, 1969), pp. 193–209; and Dean E. Neubauer, "Some Conditions of Democracy," in ibid., especially p. 225.

10. Economic development can also create attitudinal resources that facilitate mass political activity. Such activity may in turn ultimately induce elites to attempt to erect political structures that can allow the regime to accommodate sustained mass involvement. See Daniel Lerner, *The Passing of Traditional Society* (New York: Free Press, 1958), ch. 2; see also Karl W. Deutsch, "Social Mobilization and Political Development," *American Political Science Review* 55 (September 1961):493–514.

11. Charles Lewis Taylor and Michael C. Hudson, *World Handbook of Political and Social Indicators*, 2d ed. (New Haven: Yale University Press, 1972). See tables 4.5, 4.7, 4.8, 5.5, and 5.10.

12. Data pertaining to per capita gross national product, literacy, media, and occupation are drawn from Taylor and Hudson, *World Handbook*. The number of years of competitive or quasi-competitive elections is estimated based on historical accounts. See, for example, Martin C. Needler, *Political Systems of Latin America* (New York: Van Nostrand, 1970).

13. A useful review of the details of U.S. tax policy and its administration can be found in Joseph A. Pechman, *Federal Tax Policy* (New York: Norton, 1971). Efforts by the IRS to distinguish, in effect, between true religion and heresy can be particularly amusing. In recent years, the agency sought to deny tax exempt status to the All One Faith in One God State Universal Life Church and denied tax exempt status to the Zion Coptic Church, Inc. Curiously, the People's Temple, led by the Reverend Jim Jones, had no difficulty acquiring exemption from federal taxation. See Eugene McCarthy, *The Ultimate Tyranny* (New York: Harcourt Brace Jovanovich, 1980), p. 205.

14. The problem of administrative discretion is discussed in Theodore J. Lowi, *The End of Liberalism*, rev. ed. (New York: Norton, 1979). See also Kenneth Culp Davis, *Discretionary Justice* (Baton Rouge: Louisiana State University Press, 1969), for a discussion of the injustices that can arise from the inevitable exercise of administrative discretion.

15. Despite a general diminution of public confidence in most other aspects of government and politics, the American public continues to believe in the significance of democratic elections. Data from a recent University of Michigan poll, for example, indicate that 91 percent of those surveyed believe that it is important to vote even when their own party has no chance to win; 87 percent believe that every single vote matters though it may be only one of millions cast; 87 percent feel that everyone should vote even in apparently unimportant local elections; and 50 percent go so far as to assert that those who do not care about the election's outcome should vote nonetheless.

16. Richard Wollheim, "A Paradox in the Theory of Democracy," in *Philosophy, Politics and Society*, ed. Peter Laslett and W. G. Runciman (Oxford: Blackwell, 1962), p. 72.

Only after they are made clear can we begin to understand how elections sometimes overcome the systemic incremental biases to produce significant policy change.

## The Constitutional Context

Federalism.  The first defining feature of the structure in which public policy is made is the federal system of government. Power is divided between the national and state levels of government, with some powers being shared. The Articles of Confederation could not pull together the diverse state and sectional interests that existed when America achieved independence. When the founding fathers met in Philadelphia in 1787 for the purpose of amending the Articles, their central problem was how to create a more centralized government that would still be acceptable to the various sectional interests.[2] There was never any serious intention of creating a unitary government: Not only would such a thought have been repugnant to many of those in attendance, but a uniform national government would have been impossible given the vast state and sectional differences. Delegates to the convention were selected on a state basis; voting was by states; the various governmental proposals, such as the Virginia and New Jersey plans, were developed by and named after states; and ratification was by states. Before, during, and after the Constitutional Convention, states' interests were an accepted fact of political life.

To the extent that a federal system reflects and recognizes in government organization the social, economic, and religious differences between states, it represents a "numerous and diverse population."[3] The "father" of the Constitution, James Madison, argued that such a population constituted a real check on the ability to form a majority that could act hastily. Different sectional interests pressure Congress to pass legislation viewed as beneficial to one section even if inimical to others. This pattern has prevailed, from Alexander Hamilton's use of the Treasury Department to boost industrial and monied interests in the late 18th century to the sunbelt/snowbelt controversy of the 1970s. Certainly the Civil War and 1896 realignments were highly sectional in nature. These and countless other events in American history are eloquent testimony to the effects of sectional diversity on the American system of government. The House of Representatives, as a focal point for those differences, has had not only to deal with substantive policy issues, but also to temper sectional demands. Such divisiveness makes it difficult to form majorities capable of enacting significant policy changes.

Separation of powers and checks and balances.  The founding fathers did not consider diversity of populace a *sufficient* roadblock to the formation of majorities. It was their firm conviction that concentration of legislative, executive, and judicial powers in the same hands would lead to tyranny. To prevent that, they embodied in the Constitution the doctrines of separation of powers and checks and balances. These doctrines have resulted in a system of government that is characterized by "separate powers sharing functions."[4] This is in contradistinction to other Western democracies, where power is centralized and functions are more specific. Thus, one distinguishing feature of the U.S. House of Representatives is that, unlike the British House of Commons, for example, it shares power with the Senate, the President, the courts, and the bureaucracy. The most immediate effect on the House of the separation of powers and checks and balances is that even when it can build majorities for innovative policies, it must consider the Senate, the President, and the courts. Neustadt and others have shown that each of these institutions has different constituencies to please, and therefore different policy solutions.[5] Policymakers in the House are likely to compromise on or water down proposals in order to enhance the possibility of final enactment,[6] or they must deal with strong policy proposals by other branches of government. The 1977 Omnibus Energy Act is a case in point. The Senate's version of the bill was very different from the House bill, and the final bill was more oriented to the status quo than the House bill would have been. Such compromises are readily associated with incremental public policy.

The multiplicity of levels and branches in the U.S. political system means that opponents of policy changes have access to a large number of power points where a defeat for the majority position spells doom for change until the next Congress forms. The history of the Elementary and Secondary Education Act of 1965 corroborates the difficulty House leaders have in building coalitions capable of enacting major policy changes.[7] In the American system, having a policy majority does not readily translate into significant policy change. Thus, those who seek to preserve the status quo have decided advantages.

Single-member-plurality electoral arrangements.    The only popularly and directly elected body provided for in the Constitution is the U.S. House of Representatives. Each member of the House represents an approximately equal number of people, and, more importantly, each is responsible to his or her constituents. The electoral method of single-member-plurality districts has enhanced and nourished localized elections. Members elected on local issues by localized, limited constituencies owe little to House leaders and can behave as they choose as long as their constituency is happy.[8]

An important policy consequence of localized elections is that the intense representation of local interests pervades the House across a broad range of issues. Representatives, hoping to enhance their reelection chances, choose committees that deal with policies affecting their constituents. Thus, committees and policy outputs are dominated by local interests. This phenomenon has been called policymaking or control by "little governments," the "iron triangles" of interest-group liberalism, pork barrel politics, and policy reciprocity.[9] Forming majorities capable of enacting major policy changes against a backdrop of institutionally localized interests is a difficult task at best, impossible at worst.

## Political Parties in Context

Fearing majority tyranny, the founding fathers intentionally created a cumbersome governmental system. And although many of the parameters of their doctrines have been changed to make the system more democratic and more centralized, the American system of government remains fragmented and cumbersome. Some of the difficulties inherent in governing within the constitutional framework presented themselves immediately, and political factions, which over time developed into political parties, came to serve a sort of coordinating role. Essentially, the parties developed in the constitutional interstices created by the separation of powers and checks and balances, because the system was too cumbersome without them.

Still, the basic features of the government also inhibited the full development of parties. Perhaps the most distinguishing characteristic of American political parties is that their three aspects—the party in the electorate, the party as a formal organization, and the party as government—are disjointed.[10] Certainly, no one claims that American parties are mass parties in the European sense of the term. Federalism, separation of powers, checks and balances, and single-member-plurality districts are in no small way responsible for the fragmented nature of the American party system.

The most basic effect of a federal form of government on the party system is that, rather than a two-party system, we have fifty such systems. Each state's party system has demographic, ideological, structural, and electoral peculiarities. Thus, the Democratic party in the electorate and as organization in New York is distinct from the Democratic party in the electorate and as organization in Georgia. The same applies to the Republican party. The heterogeneity of the state party systems means that at the level of party as government, *unlike*-minded people wearing the same party label come together in the House of Representatives. The federal system brings into the national legislature the built-in differences among states and districts.

While this may be useful in maintaining system equilibrium, it has most often been an extremely poor basis for building coherent congressional parties. The New Deal coalition of rural, southern, agricultural interests and urban, northern, industrial interests is a case in point. Long after this coalition had succeeded in enacting its major policy changes, it continued to serve as an electoral base for the Democratic party. But this historic coalition was often divided on major policy issues—for example, civil rights and social welfare. American political history teems with examples of successful electoral coalitions that could not make major policy changes because of ideological differences. It is not difficult to surmise how such coalitions lead to status quo or incremental policy.

Separation of powers and checks and balances also enhance the fragmentary, disjointed status of American parties. Parties formed out of numerous and diverse state party systems emphasize electoral success as opposed to policy cohesion (and thus policy success). When they succeed in staffing offices (both appointive and elective) in various branches of government, they are further fractionalized. Thus, for example, one faction of the party may be dominant in presidential politics, another in congressional politics, and, since both have powers over the courts, an equal division of court appointments may result. The Democratic party from 1876 to 1976 was characterized by just such an arrangement. The northern wing dominated presidential politics and elections; the southern wing, congressional leadership posts; and both wings influenced court appointments. Such a system may enhance representation of differences, but it does little to provide House majorities capable of effecting public policy changes.

The constitutional arrangement of single-member-district-plurality elections also aids in fragmenting the party system. House members elected on local issues by a localized party in the electorate build local party (or personal) organizations. Once elected, the representatives, who owe little to national party leaders, have few disincentives to behave in nonpartisan ways. Throughout most of the House's history, party leaders have only been able to persuade, not force, members to vote "correctly." Party leadership, lacking much ability even to threaten sanctions, is likely to be unsuccessful in building consistent partisan majorities. It should not be surprising that the highest levels of party voting in the history of the House occurred at a time when the speaker's sanctions over members were greatest.[11] Representatives elected by local majorities can vote those interests regardless of the national party position, and House leaders do not "persuade" from a position of power. The institutionalizing of local and state diversity in the American system of government allows the diversity to work its way up from party in the electorate through party organizations to congressional parties almost unchanged. Thus, at the top, as at the bottom, the party system reflects the cumbersomeness and fractional nature of the system of government. Whatever policy parties are able to enact under these conditions is bound to be incremental in nature, and changes in the status quo will be hard to achieve.

## Effects on House Internal Organization

Like all organizations, the House of Representatives has adapted to its environment by creating internal structures designed both to meet the pressures and demands from its various constituencies and to perform its policymaking function. Given the enormous range of interests in the United States and the concomitant pressures generated, the House has developed a division of labor—a complicated committee system. When the country was in its infancy and government was limited, the House formed ad hoc committees; by the era of Jacksonian democracy there was a standing committee system in place.[12] As the country grew more industrialized and governing became more complicated, the House responded by expanding and enlarging the committee system. The committees themselves have policy domains; thus, some of the first established dealt with war, postal services, roads, and ways and means to raise revenues to support the government. These committees—in Goodwin's words, "little legislatures"[13]— are decisionmaking structures. Reconstruction policy after the Civil War and Wilson's claim in 1885 that "congressional government is committee government" are testimony to the early power of committees. Decentralizing power to committees was a necessary response to pressures for government action in certain policy areas; but to the extent that committees decided policy, the power of party leaders was limited.

The ability of members to choose (within limits) the committees they serve on determines to a large extent which direction the committees' policy choices will take. The decentralized committee system, which allows members to represent local interests, has become a powerful force for stability. In the modern House, committees are entities unto themselves: They are stable, having little membership turnover, and new members are socialized to the committee norms that affect policy decisions.[14] The slow turnover and stable decision norms enable committee leaders to prevent House majorities from enacting major policy changes. Specialization and expertise, the bases of power, take years for new members to acquire, thus enhancing both the committee's power and policy stability. For example, even though majorities of the populace and the House itself have favored such policies as medical aid for the aged and federal aid to schools since the 1930s, committee leaders were able to obstruct enactment for almost thirty years, until the 89th House.[15]

What division of labor pulls apart, the majority congressional party tries to pull together. But, as has been shown, congressional parties are limited by the governmental structure established by the Constitution and by the fact that members are elected by local parties (or groups) on local issues. Members responsible to and punishable only by local electorates tend to be responsive to constituents, not parties. Under such conditions, party strength tends to be low. Even when party voting was at its peak in the U.S. House of Representatives, it was low compared to other Western democracies.

Even under ideal conditions, the congressional parties in the House have limited integrative capacity. This means that policy decisions are likely to reflect localized committee interests under normal conditions, thereby limiting the national party leaders' attempts to lead majorities toward forceful policy solutions to pressing problems. House voting patterns show that different coalitions form on different policy issues,[16] cutting across regional, party, social, and economic lines and making party leaders' jobs a "ceaseless maneuvering to find coalitions capable of governing" in specific policy areas.[17]

Another factor, the American cultural emphasis on equality, also affects the House's ability to legislate quickly. Because each member represents a separate and equal constituency, members receive the same pay and have the same rights to introduce bills, serve on committees, and so forth. Equality in this sense limits the House's ability to organize on a hierarchical basis; since hierarchy is limited, the House has established elaborate procedural rules and precedents to control the passage of legislation from speaker to committee to floor.[18] This system emphasizes the individual member's right to affect legislation at the various decision points in the legislative process. The result is to slow down the policy process and to encourage compromise to avoid parliamentary snafus, both of which favor incremental solutions to policy problems. Over time, the relationship between committee power and party strength has waxed and waned, but the general rule has been that committees are strong while congressional parties are weak.

In sum, major public policy changes occur rarely in the House of Representatives, for the following reasons: (1) Members are normally elected by local interests on local issues; (2) once elected, members choose committee assignments (within limits) based on those local interests and issues, thus localizing rather than nationalizing policy alternatives; (3) the committee system is powerful, in part because it is stable; (4) the congressional parties are normally weak and divided, thus they cannot put together coalitions that can override the localism of committee decisions; and (5) the organization, rules, and procedures of the House facilitate the interests of those who wish to preserve the status quo.

It should be mentioned that there are many historical periods in which inertia or incrementalism are the preference of both the majority of the public and the majority of the House. When this is the case, the congressional system is in harmony with political pressures. As Burnham has argued, however, political systems must over time adjust to majority pressures for change.[19] It is from this perspective that we look to elections to see how the U.S. House of Representatives has at times overcome these powerful biases toward incrementalism to produce significant policy changes.

## A Theory of Policy Change

It is obvious that elections do not generate changes in the basic structure of federalism, separation of powers, checks and balances, and single-member-plurality elections: The structural characteristics have survived many elections. But certain critical elections reflect partisan realignments that radically alter the standard policymaking process. To understand how these realigning elections effect major public policy changes, it is necessary to remember the generally localized nature of congressional elections. In each American realignment, elections are dominated by national issues. Prior to realignments, cross-cutting issues arise that do not fit within the framework of the existing two-party system. Ultimately, the parties take positions on the issues that offer clear-cut alternatives to voters. (In the case of the Civil War realignment, the Republicans replaced the Whigs before the choice was clear.) When the realigning elections occur, the result is a new congressional majority party elected on its positions on national, not local, issues. Moreover, the new majority party maintains uninterrupted control of the presidency and both branches of Congress for at least a decade.[20]

The effect of these elections in the House is that they reduce the major drawbacks to party voting in that body. First, elections that are decided on a localized basis make the congressional parties amalgams of differing interests, with differences of opinion on a whole series of issues. In recent times, for example, Democrats disagreed over civil rights, social welfare, and Vietnam policies, among others. As long as elections are decided on the basis of local factors, policy differences are accommodated and incrementalism results. During realignments, representatives are elected on the basis of party positions on national issues. Thus, the majority party is united on the issues of the realignment. Local factors do not mitigate policy choices, and a unified majority party votes in major policy changes.

Second, the influx of new members into the House during realignments eliminates committee stability, and new leaders support the party position for major policy innovations. The result is increased party voting, especially on issues of the realignment.

If our notion of realignments is correct, we should be able to show that in each of the realignments—Civil War, 1890s, and 1930s—the following occurred: (1) The dominant parties took polar positions on the cross-cutting issues, (2) there was an influx of new members, (3) the new majority party controlled the presidency and the Congress for at least a decade, (4) committee turnover was high, (5) party voting increased, (6) party structures voted on the realignment issues, and (7) there were significant policy changes. Since our purpose is to show that realigning elections share these seven features, we present data from all three major realignments at the same time.

## The Theory Tested over Three Realignments

In each major realignment, a major cross-cutting issued dominated the election. The second American party system was broken up by the rise of slavery and, ultimately, the secession issue. The two dominant parties of the 1832–1856 period were the Whigs and the Democrats. Each party had northern and southern wings, which ultimately could not accommodate the slavery issue. The Missouri Compromise and the Compromise of 1850 were valiant efforts to patch over differences of opinion, but the introduction of the Kansas-Nebraska Act led to the demise of the Whigs. The Republican party replaced the Whigs as the second major party in the 1856 elections, and by 1860 the Democrats were the proslavery party, the Republicans the antislavery party. Thus, the electorate was offered a clear choice between parties and policies.

The cross-cutting issue of the 1890s realignment was whether the future for America lay in industry or in agriculture. Industrialization in the aftermath of the Civil War generated the displacement of farmers and a change from a society of

Table 1

**Partisan platform differences on major issues in three realignment eras**

| Era | Slavery | Capitalism | Depression |
|---|---|---|---|
| | | Issues | |
| Civil War | | | |
| 1848 | 0 | | |
| 1852 | .10 | | |
| 1856 | .24 | | |
| 1869 | .71 | | |
| 1890s | | | |
| 1884 | | .08 | |
| 1888 | | .04 | |
| 1892 | | .44 | |
| 1896 | | .55 | |
| New Deal | | | |
| 1920 | | | .02 |
| 1924 | | | .30 |
| 1928 | | | .19 |
| 1932 | | | .26 |

*Source:* Adapted from Ginsberg (1972), p. 612.

local, self-sufficient communities to a highly interrelated industrial society. The overarching issues were the questions of gold, silver, the protective tariff, and American expansionism. Agricultural interests favored the inflationary coinage of silver at a sixteen-to-one ratio to gold, free tariffs, and limited expansion. Industrial interests favored exactly the opposite. The rise of the profarmer Populist party indicates the existence of cross-cutting issues in the 1896 realignment. The Democrats, under William Jennings Bryan, adopted the Populist position while the Republicans adopted a pro-industrial position.

The cross-cutting issue during the New Deal realignment was the result of a single event—the Great Depression. The question was whether the government would act to combat the effects of the depression. The Republican incumbent, Herbert Hoover, would not adopt policies to aid farmers, workers, cities, and the unemployed; the Democrats, on the other hand, proposed relief funds and programs to aid those most affected. Once again, voters were offered clear choices between candidates and parties.

To demonstrate this point, Table 1 shows the party differences on these issues in each of the realignments. The differences are those in the party platforms as presented by Ginsberg.[21] The higher the value, the greater the disagreement. The table clearly shows that the Civil War and 1890s realignments were

Table 2

**House member and committee turnover and length of undivided partisan control of government on three realignments**

| Eras | % member turnover | % turnover on Ways and Means | Years of undivided party control |
|---|---|---|---|
| Pre-Civil War | 49.6 | 38.5 | 2 years since 1840 |
| Realignment | 56.4 | 67.9 | 14 years (1860–1874) |
| Pre-1890s | 38.7 | 26.5 | 2 years since 1876 |
| Realignment | 43.4 | 76.5 | 14 years (1896–1910) |
| Pre-New Deal | 19.5 | 15.0 | 10 years since 1912 |
| Realignment | 27.8 | 80.0 | 14 years (1932–1946) |

characterized by deepening party differences in regard to the cross-cutting issues leading up to the critical elections. For the New Deal realignment, the pattern is somewhat different. The parties differed in 1924, but it was not until 1932 that the Democrats could convince the electorate to send a new majority party to Congress. In addition, the magnitude of these figures suggests that the parties were less polarized in the positions they took during the New Deal than they were during the Civil War and 1890s realignments.[22] Still, the first part of our theory holds: In each realignment era, the major political parties took opposing positions on the issues of major concern. Thus, when voters went to the polls in the elections of 1860, 1896, and 1932, they were offered a clear choice.

Points 2, 3, and 4 of the test of our theory are concerned with the implications of how voters responded to these choices. To test these points, we must show that realigning elections produce an increase in new members, high turnover on committess, and new majority control in Congress and the presidency for at least a decade. Table 2 presents these data for each realignment (using Ways and Means as an example of the broader pattern of committee turnover). The table suggests that, consonant with our theory, realigning elections are characterized by high turnover in membership and on committees, and that realignment brings the new majority party a stable electoral base for fourteen years.

Our theory also says that under electoral conditions where parties take distinct stands on national issues, the new members in the House will vote along party lines because they have a mandate to act. Party voting in the House will increase because members are not cross-pressured by local interests differing from national party positions. Thus, we should expect to see party voting increase during the realignment relative to the period of politics preceding it (point 5). Table 3 shows the average percentage of party votes in the five Houses preceding the realignment and the percentage of party votes in the realignment Houses.

Table 3

**Percentage of party votes in pre-realignment and realignment eras**

| Era | 50 v. 50 | | 90 v. 90 | |
|---|---|---|---|---|
| | Pre | Realignment | Pre | Realignment |
| Civil War | 66.4 | 74.7 | 8.9 | 20.9 |
| 1890s | 53.8 | 76.4 | 21.1 | 50.1 |
| New Deal | 48.7 | 69.4 | 7.9 | 16.4 |

Party votes are defined in two ways. First, the percentage of votes that pitted a majority of one party against a majority of the other (50 v. 50) is presented. Second, a more stringent criterion is used, defining party votes as those in which 90 percent of one party opposed 90 percent of the other (90 v. 90).

The results clearly indicate a rise in partisan voting during each realignment. While these results help to corroborate our theory, it would be better if we could show that party voting increases dramatically on the cross-cutting issues associated with realignments. Thus, we created a set of scales for each of the following realignments and issues: Civil War—slavery, secession, and civil rights; 1890s—monetary policy; and New Deal—social welfare.[23] The hypothesis is that on each of these dimensions in the prealignment period, party will not predict voting. We measure the extent of the relationship by correlating a representative's party identification (0 = Democrat, 1 = Republican) with his or her voting score. The higher the correlations (+1.0 = highest), the stronger the relationship and the greater the party structuring of the vote. Table 4 presents the results.

The results support the hypothesis. In each realignment, the correlation between party and support for or opposition to the dominant issue dimension increases. During the Civil War and 1890s realignments, the Republicans became more antislavery and progold, respectively. In the 1930s realignment, the Democrats became more pro-social welfare. In short, during each realignment, party structured voting in the House, especially on the realignment issues.

Point 7 asserts that during each realignment, clusters of major policy changes occur. In one sense, this is obvious. The Civil War realignment ultimately resulted in the end of slavery, the passage of the thirteenth, fourteenth, and fifteenth amendments, and an increased governmental role in modernizing the economy. The 1890s realignment resulted in noninflationary money, protective tariffs, the annexation of Hawaii, and the Spanish-American war—in short, it assured America's industrial future. The New Deal introduced the welfare state to America. Social security, unemployment assistance, prolabor legislation, agricultural assistance, and government management of the economy are but a few of the legacies of the New Deal. In sum, in each of these realignments, election results were transformed into major public policy changes. Elections did matter.

Table 4

**Correlation (r) between party voting and the cross-cutting issue in three realignment eras**

| Era | | | | | | | |
|---|---|---|---|---|---|---|---|
| Civil War | Issue: | Slavery/Secession/Civil Rights | | | | | |
| | Year: | 1853 | 1855 | 1857 | 1959 | 1861 | |
| | Congress: | 33d | 34th | 35th | 36th | 37th | |
| | r: | .51 | .41 | .89 | .87 | .88 | |
| 1890s | Issue: | Currency | | | | | |
| | Year: | 1891 | 1893 | 1895 | 1997 | 1899 | |
| | Congress: | 52d | 53d | 54th | 55th | 56th | |
| | r: | .02 | .42 | .71 | .96 | .96 | |
| New Deal | Issue: | Social Welfare | | | | | |
| | Year: | 1925 | 1927 | 1929 | 1931 | 1933 | 1935 |
| | Congress: | 69th | 70th | 71st | 72d | 73rd | 74th |
| | r: | 0 | 0 | 0 | .72 | .89 | .94 |

## Discussion

Having defined what we mean by elections "mattering," we are able to identify the conditions necessary for the affirmative answer to the query "Do elections matter?" To recapitulate, elections matter in terms of producing significant public policy changes when the major political parties take opposing positions on new issues that do not fit into the existing party cleavages. At such times, voters may clearly choose one alternative by voting out incumbents and filling Congress with large numbers of new members. This naturally produces high committee turnover and weakens the effect of traditional strategies on committee policy decisions. To qualify as a critical or realigning election, the voters' choice would have to be deep-seated enough to be reaffirmed in subsequent elections. The new majority party would control both the presidency and Congress for at least a decade. This depth of commitment would overcome the localizing forces in Congress, freeing members to coalesce under the aegis of the party to enact major policy initiatives in response to the important issues of the time.

The confirmation of these conditions in the three realignment eras studied here leads us to apply this theory in two other ways. First, we shall consider the importance of elections in which these conditions do not obtain. Second, we shall comment on the possibility of avoiding strictly post hoc analysis.

As mentioned earlier, other definitions of "mattering" should lead to the specification of different sets of conditions or different theories. In the broadest sense, individual political careers are affected by each election. And, related to our analysis, elections may be important in continuing the arrangements brought about by a realignment. As we state, it is necessary for the new majority party to maintain its majority status for at least a decade to assure the permanence of the policy changes. Clearly, this implies the necessity of forging a series of electoral victories. But elections are important even beyond the immediate postrealignment decade because they reflect the continuation of a viable consensus formed during the last realignment. These interrealignment elections permit incremental adjustments until such time that small changes are insufficient to deal with the pressures of the day.

Given this framework, we can examine other seemingly important elections to ascertain whether they were in fact critical. Elections that have been associated with major policy changes or actually labeled "realignments" include those involving Woodrow Wilson and the Progressive movement and Lyndon Johnson and the Great Society. The Progressive era—roughly 1912 to 1916—gave rise to reform politics such as nonpartisan city elections and a new theory of administration which led to new federal bureaucracies such as the Federal Trade Commission and the Food and Drug Administration. In addition, there was an increase in the democratization of politics characterized by such reforms as the initiative, referendum, and recall. The sum of all policy changes associated with Wilson and the Progressives did mark a break with previous policy, but the electoral conditions of the realignments discussed above differ somewhat from those of the Progessive era.

The major difference is that Wilson was elected as a minority president. Theodore Roosevelt ran on a progressive Bull Moose ticket and garnered more votes than William Howard Taft, the Republican candidate, but Wilson was elected president with about 40 percent of the vote. The Democrats won control of the House in the 1910 election and with the help of progressive Republicans stripped the speaker of his power over the legislative process. At both the congressional and presidential levels, progressive Republicans aided Democrats. The Progressive era congresses were characterized by bipartisan support for much of the legislation associated with Woodrow Wilson. Under this condition, party labels were not clearly applicable to different policy positions.

Another important difference was that the Democrats lost control of Congress in 1918, and the Republicans won a landslide victory in 1920. Thus, the Democrats had complete control over government for only six years (1913–1919).

On the other hand, the policy changes associated with the Progressive era were the result of electoral turnover in 1910 and 1912 and were largely voted through by the new Democratic majority voting cohesively. In addition, Wilson had a program that distinguished him and his party from the regular Republicans. Thus, votes for Wilson or Roosevelt in 1912 and votes for Democratic congressional candidates strongly suggested support for Progressive policies. In sum, the Progressive era meets some but not all of the conditions associated with the three major realignments.

The Great Society—roughly 1964 to 1968—also involved major policy shifts. The Johnson-Goldwater election of 1964 offered voters, in Goldwater's words, "a choice not an echo." And, with the overwhelming victory of Johnson, the stage was set for dramatic changes in civil rights policy. Congress passed major civil rights legislation in 1964 and 1965, laying the groundwork for progress in voting rights, equal access to public accommodations, and school desegregation.[23] Furthermore, Congress followed Johnson's initiatives in establishing the Office of Economic Opportunity as the instrument for achieving the goal of eliminating poverty.

Congress was able to do this because Johnson saw his election as a clear choice for his policies and pressed hard for their enactment. He was aided by a massive influx of new members of Congress swept into office with him (89th Congress).

Additional evidence of the importance of civil rights policies comes from the presidential voting patterns of 1964, whereby the once solidly Democratic South dramatically switched to the Republican column. Goldwater's few electoral votes came from states that had not returned a Republican majority since Reconstruction.

Thus, the evidence for the election of 1964 being a critical election hinges on the facts that (1) the dominant parties' nominees took and communicated polar positions on civil rights policies, (2) the voters swept in a large new Democratic majority in Congress with Lyndon Johnson, (3) this produced significant levels of turnover, and (4) significant policy changes occurred.

But because of the size of the Democratic majority and the nature of the civil rights issue, party voting became less important. The massive Democratic majority was able to overcome the defections of its southern nominal copartisans to build winning coalitions. At the same time, nonsouthern and distinctly minority Republicans found it more difficult to join with conservative southern Democrats in thwarting civil rights legislation, because of public opinion and intense media coverage of the movement.

Finally, civil rights as a cross-cutting issue faded rather quickly. Dramatic legislative battles were won, and the less dramatic drudgery of bureaucratic implementation followed. At the same time, massive, overt resistance withered, to be replaced by grudging acceptance by some and more subtle second-generation discrimination by others. Television coverage shifted from Bull Conner's police dogs attacking civil rights demonstrators to the carnage of a futile war in Southeast Asia. The result was that the new majority which had forged the policy changes disintegrated. The Democratic majority in the House was maintained, but the presidency was lost in 1968. Richard Nixon was then able, using administrative means, to mute the ongoing process of policy change started during the Great Society. In this light, the Great Society appears to have been the completion of the New Deal—a final effort to expand the fulfillment of the promise of social and economic well-being to all in the United States.

The theory we outline should allow us to avoid having to wait thirty years to ascertain whether or not an election was critical. This is relevant today as people question whether Ronald Reagan and the Republican majority in the Senate are evidence of the somewhat belated fulfillment of the prediction of an "emerging Republican majority."

In evaluating the Reagan elections and subsequent elections, we suggest looking back to our seven points. Have the Republicans and Democrats taken polar positions? Clearly, Reagan represents a Republican contingent that harkens back to the 1950s. But it is not clear that the Democrats are identified with a coherent polar position or, for that matter, that Reagan can hold together the Republican party.

Party voting has not jumped dramatically over the levels seen in the pre-Reagan Houses. Furthermore, the conservative coalition of Republicans and southern Democrats has been quite active and extraordinarily successful. The partisan polarization seen in previous realigning elections is not apparent.

Turnover was up somewhat both in the House and on committees early in Reagan's administration. However, subsequent turnover in the House has not redounded to the Republicans' benefit. In 1982, the President's party suffered the worst losses in the House—twenty-six seats—of any party at the two-year point since the GOP lost seventy-five seats two years into Warren Harding's presidency (1922). It was able to recapture only fourteen seats in the 1984 elections, a number well below even the party's most pessimistic predictions. Thus the GOP has failed to gain control of both the legislative and executive branches at all, much less for a significant period of time, to enact and implement significant policy changes of the sort associated with realigning elections.

In sum, we still cannot predict critical elections. But, by careful observation, with the theory presented here in mind, we can perhaps be more cognizant of elections that matter as they are occurring.

## Notes

1. Walter Dean Burnham, *Critical Elections and the Mainsprings of American Politics* (New York: Norton, 1970); Barbara Sinclair, "Party Realignment and the Transformation of the Political Agenda: The House of Representatives, 1925–1938," *American Political Science Review* 71 (September 1977):940–54; David W. Brady, "Critical Elections, Congressional Parties and Clusters of Policy Change," *British Journal of Political Science* 8 (January 1978):79–99; David W. Brady with Joseph Stewart, Jr., "Congressional Party Realignment and Transformation of Public Policy in Three Realignment Eras," *American Journal of Political Science* 26 (1982):333–60.

2. Robert A. Dahl, *A Preface to Democratic Theory* (Chicago: University of Chicago Press, 1956).

3. Ibid.

4. Samuel P. Huntington, "Political Development and Political Decay," *World Poli-*

*tics* 17 (April 1965):386–430.

5. Richard E. Neustadt, *Presidential Power* (New York: Wiley, 1976); John R. Schmidhauser and Larry R. Berg, *The Supreme Court and Congress: Conflict and Interaction, 1945–1968* (New York: Free Press, 1972).

6. James E. Anderson, *Public Policy Making*, 3d ed. (New York: Holt, Rinehart and Winston, 1984).

7. Frank J. Munger and Richard F. Fenno, Jr., *National Politics and Federal Aid to Education* (Syracuse: Syracuse University Press, 1962).

8. Thomas E. Mann, *Unsafe at Any Margin: Interpreting Congressional Elections* (Washington, D.C.: American Enterprise Institute, 1978).

9. Theodore J. Lowi, *The End of Liberalism*, 2d ed. (New York: Norton, 1979); Emmette S. Redford, *Democracy in the Administrative State* (New York: Oxford University Press, 1969).

10. Frank J. Sorauf, *Party Politics in America* (Boston: Little, Brown, 1968).

11. David W. Brady and Phillip Althoff, "Party Voting in the U.S. House of Representatives, 1890–1910: Elements of a Responsible Party System," *Journal of Politics* 36 (August 1974):753–73.

12. Joseph Cooper, "Congress in Organizational Perspective," in *Congress Reconsidered*, ed. Lawrence C. Dodd and Bruce I. Oppenheimer (New York: Praeger, 1977).

13. George Goodwin, *The Little Legislatures: Committees of Congress* (Amherst: University of Massachusetts Press, 1970).

14. Ralph Huitt, "The Morse Committee Assignment Controversy: A Study in Senate Norms," *American Political Science Review* 51 (June 1957):313–29; Huitt, "The Outsider in the Senate: An Alternative Role," *American Political Science Review* 55 (September 1961):564–73; and Richard F. Fenno, Jr., *Congressmen in Committees* (Boston: Little, Brown, 1973).

15. Gary Orfield, *Congressional Power: Congress and Social Change* (New York: Harcourt Brace Jovanovich, 1975).

16. Aage Clausen, *How Congressmen Decide: A Policy Focus* (New York: St. Martin's, 1973); Sinclair, "Party Realignment."

17. V. O. Key, Jr., *Politics, Parties and Pressure Groups* (New York: Crowell, 1967).

18. Cooper, "Congress in Organizational Perspective."

19. Burnham, *Critical Elections*.

20. Jerome M. Clubb, William H. Flanigan, and Nancy H. Zingale, *Partisan Realignment: Voters, Parties, and Government in American History* (Beverly Hills: Sage, 1980).

21. Benjamin Ginsberg, "Critical Elections and the Substance of Party Conflict: 1844–1968," *Midwest Journal of Political Science* 16 (November 1972):603–25.

22. See also Brady with Stewart, "Congressional Party Realignment."

23. For a fuller discussion, see ibid.

## 1.3

# Political Parties and Regulation

## Richard Barke and Alan Stone

American political elections (with the exception of some local contests) have been fought out through the mechanism of political parties. Whether one votes for president, senator, representative, governor, or mayor, electoral choices are conducted through political parties. Of course, as some of the essays in this book and other writings suggest, the personal characteristics of candidates and other factors can play important roles in determining for whom one will vote. Neverthless, candidates do talk about issues and do claim to represent their party's position on those issues. Candidates pat themselves on the back and question their opponents' experience, wisdom, and sometimes even honesty, but most of their energies are devoted to showing their differences in policy preferences and how these differences reflect fundamental conflicts in party orientation. Thus, in recent times, Democratic candidates have attempted to show that their party represents the interests of the poor and the downtrodden, while Republican candidates have sought to represent their party's policy preferences as responsible and tending to get government off people's backs.

There are mavericks in both major parties, but the dynamic described above characterizes most American electoral contests. Public issues, political parties, and elections are supposed to be linked in this fashion. These linkages suggest one way in which to determine whether elections matter. Candidates would have us believe that, as agents of their respective parties, they represent vastly different political philosophies. One would expect these alleged philosophical differences to show up in legislative voting. Certainly one policy area in which to test these differences is regulation: In virtually every peacetime national election since the turn of the century, there have been regulatory issues. From

Richard Barke and Alan Stone teach at the University of Houston.

demands for trustbusting and pure food and drug legislation early in this century to the recent Reagan–Carter and Reagan–Mondale debates on "overregulation," environmental protection, and the proper scope of the free market, regulatory issues have been important in elections. One would expect that if there really are significant philosophical differences between the two major political parties, they would certainly be reflected in something as central as government restrictions and limitations on decisionmaking in the marketplace—the very essence of regulation.

Oddly, most theories developed by political scientists and economists share the view that parties and elections play virtually no role in legislative regulatory outputs. Yet none of these theories has been accompanied by empirical examination of whether elections and party differences matter; it is simply assumed that they do not.[1]

Political scientists have, of course, been very attentive to the effects of party and elections upon policy outputs and have offered many case studies and analyses of the role of political parties in the legislative process. Some of these studies have shown that party differences account for little in other policy areas.[2] The failure to categorize systematically the effect of party on regulatory policy stems in part from the powerful theoretical influence of Theodore Lowi's work as applied to the regulatory arena. In an article published in the journal *World Politics*, Lowi argued that regulatory politics is characterized by interest groups contending over outcomes, using bargaining and compromise to attain the ultimate legislative result. Drawing on case studies by David Truman and others, Lowi concluded that the theory of pluralism best describes regulatory politics.[3] Inferentially, political parties and elections did not play significant roles in regulatory politics; rather, they moved to center stage in the more ideologically charged arena of redistributive policies.

Lowi extended this view in his book *The End of Liberalism*, in which he argued that, since the advent of the New Deal, regulatory statutes have been increasingly discretionary, devolving real decisionmaking power to administrative agencies: "Modern law has become a series of instructions to administrators rather than a series of commands to citizens."[4] Since the stakes in legislative action, as opposed to administrative action, are reduced from what they were in prior eras, political party differences again play little role in regulatory issues. Legislative voting differences stem from the fact that Republicans and Democrats can, but do not necessarily have to, represent different interest groups.[4] Thus, according to Lowi, a political party may be a surrogate for interest groups, but the principal focus in regulatory politics should be on interest groups. It is possibly because of the widespread acceptance of Lowi's views—which mesh well with Truman's and even C. Wright Mills's in the regulatory arena—that political scientists have not systematically looked at the role of political parties in this area. Yet, as we will show, political parties can play a significant role in regulatory legislation, albeit a complex one. Later we will develop categories of regulatory issues that help to explain when party differences are important in legislative voting on regulatory issues and when they are not.

## Parties and Regulatory Issues

What is the relationship between party and policy in general? Does party *matter*? The evidence is mixed. Party affiliation seems to be the most important single factor in congressional decisions, but it often works indirectly—for example, by affecting a congressman's relationships with other political actors.[6] The importance of party also appears to differ across policy areas, for reasons that we will soon discuss.[7] Our point here is that any *a priori* expectations about the role of party in regulatory legislation must be tempered by the findings of other political scientists regarding party and policy in general. As David Price concluded, "Organizationally and ideologically diffuse, American parties have displayed only a limited capacity to bind together the branches of the federal government— and disparate elements within the legislature—in pursuit of well-defined policy goals.[8]

Given this complexity, any claim that parties make a difference in regulatory policy must identify the mechanisms by which such influence occurs. Parties may, for example, mobilize voters or interest groups, polarize congressional committee or subcommittee members, divide the members of Congress during a floor vote, challenge or respond to the president, restrict the legislative agenda in an effort to appease the ideologically diverse parts of the party's coalition, and so on. We have sufficient evidence about several of these functions to suggest whether parties might be expected to perform these tasks more or less consistently on regulatory matters than in other issue areas.

As an example, we can examine attempts by both parties to inform and attract voters and interest-group support by means of their party platforms. While platforms are rarely read by voters and may be full of inconsequential promises, they are likely to reveal something about how the coalition of interests and ideologies that parties comprise views contemporary issues. At the very least they are scrutinized by competitors looking for political flaws to exploit. At the aggregate level, Ginsberg's study of platforms from 1844 to 1968 indicates that since 1884 the issue of "internal sovereignty" ("exercise of the power and increase of the sphere of action of the central government *vis-à-vis* states, localities, and individuals")—the category most congruent with regulatory intervention—has been among the consensual of issues.[9]

An examination of party platforms that preceded particularly important regulatory changes shows the difficulty in generalizing about overall party positions on regulatory issues. In the 1912 presidential campaign, which immediately preceded formation of the Federal Reserve Board and the Federal Trade Commission and passage of the Clayton Act, both parties called for strengthening of the Sherman Act (although only the Republicans specifically proposed an FTC) and opposed a central bank that would threaten the independence of individual banks. Although Democrats were specific about the need for utility and transportation regulation and pure food legislation, they also were emphatic about the primacy of the states in seeking remedies to national problems. It is also unclear which party was more "proregulation" in the 1932 platforms (which anticipated formation of the Federal Communication Commission, the Federal Deposit Insurance Corporation, the Securities and Exchange Commission, and such major legislation as the Public Utilities Holding Act and the Motor Carrier Act). For example, the Republicans claimed credit for creation of the Interstate Commerce Commission and specifically called for strengthening and expanding utility and transportation regulation, whereas the Democratic platform of 1932 called for full regulation of holding companies and securities exchanges.

More recently, the language used in party platforms has suggested greater differences between Democrats and Republicans on regulatory issues, but the substance has remained similar. In 1964 both parties called for rigorous enforcement of antitrust laws and careful and balanced development of natural resources. And while the Republicans promised an "end to power-grabbing regulatory actions, such as the reach by the FTC for injunctive powers and the ceaseless pressing by the White House, the Food and Drug Administration, and the FTC to dominate consumer decisions in the market-place," the Democrats pledged to "promote efforts on behalf of consumers by industry, voluntary organizations, and state and local governments" and, where appropriate, to provide consumers with "essential information." This partisan difference on consumer legislation seems to have been more semantic than real.

Partisan ability to mobilize interest groups may also be restrained by the relative visibility of regulatory issues. Those who face government control from new regulatory legislation are likely to be quite aware of the matter without the assistance of the Democrats or Republicans. A party's ideology (as expressed by its platform or by the behavior of its coalition) may be much too broad to be useful to concerned groups of voters, to whom regulatory issues are salient enough that details are important. For example, the trucking and airline industries were far from united on many aspects of the deregulatory packages of the late 1970s, so a party would have been hard-pressed to have found (or reluctant to have proposed) a position that would gain majority support while not antagonizing a sizeable minority. Given the specific and complex demands that interest groups present to regulatory lawmakers, parties have been generally incapable of exploiting regulatory issues to attract particular interest groups.

## Presidential Party and Regulation

Should we expect the President's party to be more effective as a predictor of regulatory policy than the larger (and thus more blunt) congressional parties? On the one hand we might expect so, since Democratic administrations are often viewed as more liberal than Republican adminstrations, and thus more supportive of "big government" and more willing to impose new regulations on private industry. On closer examination, however, we find several problems with such an interpretation. It is difficult to ascribe the growth or contraction of the regulatory bureaucracy solely to a president or his party, since recent Republican presidents have been countered by Democratic Congresses which some would say have forced new agencies onto unwilling administrations. The historical record on congressional behavior, however, does not support this explanation.

It is certainly true that presidents set the tone for regulatory agencies by recommending their budgets, suggesting or supporting new legislation, directly intervening in agency actions, or through Office of Management and Budget reviews.[10] Much of the historical expansion of the federal regulatory apparatus occurred while Democrats Woodrow Wilson and Franklin Roosevelt occupied the White House. Yet expansion also took place under the Nixon Administration, when even a majority of Republicans in Congress supported the formation of the Occupational Safety and Health Administration, the Consumer Product Safety Commission, and the Environmental Protection Agency. And although the deregulatory bandwagon of the late 1970s began rolling under Gerald Ford, Jimmy Carter (with the support of a Democratic Congress) made the greatest recent strides in dismantling parts of the regulatory state.[11] Whereas the Reagan Administration continued and expanded Carter's moves in some areas of deregulation, the Reagan program included the retardation or reversal of the deregulation movement in other areas, especially surface transportation.

Finally, the most overtly partisan aspect of presidential control over regulation is in appointments to regulatory agencies. The statutes of all independent regulatory commissions try to guarantee some bipartisanship by requiring that these commissions have no more than a simple majority of members from one party. In practice, most presidential appointments have been "independents," or minority partisans who are ideologically compatible with the President. In other words, the party of the appointee seems to have had little practical effect, as presidents have intended and as Senate confirmers have allowed.

Political party is thus not of direct and obvious utility in explaining legislative regulatory behavior, but it can be of considerable importance in understanding many regulatory issues.

## A Framework of Regulatory Legislation

Very few regulatory statutes are subject to roll call in either chamber of Congress. Most appear to be settled consensually, usually at subcommittee or committee levels, and entail minimal floor discussion. Yet our research indicates that political party or division within a party (e.g., northern and southern Democrats) plays a role in many cases. Moroever, the instances in which the standard pattern applies and those in which party or some other division is important in floor votes do not transparently depend upon the subject of the regulation. For example, most railroad regulatory legislation conforms to the standard pattern, but there has been at least one important exception in which a bitter division occurred, which we will describe shortly.

Clearly, a theory of regulatory legislation must account for instances of both the standard pattern and deviations from it. To provide such a comprehensive explanation, we will construct a typology of regulatory legislation embracing three categories, each with its own pattern of politics. Then we will explain and illustrate each type, providing a framework for understanding when each may occur as well as the prevalence of the standard pattern.

We begin by noting a lesson that political scientists should learn from social anthropologists. In describing and conceptualizing human behavior in areas as diverse as religious ritual and legislative action, attention must be paid to both subjective and objective components. Because human beings act purposively, the interpretation of human action, such as voting in Congress, must embrace the subjects' interpretation as well as the investigator's own frame of discourse.[12] The difficulty with a framework such as Lowi's in describing legislative regulatory behavior is its failure to embrace the subjects' purpose in undertaking action. More concretely, the legislator confronted with a problem that is objectively described as regulatory may in fact be considering it in very different terms that are not translatable to the objective regulatory framework. And this disjunction may in turn lead the legislator to undertake action different from that anticipated pursuant to the objective category. Categories of human behavior, such as legislative action, should therefore embrace both objective behavior and the subjective understanding of it.

With the foregoing in mind, we propose three categories of legislative regulatory issues—subsumptive, conjunctive, and discrete—that include the variety of legislative responses to such issues with respect to political party and other variables.

1. *Subsumptive* regulatory issues are those in which the regulatory aspects are considered (subsumed) as part of more embracing issues, such as those affecting the economy or society as a whole. For example, during the 1980 presidential election campaign, "overregulation," particularly in the environmental and safety areas, was widely held to have serious adverse effects upon the American economy.[13] Thus, what are objectively described as regulatory issues were treated as being *subsumed* under the large problem of the economy as a whole. At times both parties (or all segments of a party) may hold consensual views about the connection between the objective regulatory issue and the "proper" solution to the larger economic or social problem, but at other times they may not. The consensus or division flows not as much from the nature of the specific issue area as it does from ideological or technical agreements or differ-

ences over approach to the wider problem and the place of regulation in the approaches. In other words, the perceived social costs of some legislative action (or inaction) may be assessed by each political party differently. Or both parties may concur. But the causes of consensus or dissensus on subsumptive issues must be found in the realm of economic or social ideology, not in interest-group politics. Whereas economic interests are virtually certain to take positions on subsumptive regulatory issues, the party battle will be joined over much broader questions.

Our research indicates, for example, that virtually all railroad regulatory legislation has been consensual and has concerned what we later define as discrete regulatory issues. A notable exception was the Reed-Bulwinkle Act of 1948, which explicitly authorized common carriers collectively to formulate rate, fare, and other agreements in rate bureaus. Such conduct would otherwise have clearly violated the Sherman Act's prohibitions on collusive agreements concerning price, rates, and other terms of trade.[14] Joint rate agreements had become a customary way of doing business, but in the late 1930s both the Justice Department's Antitrust Division and the state of Georgia instituted Sherman Act proceedings challenging the practice. In view of the clear violation, only legislative action exempting such agreements from the coverage of the Sherman Act prohibition could legalize the actions of rate bureaus. In this way the problem moved onto the legislative agenda.

Several roll-call votes in both chambers were taken on the Reed-Bulwinkle bill, including votes that overrode President Truman's veto. The votes were clearly along party lines, with Republicans generally favoring the bill and a majority of Democrats opposing it. In the Senate the veto was overridden by a 63–25 vote (Republicans 47–3, Democrats 16–22), and in the House by a 297–102 vote (Republicans 228–4, Democrats 69–96, others 0–2). Political party, then, played a significant (but not predictive) role in this outcome, unlike virtually all other transportation regulation enactments.

The reason for this outcome must be traced back to the recession that began in late 1937, and the subsumption of antitrust regulatory policy to the larger issue of economic recovery.[15] The confidence espoused in early 1937 that New Deal spending policies were at last moving the nation toward steady recovery was shattered by the severe and rapid economic downturn that began in the fall of 1937. Even before the onset of this recession, New Deal policymakers had charged that prices in key industries were rising too rapidly and were monopolistically controlled. When the recession began, the argument was amended to explain the economic downturn almost entirely on the basis of monopolistic pricing. In brief, many New Dealers charged that arbitrary and unreasonable price increases had "siphoned off all the gains [of the recovery] to wealthy savers [who] failed to find profitable investment outlets, and the result was a new failure of purchasing power. Yet instead of lowering prices, business men had again reacted by laying off workers, reducing output, and postponing investments, a process that cut purchasing power that much more and made the recession worse."[16]

Gradually this line of reasoning was accepted by the administration, so that antimonopoly policy became a major weapon in the fight against depression. The Administration, in carrying out its new policy, embarked on a multipronged attack that included the most massive antitrust campaign in history, a lengthy investigation by the Temporary National Economic Committee into the effects of economic power, and firm opposition to proposed legislation that would exempt economic activity from antitrust coverage.

The Democratic campaign and philosophy carried over into the immediate postwar period. Most Republicans and many conservative Democrats viewed the problem rather differently. To them, the excessive government intervention into business affairs characteristic of the New Deal discouraged business investment, especially long-term capital investment. Accordingly, their solution to the problem of depression and recession was greatly to reduce government intervention in business activity. We can thus see why the Reed-Bulwinkle bill was a subsumptive regulatory issue in which political party was important.

2. While subsumptive regulatory issues contain a notion of hierarchy between the regulatory issue and other issues that are held to be of greater objective importance, *conjunctive* regulatory issues involve the perceived connection between the regulatory issue and large voting blocs such as labor or blacks. Sometimes such blocs constitute faithful members of a party's coalition. At other times a party may attempt to recruit and mobilize a potential bloc, such as the urban poor. This notion is akin to David Truman's concept of converting a potential group into an actual one.

A legislator considering conjunctive issues is involved in a weighing process. Minimum wage regulation, for example, is a regulatory issue, but it is also a labor issue. Similarly, the 1964 statute that barred discrimination on grounds of race or color in public accommodations was a regulatory issue, but it was also a civil rights issue. Conjunctive regulatory issues link a narrow regulatory issue to broader issue areas of concern to large categories of people such as unionized workers or racial minorities. Yet the narrow regulatory issue may directly affect only a small percentage of this broad category. Thus, a very small percentage of unionized workers were directly affected by minimum wage legislation, and even in the case of civil rights, by 1964 less than a majority of racial minorities were barred from public accommodations on grounds of race. The symbolic component of the link to political groups in such issues is very strong, however.

Two important consequences follow from these observations about conjunctive regulatory issues. First, such issues tend to be very salient to the political actors. Organized labor views the issue of minimum wage increase as very important because of its symbolic link with the larger policy stance, just as civil rights groups link any civil rights regulatory issue to the wider struggle for civil rights. Second, the salience to each group of the particular solution is known to legislators for precisely the same reason: They are aware of the importance to the involved groups of any question linked to the wider interest. The high salience of an issue combined with legislators' awareness of it leads us to infer that the likelihood of compromise on such an issue is low. Rather, each legislator is apt to vote in a manner consistent with the actual or potential voting-bloc support. Thus, a congressman who was strongly supported by organized labor will vote for minimum wage legislation whereas one who was strongly supported by small business groups will oppose such legislation. From what we know of support patterns (e.g, organized labor and northern Democrats), it is not surprising, therefore, that divisions on conjunctive regulatory issues often occur on party or regional lines.

Voting on conjunctive regulatory issues is based on perceived *political* costs and opportunities, whereas voting on subsumptive issues is based on perceived *social* costs and opportunities.

3. The final result of a congressional roll-call vote on a conjunctive issue may resemble the pattern of party and regional divisions observed for subsumptive issues. This does not imply that the dynamics underlying the congressional vote are similar; compromise solutions are not always reached in subsumptive or conjunctive regulatory issues. In contrast, *discrete* regulatory issues involving competing interest groups are usually settled in the form of compromise at the committee or subcommittee level, so that floor votes on such issues are predominantly consensual. Consequently, political parties tend to be less important in such issues, and interest groups assume the roles of principal actors.[17] Legislators, in effect, act as negotiators in transactions. There is no assurance that a satisfactory compromise can be reached, so it is not uncommon for discrete regulatory issues to drag on through many sessions of Congress before being resolved. This tendency is enhanced by the fact that, in the world of legislative negotiations, delay is relatively costless to the negotiators.

Since the largest number of regulatory issues are of the discrete type, it is not surprising that Lowi and others have concluded that regulation is almost always characterized by interest-group bargaining and compromise.

Discrete regulatory issues are those that are neither subsumed under larger social and economic issues and policies nor perceptually linked with large voting blocs. Of course, every interest group asserts that its preferred outcome serves the national interest, but the desired outcome is of direct benefit to the vocal interest group. Symbolic significance, such as we see in the case of minimum wage regulation, counts for very little. Banking regulation is of major concern to groups that directly focus on the financial industry, and communications regulation is of direct and major importance to that industry and to users of such services. Most regulatory bills are of considerable concern to many interest groups, each with a somewhat different desired outcome.[18] For example, in banking regulation, five federal agencies, large and small commercial banks, savings and loan associations, the housing industry, money market funds, credit unions, and many more interests have sought different and conflicting goals in regulatory proposals. In many cases, such as banks and savings and loan associations, any particular House district contains many of these conflicting interest groups. Although contrary incentives are present, this factor leads legislators to avoid making discrete regulatory policy for fear of affronting an important district interest.

Thus, from the perspective of most legislators, there are incentives to inaction as well as incentives to action. But legislators may—and indeed usually do—engage in a bargaining process, both among themselves and with conflicting interest groups, in which the terms of the statute are modified. This is their solution to the cross-incentive problem. Often, compromises are not easy to reach, and for this reason the time between the introduction of a bill and its signing into law may be very lengthy. But exactly how do legislators determine what the optimum policy solution should be? How do they respond to the pull of different, often competing, motivations?

One response is to do nothing, but this can sometimes antagonize every group. When no group's feelings on a matter are particularly intense, or when no acceptable conciliation can be worked out, inaction might be an appropriate response. But otherwise something will be done or attempted. In so doing, legislators are prone to adopt a mini-max strategy designed to minimize their possible losses. This strategy accords with Kingdon's observation that a legislator tends to look for consensus, either generally or within the field of forces with which he or she shares an electoral connection—party, constituent interest groups, and so on.[19] For example, a representative from New York City will strive for consensus among labor and industrial groups but may not be concerned about the interests of wheat farmers.

A simple demonstration will illustrate a mini-max strategy. Let us assume that there are five interest groups in a constituency, each with equal strength. Let us further assume that there are only two issues, and that a legislator wishes to adopt a minimum winning coalition, rather than a mini-max strategy. his coalitions on the two issues may then be (1) $A + B + C > D + E$ and (2) $A + D + E > B + C$. But by arranging matters in this way, he may have succeeded in antagonizing B, C, D, and E and only pleasing A, unless he is certain that B and C value the gain in issue 1 more than they value the loss in issue 2. But in the real world of costly information, a legislator will not know how salient each issue is to each interest group. The difficulty is greater as we include more issues in the legislator's considerations. Additionally, from the perspective of B and C, the cost of losing on issue 2 is even greater than the specific costs occasioned by that particular decision, for they can no longer assume that the legislator will fulfill their requests in the future and must therefore make costly alternative plans to cope with his decisions on future issues. Consequently, undertaking a minimum winning coalition strategy in situations in which there are conflicting views is a very high-risk enterprise from a legislator's point of view.

In such situations a mini-max solution is a much more rational one from a legislator's perspective. He seeks to achieve a policy solution that will not dissatisfy any of the interests, or at least very few of them. In banking legislation, the legislative response has been to reach a solution that somewhat satisfied each group as well as the aspirations of legislators to make "good" public policy. It is for this reason, as economist Gary Becker notes, that "empirically, even small but vocal minorities often have to be appeased: minority opposition is not automatically muted simply because the majority has 51 or 75 percent of the vote."[20] But does this mean that the mini-max strategy requires that the policy a legislator advocates must embrace every interest? No, it does not, for as we will see, the concept of marginality employed in economics is appropriate here.

Why should the legislator in the example above seek to satisfy all five interests somewhat, rather than just four of them in each case? The likely answer is that a legislator, as Becker notes, is apt to use marginal analysis. A legislator is apt to ask what the additional benefits are by satisfying an additional interest compared to the additional losses incurred by so doing. Thus, he may find in issue 1 that adjusting his policy proposal so that A, B, C, and D are satisfied and only E is dissatisfied minimizes his loss (E), because E might require a policy adjustment that will displease A and B. Again, in issue 2 he might be able to arrange the policy proposal through compromise that will allow him to add both B and C without endangering the loss of A, D, or E. Of course, there are several possible hypothetical outcomes, but they all point to the use of marginalism as the better way to maximize interest group support while using the mini-max solution. This dynamic mode of operation also involves risks associated with imperfect information about the intensity of interests on regulatory proposals and compromise solutions, but it is clearly a better way to attract and retain support on discrete regulatory issues than simply building minimum winning coalitions, issue by issue.

## Categories of Regulatory Issues: Illustrations

As the preceding discussion has shown, one of the distinctive characteristics of the major types of regulatory legislation is the feasibility of compromise among congressmen. Subsumptive regulatory issues often evoke controversies over large questions (such as the state of the economy or American society) that overshadow the regulatory content of proposed legislation. Compromise is very unlikely since sweeping and generally deeply held ideological forces will dominate congressional considerations. We can identify subsumptive regulatory issues

Table 1

**Congressional roll-call votes on energy regulation legislation**

| Year | Content | Southern Democrat | Northern Democrat | All Democrat | Republican | Total |
|------|---------|-------------------|-------------------|--------------|------------|-------|
| 1973 | Suspend auto emission standards | 56–24 | 22–113 | 78–137 | 102–73 | 180–210 |
| 1975 | Set domestic crude oil price limits | 9–6 | 32–3 | 41–9 | 6–27 | 47–36 |
| 1975 | Emergency natural gas price exemptions; eventual deregulation of natural gas | 12–3 | 13–25 | 25–28 | 33–4 | 58–32 |
| 1975 | Strategic oil reserve; domestic oil price controls; mandatory allocation; auto fuel economy standards | 44–35 | 180–5 | 224–40 | 31–108 | 225–148 |
| 1976 | Energy conservation standards in buildings | 4–9 | 33–4 | 37–13 | 15–22 | 52–35 |
| 1976 | Deregulate natural gas sold by small producers | 25–61 | 147–40 | 171–101 | 33–93 | 205–194 |
| 1978 | Decontrol natural gas by 1985 | 12–7 | 28–15 | 40–22 | 17–20 | 57–42 |

by their hierarchical relationship to macroeconomic or other large social policies, and by the rarity of unanimity among congressmen. Thus, subsumptive issues are often decided by narrow vote margins. Further, because of the ideogical heterogeneity within the congressional Democratic and Republican delegations, we should also see little intraparty or interparty unity.

One recent subsumptive regulatory issue is energy regulation. Specifically, the question of whether to deregulate the price of natural gas involved much more than the technical solution to the problem of getting fuel from producers, suppliers, and distributors to consumers. Natural gas pricing policies have immediate effects on redistribution of income (by region, income group, etc.), foreign policy, and future industrial growth. A sample of congressional roll-call votes in Table 1 reveals the nature of such energy regulation legislation. Each bill listed involved issues with major implications for the operation of large segments of the American economy and the cost of energy to private and commercial consumers. Like the Reed-Bulwinkle bill in the 1940s, many of the regulatory questions about energy in the 1970s were imbued with enough significance so that regulation *per se* was not the subject of dispute, and regional and party differences divided both Congress and the two political parties.

Table 2

**Congressional roll-call votes on minimum-wage increase legislation**

| Year | Southern Democrat | Northern Democrat | All Democrat | Repub- lican | Total |
|------|------------------|-------------------|--------------|--------------|-------|
| 1960 | 54–39 | 171–1 | 225–40 | 116–32 | 341–72 |
| 1961 | 54–38 | 154–5 | 208–43 | 133–35 | 341–78 |
| 1966 | 40–51 | 174–4 | 214–56 | 89–38 | 303–93 |
| 1972 | 52–26 | 160–2 | 212–28 | 118–50 | 330–78 |
| 1973 | 57–24 | 151–2 | 208–26 | 79–104 | 287–130 |
| 1974 | 70–10 | 150–1 | 250–11 | 155–26 | 375–37 |
| 1977 | 71–15 | 177–5 | 282–20 | 61–76 | 309–96 |

As for conjunctive regulatory issues, in which a narrow regulatory question is linked to a broad area of particular concern to a group or class of people, the regulatory issue is salient to that group and therefore to congressmen, making compromise difficult. Thus, we would expect conjunctive regulatory issues to be resolved in nonconsensual congressional votes, but because of the political organization and experience of the affected groups, narrow vote margins should be relatively rare. Similarly, party and regional patterns should be observed in roll-call votes, but such differences should be less emphatic and less consistent than with subsumptive regulatory issues.

Minimum wage regulation is a good example of a conjunctive issue. The regulatory issue is connected to another issue of particular interest to large categories of people. With minimum wage regulation, the question for congressmen is not simply whether government should regulate wages, but also how organized labor, business groups, and particular industries will respond to an increase in the minimum wage. Whereas Democrats may be more likely than Republicans to be ideologically disposed to favor such legislation, they may also be likely to consider the argument that minimum wage increases will increase teenage unemployment. A sample of congressional roll-call votes on minimum wage increases (Table 2) indicates consistency over the years in several patterns: Most votes passed by similar margins, Republicans and Democrats voted in similar proportions for increases, and southern Democrats were always less supportive than northern Democrats. While these data do not prove our generalizations about conjunctive regulatory issues, they suggest that this type of legislation, marked by the attention of voting blocs, generally is passed by nonunanimous (yet somewhat consensual) votes.

Finally, discrete regulatory issues, which produce direct benefits or costs to regulated industries or their customers, are usually resolved in compromises that result from the active participation of well-defined groups in procedures re-

Table 3

**Congressional roll-call votes on consumer regulatory legislation**

| Year | Content | Southern Democrat | Northern Democrat | All Democrat | Repub-lican | Total |
|------|---------|-------------------|-------------------|--------------|-------------|-------|
| 1962 | Drug act | 19–0 | 29–0 | 48–0 | 30–0 | 78–0 |
| 1965 | Cigarette labels | 15–1 | 31–4 | 46–5 | 26–0 | 72–5 |
| 1965 | Auto safety | 84–0 | 162–0 | 246–0 | 125–0 | 371–0 |
| 1965 | Packaging & labelling (House) | 62–4 | 135–1 | 197–5 | 103–3 | 300–8 |
| 1966 | Packaging & labelling (Senate) | 19–1 | 38–0 | 57–1 | 15–18 | 72–19 |
| 1966 | Tire safety | 17–0 | 37–0 | 54–0 | 25–0 | 79–0 |
| 1967 | Flammable fabrics | 66–0 | 125–0 | 191–0 | 154–0 | 345–0 |
| 1967 | Truth in lending | 18–0 | 38–0. | 56–0 | 36–0 | 92–0 |
| 1967 | Auto safety | 72–0 | 113–1 | 185–1 | 159–1 | 344–2 |
| 1969 | Cigarette advertising | 10–5 | 31–0 | 41–5 | 29–2 | 70–7 |
| 1969 | Toy safety | 69–0 | 113–0 | 186–0 | 145–0 | 327–0 |
| 1971 | Auto repair costs | 16–0 | 34–0 | 50–0 | 39–4 | 89–4 |
| 1972 | Auto repair costs | 47–10 | 103–1 | 150–11 | 104–27 | 254–38 |
| 1972 | CPSC | 52–24 | 141–3 | 193–27 | 126–23 | 319–50 |
| 1973 | Lead paint | 65–1 | 136–0 | 201–1 | 167–10 | 368–11 |
| 1974 | CPSC | 45–28 | 150–1 | 195–29 | 98–65 | 293–94 |
| 1975 | DES (Diethylstilbestrol) | 8–7 | 36–3 | 44–10 | 17–19 | 61–29 |
| 1975 | Truth in leasing | 71–10 | 170–6 | 241–16 | 98–25 | 339–41 |
| 1975 | Agency for consumer protection | 28–55 | 160–25 | 188–80 | 20–119 | 208–199 |
| 1980 | Commercial motor vehicle safety | 16–2 | 27–5 | 43–7 | 26–9 | 69–16 |

moved from the most visible partisan political arena—the floor of Congress. Thus we expect these discrete issues to be settled by consensual floor votes, with the corollary that the parties are united in their support for the legislation. Since the political nature of the issues promotes a resolution at a less visible level, there is little incentive for parties to press for ideological or programmatic rigor on final roll-call votes.

Consumer and product safety regulatory legislation in the 1960s provides an example of a discrete regulatory issue and how it can evolve into a conjunctive or subsumptive issue over time.[21] From a selected sample of congressional roll-call votes in Table 3, we can see how this has occurred. The early bills were marked by compromises and weakening of original legislation, which resulted from intense lobbying by particular industry groups and self-proclaimed consumer groups. For example, the 1962 drug amendments were passed only after provisions forbidding patents on drugs were scrapped (and after the thalidomide crisis mobilized presidential and public support for action).[22] The 1965 Cigarette Labeling and Advertising Act was largely the result of a retreat from an FTC cigarette package warning label (which included the words "dangerous," "death," and "cancer") to a warning using the word "hazardous." The Truth-in-Lending Act of 1967 was unanimously passed largely because of the "widespread conviction among lenders that the act did *not mean* a thing and would not alter consumers' purchasing or borrowing patterns at all."[23] While not all of the consensual consumer votes of the 1960s can be categorized as discrete issues, the discrete pattern generally applied during that time. Consumer issues were marked more by the involvement of particular interest groups than by larger concerns.

During the 1970s, however, the nature of consumer and product safety regulation underwent a dramatic shift from a series of ad hoc corrections to specific problems to a political movement and a symbol of government involvement in private decisions. First, consumers became organized. The Consumer Federation of America, formed in 1968, now consists of about two hundred member organizations and employs full-time lobbyists in Washington. With this development activist consumers became, at least potentially, a voting bloc capable of linking congressional behavior on consumer legislation to the electoral behavior of a very large group of affected people—thus making consumer legislation less discrete and more conjunctive.

Second, proconsumer regulation fell under the scrutiny of the deregulatory campaigners of the 1970s. Various scholars and government agencies began to estimate the burden on the American economy of the regulatory controls imposed during the 1960s, and new legislation was subjected to debate in cost-benefit terms.[24] For example, in 1978 the cost of automobile safety features was estimated to add between $250 (according to the National Highway and Traffic Safety Administration) and $666 (according to the Joint Economic Committee) to the price of a new passenger car. These figures were then related to broader issues, such as the competitiveness of American automobiles against foreign imports and the resultant effects on the automotive sector of the economy. Consumer protection had become much more than a regulatory issue; it was now a macroeconomic issue.

The roll-call data in Table 3 suggest that these shifts were realized in congressional behavior. Although the nature of the particular regulatory issues was not constant here, there appears to be a clear trend in congressional voting patterns away from the discrete (consensual) issue responses of the 1960s to more conflictual votes in the 1970s.

## Conclusion

We began by asking whether electoral and partisan politics affect regulatory policy. As the foregoing has shown, the answer is complex. If electoral politics do have an effect on the direction of regulation, it is most likely only at the subsumptive or conjunctive level. While these types of issues are often the more visible regulatory considerations (due to their ideological or large-group connotations), they are overshadowed in quantity by discrete issues. Most regulatory questions are resolved in Congress by quiet compromises among those affected, in arenas where neither political parties nor electoral matters are likely to intrude.

## Notes

1. One notable exception to the general disregard of party was economist George Stigler. He argued that information and organizational costs for political participants provide incentives to find "representatives organized in (disciplined by) firms which are called political parties or machines," and that "the industry which seeks regulation must be prepared to pay with the two things a party needs: votes and resources." ("The Theory of Economic Regulation," *Bell Journal of Economics* [Spring 1971]:11-12.) In drawing the conclusion that smaller industries are thus "effectively precluded from the political process," he greatly overestimated the power of parties and oversimplified the regulatory process. And, like many others, Stigler offered no evidence of the central role of parties as the distributors of regulatory favors.

2. For example, Charles O. Jones, *Clean Air: The Policies and Politics of Pollution Control* (Pittsburgh: University of Pittsburgh Press, 1975), ch. 7; and Mark V. Nadel, "Making Regulatory Policy," in *Making Economic Policy in Congress*, ed. Allen Schick (Washington, D.C.: American Enterprise Institute, 1983). Nadel distinguishes between the role of parties in economic regulation and in social regulation.

3. Theodore J. Lowi, "American Business, Public Policy, Case Studies and Political Theory," *World Politics* 16 (July 1964):677-715. See also David Truman, *The Governmental Process* (New York: Knopf, 1951).

4. Theodore J. Lowi, *The End of Liberalism* (New York: Norton, 1970), p. 106. In the second edition of his book (1979), Lowi complained about the "congruence of values and ideologies" that have characterized recent administrations, agencies, and congressional parties (p. 90).

5. Ibid., p. 51.

6. See, for example, William J. Keefe, *Parties, Politics, and Public Policy in America*, 3d ed. (New York: Holt, Rinehart, and Winston, 1980), ch. 5.

7. Aage R. Clausen, *How Congressmen Decide* (New York: St. Martin's, 1973); Richard F. Fenno, Jr., *Congressmen in Committees* (Boston: Little, Brown, 1973).

8. David E. Price, "Congressional Committees in the Policy Process, in *Congress Reconsidered*, 2d ed., ed. Lawrence D. Dodd and Bruce I. Oppenheimer (Washington, D.C.: Congressional Quarterly Press, 1981), p. 161.

9. Benjamin Ginsberg, "Elections and Public Policy," *American Political Science Review* 70, 1 (March 1976):41-49.

10. For example, the Carter Administration, through its Regulatory Advisory Review Group, selectively intervened in the publication of new regulations, but only ten to twenty per year. In March 1978 Carter issued Executive Order 12044, which required the "nonindependent" federal agencies to analyze the economic consequences of large-scale proposed regulations.

11. See the discussion between Stuart Eisenstadt and Calvin Collier (*Regulation* [September/October 1980]) on the 1980 Carter and Reagan platforms. The basic disputes were more over how to deregulate than over whether to do so.

12. See W. G. Runciman, *Social Science and Political Theory*, 2d ed. (Cambridge: Cambridge University Press, 1969), pp. 11-21, and I. C. Jarvie, *The Revolution in Anthropology* (Chicago: Henry Regnery, 1967), ch. 5.

13. Alan Stone, "State and Market: Economic Regulation and the Great Productivity Debate," in *The Hidden Election*, ed. Thomas Ferguson and Joel Rogers (New York: Pantheon, 1981), pp. 247-54.

14. See *United States v. Socony-Vacuum Oil Co.*, 310 U.S. 150 (1940).

15. The following summary is drawn primarily from Ellis W. Hawley, *The New Deal and the Problem of Monopoly* (Princeton: Princeton University Press, 1966), part 4; David Lynch, *The Concentration of Economic Power* (New York: Columbia University Press, 1946), chs. 1, 2, 7, and 9; and John G. Schott, *The Railroad Monopoly* (Washington, D.C.: Public Affairs Institute, 1950), chs. 1 and 10.

16. Hawley, *The New Deal*, pp. 387-88.

17. The role of interest groups in the regulatory process is discussed in Roger G. Noll and Bruce M. Owen, *The Political Economy of Deregulation* (Washington, D.C.: American Enterprise Institute, 1983), but their concern is primarily with the incentives for interest groups to participate at the agency level rather than at the legislative level. Their discussion focuses more on the behavior of groups than on their effectiveness. We would expect significant differences in the role of interest groups at the agency and congressional levels in view of the greater economic and procedural opportunities for group participation in the administrative process.

18. These issues would fit into the high pubic salience/high-conflict policy areas discussed by David E. Price, "Policy Making in Congressional Committees: The Impact of 'Environmental' Factors," *American Political Science Review* 72 (June 1978):548-74.

19. John W. Kingdon, *Congressional Voting Decisions* (New York: Harper and Row, 1973), ch. 10.

20. Gary Becker, "Comment on Sam Peltzman's 'Toward a More General Theory of Regulation,'" *Journal of Law and Economics* 19 (August 1976):245.

21. Price, "Policy Making," p. 562.

22. Richard Harris, *The Real Voice* (New York: Macmillan, 1964).

23. Alan Stone, *Economic Regulation and the Public Interest* (Ithaca: Cornell University Press, 1977), p. 241. Emphasis in original.

24. See the studies in James C. Miller III and Bruce Yandle, eds., *Benefit-Cost Analyses of Social Regulation* (Washington, D.C.: American Enterprise Institute, 1979).

## 1.4

# The Impact of the Voting Rights Act on Southern Welfare Systems

## Richard F. Bensel and M. Elizabeth Sanders

The American South has been something of an anomaly in most studies of the connection between voting and policy outcomes.[1] For one thing, the region never seems to participate in "critical elections," those periodic reorganizations of national party coalitions that result in major adjustments of the policy concerns of the American state. The South remained solidly Democratic from the end of Reconstruction until the middle 1960s, largely unaffected by the realigning elections of 1896 or 1932 (and some would include, 1912). By reconciling a traditional identification with the Democratic party and Republican voting predilections, southerners have also mocked the common assumption that party identification, viewed nationally, can account for incremental policy change over shorter spans of time. In sum, the South has not fit well into the conventional vision of a national polity organized by national parties and linked, through opinion surveys, into a national dialogue.

In the space available to us here, we cannot offer a fully developed alternative interpretation of the connection between voting and policy that reconciles the southern anomaly. We can, however, suggest what a political economy approach to analysis would look like as a supplement to more traditional interpretations. We can also point out that much of "southern exceptionalism" can be traced, at an intermediate level, to the highly manipulated shape of the electorate. Much of this manipulation, of course, has had as its object the exclusion or inclusion of blacks in the voting rolls. Major changes in southern policy preferences can, for example, be traced to black voting during Reconstruction, disfranchisement at

Richard F. Bensel and M. Elizabeth Sanders teach at the New School for Social Research.

the turn of the century, and reentry into the electorate with passage of the 1965 Voting Rights Act.

In this study, we trace the impact of the last of these manipulations on the local delivery of welfare benefits. The dramatic transformation of southern welfare policy that followed in the wake of suffrage expansion did not herald the region's entrance into the national mainstream, but this transformation did dramatically weaken the political underpinnings of a hitherto feudalistic agricultural economy. Furthermore, while southern politics has retained its anomalous place in the national system, the impact of suffrage expansion on welfare delivery fulfills most expectations of the connection between voting and policy in classical democratic theory. Southern welfare policy changed in a way that met the clearly defined and almost universally held demands of the electorate.

## Welfare in the Plantation Economy

Before 1965, the situation of low-income families in the South—particularly black families—was dismal.[2] Although the impoverished southern economy could not have supported a generous social welfare system in any event, it is hard to escape the conclusion that elites in the region went to extreme lengths to discourage welfare dependence. The plantation economy traditionally rested on four political devices which served to maintain a large pool of very low wage, unskilled labor. Perhaps the most important of these devices was a panoply of restrictive suffrage laws that reduced the laborers to political impotence. The second was a primitive system of public education (education, it was widely believed in the plantation South, only spoiled good field hands). In addition, the agrarian elite discouraged the development of a high wage, skilled industrial base that might either lure away their own workers or attract outsiders into their "closed" society. Finally, there was the welfare system—or, rather, the lack of one.

Welfare benefits in the South have always been extremely low. Even in 1976, the average AFDC (Aid to Families with Dependent Children) payment in Alabama was $100 per family, compared to a national average of $229.[3] While the South could plead poverty as a reason for low payments, there was little justification for keeping eligible people off the welfare roles. Since the federal government paid more than three-fourths of the cost of the AFDC program in the South, it was relatively inexpensive to admit new recipients to the rolls. Similarly, commodity foods or food stamps were available at little or no cost to local governments. Even low-income public housing was largely subsidized by the federal government; local governments had only to create housing authorities, document need, and obtain land for the housing projects. In spite of the availablity of externally subsidized welfare benefits, the typical southern black-belt county in the early 1960s had no food program, no public housing, and only a small minority of the eligible population enrolled in the AFDC program.[4] In addition, welfare was not available to intact families (those with unemployed, able-bodied fathers) and "general relief" programs—programs for "emergency" aid and so forth, supported out of local funds—were funded only at token levels. In 1964 in the twenty black-belt counties of Alabama, where well over half of the families had incomes below the poverty level, on the average only 13 percent of the poverty population was receiving some form of public assistance.[5] Without surplus commodity or food stamp programs, without a general relief program, without subsidized housing, and with highly selective eligibility determination for child aid, the working class in the South had little or no alternative to work— under whatever conditions employers chose to offer. This was undoubtedly the way the system was intended to operate.

AFDC, like other welfare programs, is heavily subsidized by the federal government but allows "standards of need" and eligibility criteria (for example, limits on the value of home and possessions for welfare recipients) to be set by the states. Determination of eligibility—the actual enrolling of a low-income person in the welfare program—is a local matter determined by county and, in Virginia, city welfare departments. Because of the discretion available to local offices, there has been considerable county-to-county variation in the percentage of the population admitted to the welfare roles, even where income levels are very similar. For example, in the mid-1960s, only 1.3 percent of the population of black-majority Fairfield County, South Carolina, received AFDC benefits, even though more than 50 percent of the county's families had incomes below the poverty level.[6] In a number of other South Carolina counties with similar economic profiles, the AFDC percentage was almost twice as great (although still quite low by national standards).

The discretion available to the local welfare office permitted the welfare system to be manipulated according to the needs of the local economic elite. Since the neediest counties in the South are found in the rural black belt, the role of welfare in the local political economy can best be illustrated by grouping these counties into two broad categories: plantation and nonplantation.

A plantation county was one devoted to large-scale production of a staple, cash crop—in most cases, cotton. In areas of the South where cotton was still king in the 1960s, farms were larger and more valuable than elsewhere, agricultural production was much more labor-intensive, and tenancy ratios were higher. For example, the average farm in the upper Mississippi delta county of Sharkey was 437 acres in 1964, and the average value of farm products sold (per farm) was $35,581. In eastern black-belt Kemper County, where cotton had been largely replaced by livestock, poultry, and timber after the 1930s, the average farm was only 162 acres and the average value of products sold was $2,719. In Sharkey County 48 percent of farms were operated by tenants, compared to only 22 percent in Kemper.[7]

Plantation counties were often willing to make selected welfare programs available to their poor populations. The upper delta plantation counties of Mississippi enrolled up to 79 percent of their poor populations in commodity food programs (donated U.S. Department of Agriculture surplus foods) in 1964, compared to an average 15 percent enrollment in nonplantation black majority counties.[8] By taking advantage of federally supported food programs, the land owner was able to pass a portion of his labor costs on to the national government.

The manipulation of local welfare systems to suit the needs of the plantation economy is an old practice in the South. In *Preface to Peasantry*, published in 1936, Arthur F. Raper described local reactions to New Deal relief programs. According to Raper, the plantation owners in two Georgia black-belt counties at first opposed the early depression relief efforts of the Red Cross. Later, however, the price of cotton dropped so low that many tenants could not settle their accounts with the landlord. At this point, he wrote, "the planters found the Red Cross to be a convenience rather than a nuisance, for they could more easily secure full settlement from their tenants when Red Cross food and clothing were available for the winter." The Red Cross "had given the landlords, in sore need of money, a chance to squeeze their tenants dry." Raper makes it clear that public relief was controlled by the landed elite in these counties. Their cooperation was often essential in vouching for the needy, and their claims that certain applicants for relief had refused work were usually devastating to the applicants' cases. While old and disabled blacks were often put on relief at a landlord's request, the plantation owners opposed a more comprehensive welfare program. As Raper wrote in 1936, "Adequate relief will disturb labor conditions in many communities because it will offer more than many of the landless farmers have been receiving from their employment."[9]

Lest any potential laborer be tempted not to work full time, food and other wage-subsidizing "relief" programs were made available in the winter and spring but closed to able-bodied recipients in the summer and fall (cotton-chopping and picking months) in the typical plantation county.[10] As a result, food-recipient ratios tended to cycle through the year, peaking in January or February and falling precipitously during the summer. For example, in January 1964 approximately 63,000 people were enrolled in commodity food programs in Mississippi's Bolivar, Humphrey, Sharkey, and Sunflower counties (see Table 1). In June of that year, according to data supplied by the Mississippi Public Welfare Department, these three counties did not distribute commodity foods. There was no significant cycling effect in the overwhelmingly white, small-farm rural counties of Mississippi, as the examples in Table 1 illustrate.

To have free food available during part of the year would, however, have been an advantage over the meager or nonexistent food programs available to the nonplantation counties of the black belt. In black-majority Claiborne County in the lower Mississippi bluffs area and in Kemper and Maxwell counties in the eastern black belt, there were no commodity food programs even in the winter of 1964. In Alabama, the black prairie soil of the south-central black belt had long ceased to support cotton cultivation; the white-majority counties of the north and

Table 1

**Food programs in selected plantation black-belt and white rural counties of Mississippi**

| | Food program recipients | | | |
| | 1964 | | 1972 | |
| | June | December | June | December |
| Plantation counties | | | | |
| Bolivar | 0 | 25,424 | 18,746 | 18,359 |
| Humphreys | 0 | 11,700 | 5,977 | 5,676 |
| Sharkey | 0 | 6,389 | 4,121 | 4,041 |
| Sunflower | 0 | 19,451 | 10,770 | 10,247 |
| Tunica | 959 | 7,488 | 6,339 | 6,289 |
| White rural counties | | | | |
| Leake | 3,322 | 2,862 | 5,936 | 6,204 |
| Prentiss | 2,064 | 3,857 | 2,784 | 2,643 |
| Tishomingo | 1,472 | 1,875 | 1,480 | 1,775 |
| Scott | 1,923 | 1,895 | 3,280 | 3,241 |
| Union | 1,815 | 2,200 | 2,256 | 2,364 |

*Source:* Mississippi Department of Public Welfare.

southeast distributed free food to their poor, but in the black-belt counties of greatest need there were no food programs. Similarly, the only black-belt county in South Carolina that had instituted a food program before the Voting Rights Act was Horry—the state's largest tobacco-growing county.[11] Tobacco, like cotton, was a labor-intensive, plantation crop.

In the black-belt counties where cotton cultivation had given way to pasture and poultry (as was the case particularly in south-central Alabama), welfare programs were not supported by the landed elite because such wage subsidies were not needed. One also suspects that in the 1960s as the civil rights movement became threatening, the denial of welfare programs was a conscious strategy by local elites in the nonplantation counties—a way to encourage an exodus of the politically intimidating black population. It is instructive to note that almost all of the most brutal acts of violence committed against black and white civil rights workers in the 1960s took place in the nonplantation black-belt counties of Alabama and Mississippi and not in the great cotton- and tobacco-growing areas of the Mississippi delta and eastern South Carolina.[12]

Because the AFDC program targeted only women and children, it had little if any wage-subsidizing role to play in the plantation economy. For that reason, AFDC rates were low throughout the South before 1965, but they were slightly

Table 2

**Agriculture and welfare policy in the Mississippi black belt, 1964**

| Counties with 1970 black majorities[a] | % Black tenancy 1964[b] | % Tenancy (total) 1964[b] | Cotton production 1964 (bales)[b] | % Food program enrollment 1964[c] | AFDC ratio[d] | % Black reg- istration 1970[e] |
|---|---|---|---|---|---|---|
| Isaguena | 16 | 10 | 22,917 | 55 | 8.0 | 86 |
| Claiborne | 30 | 21 | 3,776 | 0 | 7.5 | 78 |
| Holmes | 40 | 31 | 61,331 | 30 | 9.3 | 83 |
| Jefferson | 40 | 21 | 1,846 | 28 | 10.4 | 81 |
| Wilkinson | 47 | 28 | 826 | 15 | 4.5 | 82 |
| Madison | 51 | 39 | 34,557 | 0 | 6.0 | 66 |
| Humphreys | 52 | 33 | 78,614 | 76 | 4.3 | 49 |
| Noxubee | 63 | 45 | 16,956 | 0 | 8.2 | 53 |
| Coahoma | 69 | 52 | 156,355 | 63 | 4.5 | 52 |
| Bolivar | 69 | 49 | 200,395 | 62 | 4.4 | 61 |
| Marshall | 70 | 54 | 46,352 | 9 | 2.2 | 71 |
| Sharkee | 76 | 48 | 56,870 | 79 | 6.6 | 52 |
| Tunica | 87 | 75 | 75,567 | 48 | 1.5 | 40 |
| Sunflower | 88 | 58 | 199,935 | 57 | 3.6 | 47 |

**Summary by level of cotton production, 1964**

| | Mean tenancy (range) | Mean food enrollment (range) | Mean AFDC ratio |
|---|---|---|---|
| More than 50,000 bales | 79% (31–75) | 59% (30–79) | 4.9 |
| Less than 50,000 bales | 31% (10–54) | 15% (0–55) | 6.7 |

a. Electoral majorities.

b. Source: 1969 Census of Agriculture, Area Reports, sec. 2 (part 33: Mississippi).

c. Source: Mississippi State Department of Public Welfare. Recipient families are divided by the number of 1960 poverty-income families from OEO, *County Profiles*. Food program data are for December 1964.

d. AFDC recipients are divided by total 1964 population (Rand McNally estimates).

e. Based on estimates reported in Elizabeth Sanders, "Electorate Expansion and Public Policy: A Decade of Political Change in the South," Ph.D. diss. Cornell University, 1978.

lower in plantation counties than in the rest of the black belt, as Table 2 illustrates.[13]

Tables 3 and 4 display welfare and voting statistics for the seven states covered by the Voting Rights Act. Since racial discrimination was presumably

Table 3

## Mean AFDC enrollment in states covered by Voting Rights Act

| State[a] | % black in county (1970) | 1964 | 1966 | 1968 | 1969 | 1972 | 1974 | 1976 | 1978 |
|---|---|---|---|---|---|---|---|---|---|
| Alabama | 75–100 | 4.4 | 3.0 | 5.4 | 9.8 | 13.1 | 13.8 | 14.8 | 15.6 |
| | 50– 74.9 | 4.2 | 3.1 | 4.2 | 6.2 | 9.5 | 10.7 | 12.0 | 12.3 |
| | 25– 49.9 | 3.7 | 2.7 | 3.1 | 4.0 | 5.1 | 5.2 | 6.0 | 5.9 |
| | 0– 24.9 | 2.8 | 2.0 | 2.1 | 2.3 | 3.0 | 2.7 | 2.9 | 2.7 |
| Georgia | 50– 74.9 | 2.1 | 3.0 | 3.7 | 6.8 | 12.3 | 13.0 | 10.9 | 8.5 |
| | 25– 49.9 | 2.3 | 2.8 | 3.4 | 4.9 | 8.7 | 9.1 | 7.6 | 5.8 |
| | 0– 24.9 | 2.0 | 2.0 | 2.2 | 2.6 | 4.1 | 4.1 | 3.5 | 2.4 |
| Louisiana | 50– 74.9 | 4.6 | 5.3 | 6.2 | 9.6 | 11.2 | 11.5 | 11.0 | 11.0 |
| | 25– 49.9 | 4.3 | 4.2 | 4.7 | 6.2 | 7.3 | 7.3 | 6.7 | 6.1 |
| | 0– 24.9 | 2.7 | 2.3 | 2.6 | 3.2 | 3.7 | 3.8 | 3.5 | 3.0 |
| Mississippi | 75–100 | 10.4 | 8.4 | 9.9 | 11.4 | 16.8 | 18.8 | 18.5 | 17.1 |
| | 50– 74.9 | 4.8 | 5.2 | 6.4 | 7.9 | 12.1 | 13.9 | 13.7 | 12.7 |
| | 25– 49.9 | 4.4 | 4.4 | 4.7 | 4.6 | 6.6 | 7.4 | 7.5 | 6.5 |
| | 0– 24.9 | 2.9 | 2.6 | 2.7 | 2.6 | 3.7 | 4.2 | 4.1 | 3.5 |
| North Carolina | 50– 74.9 | 2.5 | 3.0 | 3.7 | 4.4 | 5.0 | 4.4 | 4.9 | 5.4 |
| | 25– 49.9 | 2.4 | 2.7 | 2.7 | 3.1 | 4.3 | 3.9 | 4.4 | 5.0 |
| | 0– 24.9 | 2.2 | 2.0 | 2.2 | 2.1 | 3.4 | 2.9 | 3.2 | 3.4 |
| South Carolina | 50– 74.9 | 1.9 | 1.8 | 2.1 | 3.1 | 6.6 | 8.3 | 9.6 | 10.2 |
| | 25– 49.9 | 1.4 | 1.3 | 1.4 | 1.5 | 4.2 | 5.3 | 5.9 | 6.2 |
| | 0– 24.9 | 1.1 | .8 | .8 | 1.0 | 2.1 | 2.5 | 2.9 | 2.7 |
| Virginia | 50– 74.9 | 1.0 | 1.2 | 1.4 | 1.7 | 3.7 | 5.3 | 6.6 | 6.5 |
| | 25– 49.9 | 1.0 | 1.1 | 1.3 | 1.3 | 3.5 | 3.9 | 4.4 | 4.1 |
| | 0– 24.9 | 1.0 | 1.0 | 1.0 | 1.0 | 2.0 | 2.1 | 2.3 | 2.0 |

*Source*: (for AFDC recipients) U.S. Department of Health, Education and Welfare, ''Recipients of Public Assistance Money Payments and Amounts of Such Payments by Program, State and County''; (for population figures) 1970 Census of Population for 1969 and 1970; for other years, Census Bureau and Rand McNally estimates.

*Note:* a. The entire states of Alabama, Georgia, Louisiana, Mississippi, South Carolina, and Virginia were targeted by the 1965 Voting Rights Act. In North Carolina, federal examiners could be sent to only twenty-eight counties.

more severe in the areas targeted by the act, and the post-1965 increase in political participation was most dramatic here, this analysis is limited to the seven southern states that came under the original 1965 act. Among those states, Virginia had the lowest welfare coverage, with only 1 percent of its population enrolled in AFDC in 1964. Although the 1960 census did not collect data that would permit us to gauge the exact size of the core eligible population (that is, poor female-headed families with children under eighteen), it is probable that the

Table 4

**Estimated percentage of black voting-age population registered**

| State | 1965 (pre-VRA) | 1968 | 1972 |
|---|---|---|---|
| Alabama | 19.3 | 56.7 | 57.1 |
| Georgia | 27.4 | 56.1 | 67.8 |
| Louisiana | 31.6 | 59.3 | 59.1 |
| Mississippi | 6.7 | 59.4 | 62.2 |
| North Carolina | 46.8 | 55.3 | 46.3 |
| South Carolina | 37.3 | 50.8 | 48.0 |
| Virginia | 38.3 | 58.4 | 54.0 |

*Source*: Voter Education Projects (1968 and 1972) and Commission on Civil Rights, *The Voting Rights Act; Ten Years After* (March 1965 estimates from table, p. 43).

core eligible population in 1964 was much larger in counties with large black populations than in overwhelmingly white counties. For example, in Alabama on average 47 percent of families in counties less than 25 percent black had incomes under $3,000 in 1959, compared to 69 percent in black-majority counties. In addition, black poor families in the South were and are more likely than white poor families to be headed by a woman with dependent children. In Alabama in 1970 (when the census did categorize the poor population by family structure), 25 percent of poor families in rural black-majority counties were headed by a woman with young children, compared to only 14 percent in predominantly white rural counties. Thus if 50–70 percent of the population in black-majority counties were poor in 1964, and about a fourth of these people were in core AFDC-eligible families (compared to an estimated 45–55 percent and 14 percent, respectively, in white counties), than a nonbiased AFDC program would have enrolled at least 5 percent of the population in overwhelmingly white counties and about three times that percentage in black-majority counties in 1964. No southern state came close to meeting that standard in 1964. As Table 3 reveals, AFDC enrollment before the Voting Rights Act was insufficient to meet the needs of the dependent poor population in every region of the South but was particularly inadequate in the black-belt counties.

## Suffrage Expansion and Welfare

Within three years after passage of the Voting Rights Act, black registration in the seven targeted states increased 93 percent, as almost 100,000 new black voters were enrolled.[14] As can be seen in Table 3, white southern officials did not respond promptly to this sudden expansion of the electorate by making public assistance available to the low-income residents of their counties. Although a 1968 federal court decision striking down "man in the house" rules resulted in

Table 5

**AFDC rates and black political success by degree of local home rule, 1972 (black-majority counties)**

| Home-rule states (local control) | With black county officials | Without black county officials |
|---|---|---|
| Alabama (n = 5) | 13.1% | 9.5% (n = 5) |
| Louisiana (n = 5) | 12.9 | 9.1  (n = 4) |
| Mississippi (n = 6) | 13.1 | 11.9  (n = 19) |
| *Mixed* | | |
| Georgia (n = 2) | 10.1 | 12.2  (n = 21) |
| North Carolina (n = 2) | 5.4 | 4.7  (n = 4) |
| *No local control* | | |
| South Carolina (n = 1) | 4.1 | 6.8  (n = 11) |
| Virginia (n = 6) | 4.5 | 3.7  (n = 6) |

some increase in AFDC recipient rates, it was not until the early 1970s that local officials were willing to enroll the bulk of the eligible population in this and other welfare programs. Southern politics—particularly black-belt politics during the period 1965–1970—was still marked by intense resistance to the civil rights movement. By the early 1970s, however, several things had become apparent to white politicians in the South. First, there would be no significant diminution of the national commitment to black voting rights (or desegregation) even under a Republican president. Second, the changing composition of the electorate and the reemergence of economic issues made it extremely difficult for an uncompromising segregationist to be elected, even in Deep South states like Alabama, Mississippi, and South Carolina.[15] Finally, throughout the black belt, courthouses and city council chambers were becoming integrated through the electoral process, and the new black officials were strongly committed to local policy change.

To affect the politics of local welfare offices and to encourage them to hire black staff members and cease discrimination against black applicants required different strategies in the seven states. In Alabama, Louisiana, and Mississippi, there was local home rule. Welfare boards responsible for hiring directors and overseeing the work of county welfare departments were appointed by county (and in a few cases city) elected officials. In these states, as shown in Table 5, counties with black officials elected by 1971 to their governing bodies had secured more sympathetic local welfare departments by 1972 than comparable (black-majority) counties where black gains at the ballot box had been less extensive.[16]

None of the other seven states had complete local home rule in the 1970s.[17] In Georgia and North Carolina there was a mixed system. Local officials in

Georgia recommended welfare board appointments to a state commission. In North Carolina, local elected officials appointed one-third of the welfare directors, the state appointed one-third, and the remaining directors were chosen by appointees in the first two categories. In South Carolina and Virginia, local welfare directors were appointed directly or indirectly by state officials. In these four states, local black political mobilization did not necessarily translate into welfare generosity in the early 1970s because of the tenuous linkage between local voters and local welfare personnel. In black-majority Fairfield County, South Carolina, for example, black officials tried for several years to secure the replacement of a state-appointed county welfare director who was extremely hostile to black applicants.[18] In Fairfield in 1972, only 2.2 percent of the population were covered by AFDC, compared to an average of 6.6 percent in all black-majority counties. In fact, Fairfield County's AFDC ratio actually declined between 1964 and 1969. Thirty-nine percent of the poor population in Fairfield were enrolled in the food stamp program—only half the average for the other black-majority counties in South Carolina.[19] Local black voters and officials were finally able to persuade the state welfare board (appointed by the governor) to appoint a new director, and the situation by the late 1970s showed significant improvement.[20]

By contrast, there were no counties in Alabama, Louisiana, or Mississippi where high black registration failed to elicit a significant expansion in welfare enrollments by 1972. However, in black-belt counties where black registration remained low and no black officials had been elected, welfare policies were probably more punitive in home-rule states than in centralized states, since in the centralized states (like South Carolina) governors who owed their election to strong black support might act to ameliorate local welfare administration statewide. In a home-rule state like Mississippi, a low level of political participation allowed punitive and elite-manipulated local welfare systems to continue. Black-majority Kemper County, with a black registration rate of only 29 percent in 1968[21] and no black officials in the early 1970s, experienced a decline in its AFDC ration between 1964 and 1974. The AFDC enrollment percentage as late as 1978 was only 5.4 percent in Kemper, compared to an average 13 percent for all Mississippi black-majority counties. Only 38 percent of Kemper's poor population were enrolled in the food program, compared to a mean 63 percent coverage for all twenty-two Mississippi black-majority counties.[22]

Further evidence that eligibility-finding by local welfare departments was related to black political mobilization is found in Table 6. For the three states that reported voter registration by race in the mid-1970s, counties are cross-tabulated by racial composition, black mobilization (registration), and AFDC ratios. As can be seen, in almost 90 percent (50/56) of comparisons, the counties with the higher rate of black political mobilization have higher AFDC ratios than counties of similar racial composition but lower levels of participation. The relationship between local political participation and welfare policy is much stronger, however, in the black-majority counties of the home-rule state (Louisiana) than in the

Table 6

## AFDC recipients by degree of black mobilization in county

| State and percent black in county | Black mobilization[a] | Average welfare enrollment[b] | | | | | | | |
|---|---|---|---|---|---|---|---|---|---|
| | | 1964 | 1966 | 1968 | 1969 | 1972 | 1974 | 1976 | 1978 |
| **Louisiana** | | | | | | | | | |
| 50–74.9% | Above 75% | 5.0 | 5.9 | 7.1 | 11.9 | 13.7 | 14.1 | 13.5 | 13.8 |
| | Below 75% | 4.1 | 4.4 | 5.0 | 6.8 | 7.9 | 8.2 | 7.8 | 7.5 |
| 25–49.9% | Above 75% | 4.4 | 4.2 | 4.7 | 6.1 | 7.1 | 7.2 | 6.6 | 6.0 |
| | Below 75% | 4.2 | 3.9 | 4.6 | 6.3 | 7.8 | 7.5 | 7.0 | 5.9 |
| 0–24.9% | Above 75% | 2.8 | 2.5 | 2.7 | 3.5 | 3.8 | 3.9 | 3.5 | 3.0 |
| | Below 75% | 2.6 | 2.2 | 2.4 | 3.0 | 3.7 | 3.7 | 3.4 | 3.0 |
| **North Carolina** | | | | | | | | | |
| 50–74.9% | Above 55% | 2.5 | 3.0 | 3.7 | 4.4 | 5.0 | 4.4 | 4.9 | 5.4 |
| 25–49.9% | Above 55% | 2.9 | 3.2 | 3.2 | 3.6 | 4.9 | 4.4 | 5.0 | 5.4 |
| | Below 55% | 1.9 | 2.1 | 2.3 | 2.8 | 3.7 | 3.3 | 3.8 | 4.7 |
| 0–24.9% | Below 55% | 2.2 | 2.0 | 2.2 | 2.1 | 3.4 | 2.9 | 3.2 | 3.4 |
| **South Carolina** | | | | | | | | | |
| 50–74.9% | Above 65% | 1.8 | 1.8 | 2.1 | 3.3 | 6.3 | 8.4 | 9.9 | 10.8 |
| | Below 65% | 2.0 | 1.8 | 2.0 | 2.8 | 7.0 | 8.3 | 9.1 | 9.3 |
| 25–49.9% | Above 65% | 1.6 | 1.4 | 1.6 | 2.1 | 4.8 | 6.1 | 6.6 | 6.8 |
| | Below 65% | 1.2 | 1.2 | 1.3 | 1.7 | 3.5 | 4.5 | 5.2 | 5.6 |
| 0–24.9% | Above 65% | 1.4 | 1.1 | 1.4 | 1.8 | 3.1 | 3.5 | 4.3 | 4.4 |
| | Below 65% | 1.1 | .7 | .7 | .8 | 1.9 | 2.3 | 2.6 | 2.3 |

a. Taken from *The Voting Rights Act: Ten Years After*, pp. 366–76.
b. AFDC recipients as a percentage of the population. For source of data, see Table 3.

other two states. For the counties with very small black populations (less than 25 percent), the level of political mobilization appears to have a slight but still positive effect on welfare enrollments.

On the average, welfare programs in the black-belt counties of home-rule states (Alabama, Louisana, and Mississippi) had expanded to encompass most of the eligible population by the early 1970s. Well over 60 percent of the poor population (as defined by the 1970 census) were enrolled in food programs in Alabama, Louisiana, and Mississipi black-majority counties in 1973, and over 100 percent of the core eligible population were receiving the AFDC benefits. In other words, the number of AFDC cases exceeded the 1970 census-enumerated number of poor families headed by women with dependent children.[23]

## Impact of the Voting Rights Act
## on the Plantation Economy

By 1978 the welfare rolls had expanded dramatically in all the states covered by the Voting Rights Act (see Table 3), and this expansion took place in the face of efforts by two Republican administrations to slow state welfare enrollments. Once southern black political participation became an accepted reality, local welfare administrators began to find large numbers of eligible welfare recipients among the local poor where previously they had denied that need existed. Furthermore, they ceased to manipulate the welfare system to suit the needs of local planters. As Table 1 shows, food programs showed no cycling effect in Mississippi plantation counties by the early 1970s. There were as many (or more) recipients in summer as in winter.

The broad pattern of adaptation of southern welfare systems to political change can be seen in Table 7 and maps 1 and 2. Before the abolition of the poll tax, literacy tests, and other barriers to suffrage, welfare enrollments inadequately reflected the size of the poor population throughout the southern states, but particularly in the black belt. Although poverty was generally much more severe in these counties, the correlation between the size of the black population and the number of AFDC recipients was low or negative in 1964. After 1965, the relationship between local poverty (as measured by the percentage of families with below poverty-level incomes) and welfare enrollments became much stronger—indicating that the welfare system had at last come to reflect genuine economic needs, albeit in a highly political context. The upper half of Table 7 suggests that the AFDC program was increasingly perceived by local officials (both black and white) as a way of benefitting the newly mobilized black population. The change is most striking in Georgia and Virginia, where the correlation between black percentage of the population and the percentage of the population on welfare rises from zero in 1964 to .81 and .67, respectively, in 1978. In the latter year also, the correlation between racial composition and welfare enrollments is higher than the correlation between poverty and welfare coverage in

Table 7

**Correlations between black percentage of the population, percentage of families with below-poverty incomes, and county AFDC recipient ratios for states covered by Voting Rights Act, 1964–1978**

| | Black population/AFDC ratio (r)[a] | | | | | | | |
|---|---|---|---|---|---|---|---|---|
| | 1964 | 1966 | 1968 | 1969 | 1972 | 1974 | 1976 | 1978 |
| Alabama | .37 | .36 | .57 | .73 | .82 | .85 | .89* | .89 |
| Georgia | −.02 | .22 | .32 | .58 | .78 | .81 | .82* | .81 |
| Louisiana | .44 | .59 | .65 | .71 | .79 | .80 | .80* | .79 |
| Mississippi | .41 | .55 | .71 | .79 | .83 | .85 | .85* | .85 |
| North Carolina | .03 | .00 | .20 | .28* | .08 | .10 | .13 | .21 |
| South Carolina | .56 | .70 | .70 | .71 | .73 | .79 | .85 | .87* |
| Virginia | −.03 | .04 | .09 | .12 | .32 | .46 | .61 | .67* |

| | Size of poverty population/AFDC ratio | | | | | | | |
|---|---|---|---|---|---|---|---|---|
| | 1964 | 1966 | 1968 | 1969 | 1972 | 1974 | 1976 | 1978 |
| Alabama | .50 | .42 | .60 | .71 | .75 | .78 | .80 | .80* |
| Georgia | .32 | .44 | .48 | .67 | .71* | .69 | .68 | .68 |
| Louisiana | .69 | .76 | .77 | .81* | .72 | .71 | .72 | .73 |
| Mississippi | .50 | .57 | .70 | .76* | .75 | .74 | .74 | .74 |
| North Carolina | −.08 | .14 | .31 | .43 | .25 | .34 | .37 | .49* |
| South Carolina | .67 | .80 | .76' | .73 | .71 | .77 | .83 | .85* |
| Virginia | .38 | .39* | .33 | .33 | .31 | .32 | .33 | .33 |

a. Correlations are rounded from five to two digits. Asterisk denotes largest correlations in sequence.

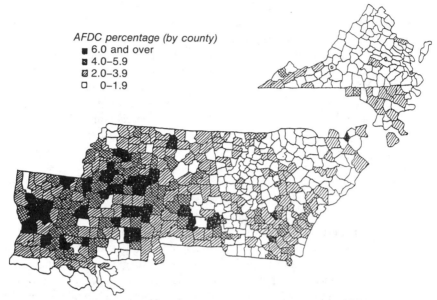

AFDC percentage (by county)
- 6.0 and over
- 4.0–5.9
- 2.0–3.9
- 0–1.9

Map 1 **AFDC recipients as percentage of total population, 1964**

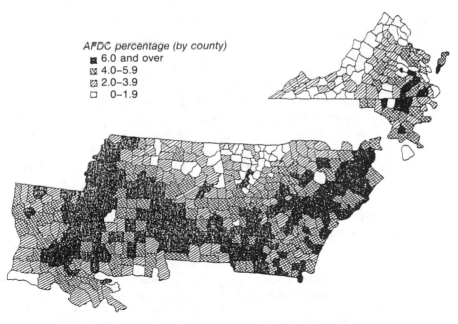

AFDC percentage (by county)
- 6.0 and over
- 4.0–5.9
- 2.0–3.9
- 0–1.9

Map 2 **AFDC recipients as percentage of total population, 1978**

every state targeted by the Voting Rights Act except North Carolina. (The correlations between black population size and AFDC are weak in North Carolina because only twenty-eight of the state's hundred counties were covered by the Voting Rights Act, and all were in the eastern black-belt section of the state.)

Expansion of the welfare rolls was most dramatic in the black belt and, particularly, in counties with substantial numbers of black elected officials. In Macon County (Tuskegee) Alabama, for example, AFDC enrollments jumped from 1.4 percent of the population in 1964 to 11.3 percent in 1978. In black-majority Greene and Lowndes counties, where blacks had also achieved control of county government by the mid-1970s, AFDC ratios climbed from 5–6 percent in 1964 to 17–18 percent in 1978. The perception of AFDC as a "black" program may make it less attractive to the poor white population. In Virginia, for example, the western Appalachian counties showed greater than average AFDC inscriptions in 1964; indeed, as map 4.2 reveals, these poor white counties constituted that state's major welfare clientele in the early 1960s. In the 1970s, however, welfare inscription ratios held steady or declined in the Appalachian counties, even as the eastern black-belt ratios were surging. Accordingly, the statewide correlation between poverty levels and AFDC ratios peaked in Virginia in 1966 and dropped to only .31/.33 thereafter. Similar patterns could be found in the white hill counties of other southern states. A plot of 1978 AFDC case loads corresponds very closely to a map of the historical southern black belt. There was no such correspondence before the Voting Rights Act.

Expansion of the welfare system eventually allowed the rural poor to subsist, after a fashion, during a period when rapid mechanization was throwing many tenants, sharecroppers, and hired farm laborers off the land. Between 1964 and 1974, the average number of hired farm workers in these seven states declined almost 50 percent.[24] Mechanization and shifts to less labor-intensive crops were spurred by a precipitous decline in the price of cotton between 1964 and 1970,[25] coincident with the rise of the civil rights movement, which probably further encouraged white farm owners to lessen their dependence on black labor. Even as these two events were producing a sharp drop in the demand for black farm workers, Congress further undermined black rural employment in 1968 by applying the minimum wage to agricultural laborers. The timing was unfortunate, for, as the preceding tables show, black political clout in the late 1960s was not yet sufficient to induce a significant expansion of the welfare rolls. In the absence of local food programs and income support, many of the black rural poor were forced to migrate or endure several years of severe privation until local policymakers finally lowered the barriers to public assistance.

The hundreds of black officials who took office in the 1970s certainly do not consider extensive welfare dependency a desirable solution to the region's economic problems (and given the restrictions on payment levels that state constitutions and laws impose, it must be very difficult for a family to subsist on AFDC, even if supplied with public housing, food stamps, and medicaid). As the authors learned in extensive interviews with Deep South elected officials in the late 1970s, the first priority of these new black office holders is job creation. Strenuous efforts are being made to recruit industry, in spite of lingering resistance to industrialization among local planters. However, if this anticipated expansion in black-belt industry does not occur, the traditional plantation economy may be replaced by a new, and thoroughly political, welfare economy.[26]

## Conclusion

In the sixteen years following passage of the Voting Rights Act the South's welfare system changed from one that provided minimal support to the poor white population, and serviced the needs of the black-belt plantation economy, to one that increasingly provides benefits to the structurally unemployed black poor. Before 1965, the governments of counties with large low-income black populations failed to provide adequate and consistently administered welfare systems. At the same time, their counterparts in the white majority hill country seemed to respond to the needs of the white poor in an objective, even-handed (albeit underfinanced) manner. The extension of the minimum wage standard to agricultural labor, the mechanization of southern agriculture, the westward migration of cotton cultivation, and the expansion of suffrage to southern blacks all combined to transform the distribution of welfare benefits. By 1981, the food stamp program blanketed the black belt and had ceased to cycle through the year in plantation counties. The increasing access of black AFDC applicants to the rolls had raised the correlation between the black proportion of the total population and welfare dependency from a median of .39 in 1964 to .83 in 1978 for the six states covered in their entirety by the Voting Rights Act. Welfare benefits had become the largest single source of income for the population of many black-majority counties.

While the combination of these political and economic events has brought to an end many of the features of the neofeudal plantation regime, the southern social welfare system still differs sharply from its northern counterpart. In northern states, the vast majority of the welfare population resides in the crumbling center cities of aging metropolises, surrounded by the affluent. In the South, a much larger proportion of the poor are rural and reside in small governmental units.

While both patterns can be explained in terms of technological and economic change (e.g., the development of a postindustrial society in the North and agricultural mechanization and diversification in the South), the southern poor have a clear political advantage over their northern counterparts for two reasons. First, the governmental bodies controlling welfare delivery systems are often small and relatively easily captured by their clientele. This is particularly the case in the home-rule states. Second, because southern states are among the poorest in the nation and the federal share of welfare expenditures is correspondingly larger, most of the expense associated with local expansion of the welfare rolls represents an infusion of outside money (from the federal treasury). Since 1965, for example, at least 75 percent of AFDC expenditures in Mississippi have originated from federal transfer payments. Because local welfare administrators are now much more willing to review applications for public assistance favorably, welfare rolls in the South have finally come to reflect local socioeconomic conditions.

Where the poor were once turned away because they were politically powerless, they now influence or, in some cases, control the political institutions that grant them aid. And, far from being a response to the needs of the local plantation economy, the resulting increase in welfare dependency has coincided with the mechanization of southern agriculture and the conversion of plantation acreage to alternative uses. The poor are significantly less relevant to the southern agricultural economy in 1981 than they were in 1965. As a result, in at least some counties, the income transfers represented by federal welfare programs comprise a major portion of all personal income within a political system heavily influenced by the poor themselves with almost no remaining connection to the traditional rural economy.

This expanding AFDC caseload in the southern plantation economy is the policy outcome of the most conventional of all democratic political activities: voting.[27] The 1965 Voting Rights Act, an exogenously determined political change, led to a rapid increase in electoral participation of the poor, particularly poor minorities, and this participation eventually led local officials to provide welfare benefits that had once been denied altogether or manipulated in the interest of local elites. However, welfare expansion did not occur during the period of greatest political upheaval, but came later after the political clout of the new black voters had been demonstrated and was accepted by elected officials as a permanent feature of local politics.

## Notes

1. This article is a substantially revised version of a paper prepared for delivery at the Annual Meeting of the Southwestern Political Science Association, Dallas, March 24, 1981. The order of the authors' names is arbitrary.

2. Concluding an analysis of the meager welfare, education, and other social services available to blacks in the 1920s and 1930s, Paul Lewinson wrote, "The Negro's votelessness has reacted unfavorably on his general social and economic welfare." *Race, Class and Party* (New York: Grossett and Dunlap, 1932), p. 197. Paul E. Mertz noted that Red Cross relief during the Great Depression was administered by "local committees of planters and businessmen. In many cases farmers used the Red Cross to furnish their tenants." Even after relief became a federal responsibility, "the fundamental problem of the poor was less the workings of specific government policies than their complete dependence on landlords in an exploitive system." *New Deal Policy and Southern Rural Poverty* (Baton Rouge: Louisiana State University Press, 1978), p. 18. Theodore Saloutos

noted that welfare was not the only New Deal program that discriminated against rural blacks in the southern economy. *The American Farmer and the New Deal* (Ames: Iowa State University Press, 1982), pp. 179–91. See also Arthur F. Raper, *Preface to Peasantry* (New York: Atheneum, 1968), pp. 254–69; Harvard Sitkoff, *A New Deal for Blacks*, vol. 1 (New York: Oxford University Press, 1981), pp. 49–57; Gilbert C. Fite, *Cotton Fields No More: Southern Agriculture, 1865–1980* (Lexington: University Press of Kentucky, 1984), p. 136; and George B. Tindall, *The Emergence of the New South, 1913–1945* (Baton Rouge: Louisiana State University Press, 1967), pp. 544–50.

3. Average 1976 AFDC payments in the seven southern states covered by the Voting Rights Act ranged from $58 in Mississippi to $194 in Virginia (calculated from tables in Bureau of the Census, *County and City Data Book* (Washington, D.C.: GPO, 1977).

4. Much of the historical and contextual material presented in this article, including the discussion of pre- and post-1965 welfare programs in the Deep South, was taken from Elizabeth Sanders, "Electorate Expansion and Public Policy: A Decade of Political Change in the South," Ph.D. dissertation, Cornell University, 1978, rev. 1980.

5. Calculated from tables in Bureau of the Census, *County and City Data Book* (1967). By 1972 an average 32 percent of the poor population were receiving public assistance, and by 1976, 75 percent of all AFDC recipients were black.

6. Data from the Mississippi Department of Public Welfare.

7. U.S. Department of Agriculture, *Census of Agriculture, 1964* (Washington, D.C.: GPO, 1964). A "plantation county" is defined here as one producing at least 50,000 bales of cotton. The term "black belt" denotes a soil type but also describes the region where cotton plantation and slave economies dominated the landscape in 1860.

8. County food program data were supplied by the Mississippi Department of Public Welfare; numbers of recipients were divided by the aggregate poor population as reported in Office of Economic Opportunity, *County Profiles*.

9. Raper, *Preface to Peasantry*.

10. Pat Watters and Reese Cleghorn, *Climbing Jacob's Ladder* (New York: Harcourt, Brace and World, 1967), pp. 132–33; Nick Kotz, *Let Them Eat Promises: The Politics of Hunger in America* (Englewood Cliffs, N.J.: Prentice-Hall, 1969); T. J. Woofter, Jr., *Landlord and Tenant on the Cotton Plantation* (Washington, D.C.: Works Progress Administration, 1936), pp. 162–63.

11. Food program information for 1964 was gathered through interviews with officials of the South Carolina Department of Social Services in June 1978. In comparison with Mississippi and South Carolina, there were no plantation counties in the Alabama black belt by the late 1910s (that is, there was no cotton or tobacco cultivation on a scale comparable with northwestern Mississippi or eastern South Carolina).

12. The same is true of lynchings in the early 1900s. Plantation counties had lower rates (of lynchings per 10,000 black population) than other counties. Southern Commission on the Study of Lynching, *Lynchings and What They Mean* (Atlanta, 1931).

13. In South Carolina, similarly, the largest cotton- and tobacco-producing counties (Clarendon, Darlington, Dillon, Florence, Horry, Lee, Marion, Marlboro, Orangeburg, Sumpter, and Williamsburg) had an average 1964 AFDC ratio of 5.06 percent, compared to an average 6.7 percent for the remaining nonplantation counties of the black belt (defined as counties with a third or more black population).

14. U.S. Senate, Committee on the Judiciary, *Hearings on Amendments to the Voting*

*Rights Act, July 1969–February 1970* (Washington, D.C.: GPO, 1970), p. 661.

15. Around the South watershed gubernatorial elections were held in 1970–71 in which racial (and usually economic) liberals were pitted against strong segregationists. In Alabama the segregationist, George Wallace, won narrowly. In Arkansas, Florida, Georgia, and South Carolina racial moderate-to-liberal candidates prevailed. The 1971 election of racial moderates in Louisiana (Edwin Edwards) and Mississippi (William Waller) also signaled a break with the past.

16. Interviews with black county officials in Alabama in the summer of 1976 confirmed that one of the achievements of black-majority counties like Greene and Lowndes was the appointment of blacks to welfare oversight boards and the hiring of black case workers in local welfare departments.

17. Information on recruitment to local welfare boards was provided by the U.S. Department of Health, Education and Welfare.

18. Interview with Fairfield County commissioner, June 1978.

19. Food program recipients (furnished by a mimeo prepared by the South Carolina Department of Social Services) were divided by numbers of poor people taken from the 1970 census.

20. In 1978, 6.9 percent of the population in Fairfield County received AFDC benefits.

21. *Hearings on Amendments to the Voting Rights Act*, p. 31.

22. All food recipient ratios reported here and below are taken from "Hunger 1973 and Press Reaction," U.S. Senate Select Committee on Nutrition and Human Needs (Committee Print), November, 1973, Appendix A.

23. For the "core" ratios reported here, AFDC recipient families were divided by the number of poor families headed by a woman with dependent children, as reported in the 1970 Census of Population and Housing. Since family structure data for the poor population are unavailable before 1970, the AFDC percentages reported in tables 2, 3, 6, and 7 are based on total population. In interpreting the tables it is plausible to assume that family structure is roughly constant for groups of counties throughout the period and that the percentage of the population with below poverty-level incomes diminishes.

24. U. S. Department of Agriculture, *Census of Agriculture, 1964 and 1974* (Washington, D.C.: GPO, 1964, 1974).

25. The average price of cotton per pound dropped from 31 cents in 1964 to 21.9 cents in 1970. Bureau of the Census, *Statistical Abstract, 1978* (Washington, D.C.: GPO, 1978), Table 1734.

26. The magnitude of the new welfare dependency in the black belt is suggested by the fact that southern black-majority counties had an average of 10.6 percent of their populations enrolled in the AFDC program in 1978 (several exceeded 20 percent). The average rate for the United States as a whole was 4.5 percent. For a description of the national geography of welfare dependency, see Richard F. Bensel, "Regional Distribution of Recipients of Aid to Families with Dependent Children," *Texas Business Review* (November–December 1980).

27. Other locally administered social welfare policies, such as food stamps, housing, and education, showed a roughly similar expansion in connection with enlargement of the low-income electorate. For evidence on the policy response, see Sanders, "Electorate Expansion and Public Policy."

# 2. THE NEW POLITICS AND THE MEANING OF ELECTIONS

Over the past three decades, sophisticated communications technology has supplanted mass organization as the ultimate weaponry of American electoral conflict. Until the mid-twentieth century, electoral contests were dominated by party coalitions capable of deploying huge armies of workers to mobilize voters. Organization has not become politically irrelevant, but declines in party strength coupled with increases in the potency and availability of the new technology have led competing groups in the 1980s to shift their reliance from large-scale organization to computers, opinion survey analyses, and electronic media campaigns directed by small staffs of public relations experts. The new political technology consists of five basic components.

1. *Polling.* Surveys of voter opinion provide the information that candidates and their staffs use to craft campaign strategies. Candidates use polls to select issues, to assess their own strengths and weaknesses as well as those of the opposition, to check voter response to the campaign, and to determine the degree to which various constituent groups are susceptible to campaign appeals. In recent years, pollsters have become central figures in most national campaigns. Patrick Caddell, who polled for the 1976 Carter campaign, once stated, "I basically had input into the schedule for all the people in the campaign, the media buys, the kind of messages, the organizational efforts, the dollar priorities." Virtually all contemporary campaigns for national and statewide office as well as many local campaigns make extensive use of opinion polls.

2. *The broadcast media.* Extensive use of the electronic media, television in particular, has become the hallmark of the modern political campaign. By far the most commonly used media technique is the thirty- or sixty-second television spot advertisement—like Lyndon Johnson's famous "daisy girl" ad—which permits the candidate's message to be delivered to a target audience before uninter-

ested or hostile viewers can cognitively, or physically, tune it out. Television spot ads and other media techniques are designed to establish candidate name identification, to create a favorable image of the candidate and a negative image of the opponents, to link the candidate with desirable groups in the community, and to communicate the candidate's stands on selected issues. These spot ads can have an important electoral impact. Generally, media campaigns attempt to follow the guidelines indicated by candidates' polls. Thus, media ads are particularly aimed at constituency groups that, according to poll data, are especially amenable to the candidate's blandishments or whose loyalties are especially in need of reinforcement. At the same time, advertisements seek to tap the electoral sentiments that are, according to poll data, especially salient.

3. *Telephone banks*. Through the broadcast media, candidates communicate with voters en masse and impersonally. Phone banks allow campaign workers to make personal contact with hundreds of thousands of voters. "Personal" contacts of this sort are thought to be extremely effective. Again, poll data serve to identify the groups that will be targeted for phone calls. Computers select phone numbers from areas in which members of these groups are concentrated. Staffs of paid or volunteer callers, using computer-assisted dialing systems and prepared scripts, then place calls to deliver the candidate's message. The targeted groups are generally those identified by polls as either uncommitted or weakly committed, as well as strong supporters of the candidate who are contacted simply to encourage them to vote. Phone banks are used extensively in pivotal contests. Before the 1980 Iowa caucuses, for example, Democratic and Republican presidential hopefuls placed more than three million phone calls to selected voters. Iowa has only 1.7 million registered voters. During the same year, former President Carter was reported to have personally placed between twenty and forty calls every night to homes in key primary and caucus states. On some New Hampshire blocks, a dozen or more residents eventually received telephone calls from the President.

4. *Direct mail*. Direct mail serves both as a vehicle for communicating with voters and as a mechanism for raising funds. The first step in a direct mail campaign is the purchase or rental of a computerized mailing list of voters deemed to have some particular perspective or social characteristic. Often sets of magazine subscription lists or lists of donors to various causes are used. A candidate interested in reaching conservative voters, for example, might rent subscription lists from *National Review, Human Events*, and *Conservative Digest*. Or a candidate interested in appealing to liberals might rent subscription lists from *The New Yorker* or *New Republic*. Considerable fine-tuning is possible. After obtaining the appropriate mailing lists, candidates usually send pamphlets, letters, and brochures describing themselves and their views to voters believed to be sympathetic. Different types of mail appeals are made to different electoral subgroups. Often the letters sent to voters are personalized. The recipient is addressed by name in the text, and the letter appears actually to have been signed

by the candidate. Of course, these "personal" letters are written and signed by a computer. Probably the first campaign to make extensive use of direct mail advertising was Winthrop Rockefeller's successful bid to become governor of Arkansas in 1966. Rockefeller's IBM 1401 and 360 computers—primitive and slow by contemporary standards—produced more than a million pieces of mail for the state's 500,000 voters. In addition to its use as a political advertising medium, direct mail has also become an important source of campaign funds. Computerized mailing lists permit campaign strategists to pinpoint individuals whose interests, background, and activities suggest that they may be potential donors. Some of the money raised is then used to purchase additional mailing lists. Direct mail solicitation can be enormously effective. During the 1980 presidential race, for example, Representative Philip Crane raised more than three million dollars, and the Republican National Committee released some eighteen million pieces of mail and raised more than twelve million dollars.

5. *Professional public relations.* Modern campaigns and the complex technology upon which they rely are typically directed by professional public relations consultants. Virtually all serious contenders for national and statewide office retain the services of professional campaign consultants. Increasingly, candidates for local office, too, have come to rely upon professional campaign managers. For example, a number of candidates for municipal office in New York City in 1982 retained consulting firms. Consultants offer candidates the expertise necessary to conduct accurate opinion polls, produce television commercials, organize direct mail campaigns, and make use of sophisticated computer analyses. Some consulting firms specialize in particular aspects of campaigning. Tarrance Associates, for example, specializes in polling, Richard Viguerie in direct mail, and Rothstein-Buckley and Roger Ailes in the broadcast media. A growing number of firms, such as Spencer-Roberts, Napolitan Associates, and DeVries and Associates, direct every aspect of an electoral campaign.

Most professional consultants prefer to work for one party or for candidates with a particular ideology. Matt Reese, for example, generally works for Democratic candidates, Stuart Spencer consults for Republicans, and Richard Viguerie serves as a fund raiser for candidates of the new right. Many firms, however, do not limit themselves to candidates of any one persuasion. Whereas David Garth is best known for his work for liberal Democrats, his firm will conduct campaigns for Republicans, under the supervision of Garth's partner, Ronald Maiorana, a former press secretary for Nelson Rockefeller. A major New York City firm, Dressner, Morris, and Tortorello, will gladly assist any candidate willing to pay the appropriate fees. Richard Morris, one of the firm's partners, declares, "We're not a political club, we're a business."

At the same time that the technology of politics has been transformed, new election rules and procedures have also fundamentally changed the character of political conflict. The most important of these changes have involved nominating processes at both the presidential and subpresidential levels. In essence, American nominating and selection processes are among the most open in the world, encouraging participation by all activists and giving ordinary citizens an extraordinary voice in candidate selection. These novel nominating processes interact with and provide an open field for deployment of the new political technologies. The two, taken together, make for a more open, unstructured politics than ever before in American history.

Chapters in this section assess the implications and consequences of the new politics. Benjamin Ginsberg and John Green examine the impact upon congressional voting of the enormous campaign contributions associated with the new politics. Richard Joslyn focuses on candidates' complex relationship with the mass media. The chapter by Peter Galderisi and Benjamin Ginsberg probes the significance of American candidate-selection processes. Collectively these essays raise the fundamental issue of how the new technology affects the question of whether elections matter. Is the marketing of political candidates no different from the marketing of soap or perfume, or is there still an important connection between elections and the quality of candidates and what they stand for?

# The Best Congress Money Can Buy
## Campaign Contributions and
## Congressional Behavior

## Benjamin Ginsberg and John C. Green

Disjunctions between democratic tenets and electoral practices often provide grist for the mills of journalists and targets for reformers. But apparent discrepancies between electoral principles and practices can also point to conflicts among the most fundamental ideals of electoral politics.

Democratic electoral processes are potentially important for at least two reasons. First, democratic elections can enhance and equalize the capacity of ordinary citizens to exercise some measure of control over leaders and public policy. Second, elections may open the way for new groups to challenge and, sometimes, replace those in power. These two roles are related in at least one important respect. The opportunity for popular influence through electoral politics is ultimately heavily dependent upon the possibility of access by new groups and forces. Ironically, however, the very practices that may be essential to insurgents, and thus to the ultimate possibility of popular influence via the ballot box, can often appear to violate democratic ideals by diminishing the equity and efficacy of electoral choice.

A prime example is the electoral fraud and corruption that was frequently associated with party building in the United States. Bribery, vote fraud, patronage practices, and so on often violated the canons of democratic ethics and denigrated the role of the individual voter. Yet these practices could also be crucial to the

Benjamin Ginsberg teaches at Cornell University and John C. Green teaches at Furman University. Research for this study was supported by a grant from the Jonathan Meigs Fund, Cornell University.

capacity of parties in a hostile institutional environment to organize the collective
energies and resources of the masses sufficiently to counterbalance the economic
and social resources of the few. The Progressive reforms that sought to end these
practices were sometimes profoundly antidemocratic in intent. And, indeed,
''corruption'' was often a code word used by the already powerful to describe the
practices of what they deemed to be undesirable elements attempting to acquire a
share of political power.[1]

A very similar problem is posed by some contemporary demands for elec-
toral reform, particularly reform of campaign finance practices. On the one
hand, the dependence of candidates on private contributions may allow well-
heeled special interests an opportunity to influence unduly the outcomes of
electoral contests and the content of national policy.[2] This potential result is
certainly incompatible with the democratic ideal of the vote as a mechanism
through which each individual can exercise an equal measure of influence on the
governmental process. Yet, at the same time, it may often be the case that
exceptionally heavy campaign spending, especially given the decline of the party
as a factor in national electoral politics, is the only means through which chal-
lengers can even hope to compete successfully against the superior institutional
resources of incumbents.[3] Like the Progressive reforms of an earlier era, reform
of spending practices may be democratic in form but profoundly conservative in
effect.

This last possibility is the backdrop to the empirical argument we will
present. Analysis of the relationship between campaign contributions and con-
gressional behavior indicates that contributions from interest groups to congres-
sional candidates have an impact on representatives' actions. Roll-call voting by
at least some United States representatives in both the 93d and 94th congresses
appears to be significantly associated with interest groups' campaign contribu-
tions in the preceding elections. At the same time, analysis of the pattern of
relationships between campaign contributions and representatives' roll-call vo-
ting indicates that these contributions are potentially more important to groups
seeking to change legislative outcomes than to interests satisfied to preserve the
status quo. These findings, in turn, have important implications for electoral
reform.

## The Data

Our analysis of the relationship between campaign contributions and congres-
sional behavior is based upon reports filed with the Federal Election Commission
(FEC) by all congressional candidates after the 1972 and 1974 congressional
elections. These reports, required under the terms of the 1971 Federal Campaign
Finance Act, have been compiled and published by Common Cause.[4] They
include the amount each congressional candidate received from any political
action committee (PAC) as well as from any individual contributor donating

Table 1

**Amount contributed to congressional candidates by category of interests, 1972 and 1974**

|                  | 1972         | 1974         |
|------------------|-------------:|-------------:|
| Agriculture      | $    35,000  | $    65,230  |
| Dairy            | 592,075      | 195,950      |
| Aerospace        | 41,422       | 35,232       |
| Trucking         | 24,000       | 121,225      |
| Oil              | 22,650       | 99,395       |
| Chemicals        | 7,525        | 27,895       |
| Food processing  | 26,000       | 62,429       |
| Banking          | 199,893      | 191,000      |
| Law              | —            | 12,957       |
| Medicine         | 828,464      | 1,504,220    |
| Labor            | 3,653,000    | 3,884,720    |
| Business         | 1,781,000    | 1,784,000    |
| Liberals         | 166,000      | 242,559      |
| Conservatives    | 149,000      | 252,805      |

more than $100.[5] Though it is possible that some candidates may have received illicit contributions that were not reported to the FEC, we must assume that these were randomly distributed. Our study takes account only of campaign contributions made by PACs. Preliminary tests indicate that the results of the study would not have been materially affected by the inclusion of contributions from individuals.

For purposes of initial analysis, we grouped the more than 500 political action committees that made contributions in one or both elections into fourteen categories. The contribution received by any individual congressional candidate from an "interest" is defined as the sum of the total dollar amounts the candidate received from all the political action committees in the particular category. The categories are a simple nominal classification of economic and social interests. We claim no particular significance for our categorization beyond the fact that it accords with many conventional classifications of the patterns of interest group alliances in American domestic politics. The data permit any number of classification schemes, and indeed, later in the analysis we break open our initial categories to deal with some of their components. Table 1 lists the fourteen categories and the total dollar amount each contributed to all candidates in the two elections.

Though the amounts contributed by these groups of interests vary considerably, the variations should not unduly effect our empirical analysis. In general, groups that contributed more money also made contributions to a larger number of candidates, so that the average contribution size does not vary greatly across the fourteen interests. Moreover, our concern is with the impact of each interest upon the representatives to whom it contributed, rather than the relative success of the interests in acquiring congressional support.

So that congressional behavior might be compared with campaign contributions, we analyzed roll-call votes in the 92d, 93d, and 94th congresses, that is, the congresses immediately preceding, intervening between, and following the 1972 and 1974 congressional elections. For each of the fourteen interest categories, we collected all the roll-call votes in each congress on which the interests in question appeared to have a stance. Any issue that seemed to divide the constituent components of an interest category was excluded, thus leaving for each category of interests the roll-call votes in each congress on which all the members of a category appeared to share a common position. These determinations were based upon an extremely time-consuming and labor-intensive review of the materials published by the relevant interest groups as well as an examination of reliable secondary sources such as *Congressional Quarterly* reports.[6] No doubt exclusion of the issues that divided particular interest categories means that some important votes were omitted from the analysis. Yet this procedure was essential to allow each category to be treated as an entity. It is not likely that an alternative system of classification could resolve this problem. Any group larger than one member is likely to exhibit divisions on some matters. Psychologists might wish to take this argument even a step further.

Using the roll-call vote on which all the members of an interest category shared a common position as a base, we calculated interest-group support scores for each representative in each of the three congresses. The interest-group support score is simply the proportion of roll calls in a given congress in which the particular representative voted in accord with the interest's position. For example, a representative whose vote supported the position held by dairy interests in 70 percent of the relevant roll-call votes in the 93d Congress simply received a dairy support score of .7 for that congress.

Our basic procedure, then, was to assess the effect of campaign contributions from interest groups on representatives' interest-group support scores. This effect was measured by comparing changes in representatives' interest-group support scores between successive congresses with the amount of money each representative received from the given interest group during the intervening election.

We acknowledge, of course, that analysis of the impact of campaign contributions on roll-call voting cannot present a complete picture of the relationships among representatives and interest groups. Roll-call voting is neither the only nor even, perhaps, the most important congressional activity. Contribution to legislative campaigns, moreover, is hardly the only technique used by organized interests to influence the actions of the Congress. It is often the case, however, that interest groups use campaign contributions in conjunction with, or to help open congressional doors for, other forms of lobbying. And it is not likely that changes in roll-call voting behavior are completely inconsistent with changes in the other aspects of a representative's support for campaign contributors.

We also acknowledge that whereas our results will be stated generally, we are empirically dealing with only three congresses and two elections. It is certainly possible to imagine characteristics of particular congressional sessions that might add to or detract from representatives' susceptibilities to interest-group influence. Beginning with the 1976 congressional election, for example, changes in federal law produced a sharp increase in the number of political action committees active in the electoral process. It may be that our results understate the effects of campaign contributions relative to 1976 and subsequent years. Studies of recent elections suggest, however, that this pattern has not changed substantially.

## Campaign Contributions and Legislative Voting

Studies of the policy implications of popular voting typically assume two broad pathways through which the behavior of the mass electorate can influence the actions of the government. First, the threat of electoral reprisal or hope of electoral reward may induce public officials to take account of their constituents' wishes even when these conflict with their own views. Second, voters' capacity to select leaders who share their own interests and preferences may mean that officials' actions will accord with the popular will even when public officials make no conscious effort to heed the views of their constituents. Thus, in the case of the legislative representation, elections may permit citizens to influence congressional policymaking through their effect upon both the behavior of representatives and the composition of the Congress.[7]

Interest groups do not cast ballots. But these two pathways correspond roughly to the two broad avenues through which their campaign contributions may influence legislative outcomes. First, campaign contributions may affect the behavior of representatives, possibly inducing them to shift their support in one or another direction. Second, through campaign contributions interest groups may influence the composition of the Congress, for example, by helping to secure the election of a group's supporters and the defeat of its opponents.[8]

A full assessment of the impact of campaign contributions on congressional policymaking would require examination of both of these avenues of influence. And, indeed, the broader study of which this analysis is a part is aimed at just such an assessment.[9] However, the capacity of any particular interest group materially to affect the composition of the Congress is usually very limited. Most congressional races are won handily by incumbent representatives. Only a relative handful of races during a given year are sufficiently close to allow any particular interest group's contribution to determine the outcome. Though there are, as we shall see, some very significant exceptions, for most campaign contributors the more promising avenue of influence is through the behavior of representatives rather than the composition of the Congress. It is probable for this reason that the bulk of interest-group campaign contributions are given to relatively secure incumbents, even though contributions would generally have a greater potential impact on the electoral fortunes of congressional challengers.[10]

## Campaign Contributions and Roll-Call Voting

Our procedure for measuring the impact of campaign contributions on representatives' roll-call voting behavior is quite simple. The data include each representative's support for each of the fourteen interest groups in the 92d, 93d, and 94th congresses. These data permit us to calculate the degree of change in each representative's support for each interest between successive congresses. The degree of change in the support shown by any representative for any interest between any two successive congresses is given by the formula $\frac{C_2 - C_1}{C_1}$, where $C_2$ is the representative's support for the interest in the second congress of a pair and $C_1$ is the same representative's support for the identical interest in the first congress of the pair.

To measure the impact of campaign contributions, we correlate the degree of change in each representative's support for each interest group with the dollar amount the representative received from the interest group in the intervening congressional election.[11] Obviously, only representatives who served in both of a given pair of congresses could be included in the analysis.[12] It should be noted that definition of the dependent variable as change in interest-group support between two successive congresses may result in some degree of underestimation of the effects of campaign contributions. However, if we were to define the dependent variable as amount of interest-group support in the single congress following an election, we would be unable to distinguish between consequences and prior correlates of campaign contributions, such as representatives' preexisting propensities to support a particular interest.

Table 2 reports the correlations between changes in representatives' interest-group support scores from the 92d to the 93d Congress with campaign contributions received during the intervening 1972 congressional election and the same correlations for change in interest-group support from the 93d to the 94th Congress, with contributions received in the intervening 1974 congressional elections.

In both years the correlations, though sometimes modest, are generally positive and significant. Taken as a whole, this pattern of associations does suggest that campaign contributions are associated with shifts in congressional support toward positions more favorable to the contributor. These patterns of association can by no means be taken to prove that interest groups directly purchase congressional votes with their campaign contributions; it may be that

Table 2

**Correlation between interest-group contributions in 1972 and 1974 congressional races and changes in roll-call voting behavior from preceding to following congress**

|  | 1972 | 1974 |
|---|---|---|
| Agriculture | .17 (66)[a] | .16 (109) |
| Dairy | −.12 (89) | .15 (88) |
| Aerospace | .28 (53) | .21 (61) |
| Trucking | −.11 (39) | .09 (80) |
| Oil | .18 (56) | −.08 (110) |
| Chemicals | .09 (52) | .10 (71) |
| Food processing | −.11 (56) | .11 (106) |
| Banking | .09 (108) | .16 (116) |
| Law | — | −.07 (49) |
| Medicine | .05 (229) | .12 (260) |
| Labor | .17 (261) | .16 (270) |
| Business | .23 (226) | .18 (231) |
| Liberals | .24 (81) | .26 (96) |
| Conservatives | .25 (46) | .21 (58) |

a. The number of cases is given in parentheses. All coefficients are significant at the .05 level or better.

campaign contributions simply create favorable dispositions toward the contributor. Or, campaign contributions may pave the way for other forms of persuasion by the contributor. Presumably, this latter possibility is what is conventionally denoted by the phrase, "buying access."[13] Yet, whatever the precise mechanism involved, there do appear to exist significant patterns of association between interest groups' campaign contributions and congressional roll-call voting.

The relatively modest strength of the aggregate associations between campaign contributions and changes in congressional support is not particularly surprising. Undoubtedly, there exist a variety of factors that can inhibit the responsiveness of at least some representatives to interest groups' blandishments. Many representatives, for example, might refuse to be swayed by contributions from groups they conceived to be pursuing goals incompatible with some broader definition of the public interest. We could not, for example, expect that contributions from nuclear energy producers would have much impact on the votes of representatives strongly concerned with the environmental and health hazards posed by atomic power. Alternatively, those representatives already firmly convinced of the merits of an interest group's position might also exhibit little or no response to its campaign contributions. Such representatives would likely maintain a high level of support for an interest whether or not it chose to contribute to their electoral races. The most obvious examples are representatives who support a particular interest because they conceive its welfare to be synonymous with the broader well-being of their own electoral constituencies. Representatives need not be given campaign contributions to support corporate interests that are major employers in their districts.[14]

Thus, whatever the factors contributing to their predilections, it would be reasonable to presume that representatives with either a strongly favorable or strongly unfavorable view of a particular interest's aims would exhibit relatively little responsiveness to campaign contributions from that group. The impact of any interest group's campaign contributions is likely to be most marked among those representatives who lack any strong positive or negative predisposition toward the group.

We have repeated the correlations between campaign contributions and changes in interest-group support scores, this time controlling for the strength of representatives' predispositions. This control simply involved partitioning the recipients of each interest's campaign contributions into three groups in each pair of successive congresses, on the basis of the strength of their support for the interest in the first congress of the pair. Taking each interest separately, the first group of representatives consists of those who ranked in or above the 80th percentile of all representatives in terms of the degree of support given the interest's position. The second group of representatives consists of those who ranked in or below the 20th percentile of support given the interest's position. The third group of representatives consists of those ranking between the 20th and 80th percentiles. Thus, essentially, the first group of representatives consists of each interest's strongest supporters prior to the receipt of campaign contributions. The second group of representatives consists of those who exhibited the least support for the interest prior to the receipt of campaign contributions. And the third group of representatives consists of those in the middle range of support before receiving campaign contributions.

Table 3 reports the correlations between the dollar amounts of campaign contributions and changes in the interest support scores of the recipients, for each of the three groups of representatives. The table clearly indicates that there is little or no association between campaign contributions and the roll-call voting behavior of those representatives who gave each interest either the highest or the lowest degree of support prior to each election. An interest's campaign contributions would appear to have little or no impact on the roll-call voting behavior of representatives with either strong positive or strong negative predispositions toward its legislative aims.

The correlations reported for the third group, on the other hand, indicate a very marked pattern of associations between campaign contributions and changes in roll-call voting behavior. It would, indeed, appear that the impact of campaign

Table 3

**Correlation between interest-group contributions in 1972 and 1974 congressional races and changes in roll-call voting behavior, controlled for representatives' support of interest prior to election**

| | Representatives exhibiting *most support* in $C_1$ | | Representatives exhibiting *least support* in $C_1$ | | Representatives *"uncommitted"* in $C_1$ | |
|---|---|---|---|---|---|---|
| | 1972 | 1974 | 1972 | 1974 | 1972 | 1974 |
| Agriculture | −.23 (22)[a] | −.13 (31) | −.01 (26) | −.03 (27) | .26 (18) | .21 (51) |
| Dairy | .03 (41) | −.02 (46) | −.07 (11) | .00 (12) | .23 (37) | .26 (29) |
| Aerospace | −.18 (12) | −.09 (16) | .02 (16) | −.04 (21) | .32 (25) | .29 (22) |
| Trucking | −.17 (20) | −.06 (22) | −.02 (10) | −.08 (10) | .14 (19) | .16 (38) |
| Oil | −.04 (21) | −.10 (24) | −.02 (12) | −.01 (26) | .27 (23) | .26 (60) |
| Chemicals | .11 (35) | −.06 (38) | −.02 (13) | −.10 (12) | .29 (20) | .30 (21) |
| Food processing | −.13 (26) | −.14 (46) | −.01 (9) | −.06 (12) | .12 (17) | .18 (48) |
| Banking | .00 (51) | −.08 (62) | −.06 (6) | .04 (8) | .13 (51) | .17 (46) |
| Law | — | −.09 (26) | — | −.06 (10) | — | .14 (13) |
| Medicine | −.06 (110) | −.05 (126) | −.05 (21) | .06 (27) | .21 (98) | .22 (107) |
| Labor | −.11 (144) | −.07 (161) | −.12 (69) | −.10 (63) | .26 (48) | .28 (46) |
| Business | −.02 (112) | −.03 (126) | −.14 (56) | −.11 (65) | .28 (58) | .21 (40) |
| Liberals | −.10 (40) | −.00 (46) | — | — | .39 (41) | .30 (50) |
| Conservatives | −.09 (21) | −.06 (30) | — | — | .42 (25) | .31 (28) |

a. The number of cases is given in parentheses. All coefficients are significant at the .05 level or better.

contributions is felt most by representatives with neither a strong positive nor a strong negative predisposition toward the contributor. It is esentially among these "uncommitted" representatives that interest groups can build support through contributions to congressional campaigns.

## Campaign Contributions and the Political Process

Among the most interesting implications of these findings is that campaign contributions may be more important to groups seeking to change existing patterns of congressional support than they are to groups satisfied with the legislative status quo. Campaign contributions appear to have little effect upon the voting behavior of representatives who already exhibit a strong positive or negative predisposition toward a given interest. Thus, interest groups relatively well-satisfied with established levels of congressional support may have less need for campaign contributions than interests wishing to increase congressional backing for their legislative objectives.

The greater importance of campaign contributions for groups seeking to change than for those wishing merely to maintain the legislative status quo can be even more clearly illustrated by a series of simple comparisons. Taking each interest separately, we have correlated representatives' postelection interest-group support scores with their preelection support scores, controlling for representatives' receipt of campaign contributions.

To the extent that campaign contributions help to maintain established patterns of congressional voting, we would expect postelection support scores to be more strongly associated with preelection support as representatives receive more campaign funds from a given interest. In other words, if campaign contributions mainly helped to preserve existing patterns of support, we would expect that the more funds representatives received, the less their support scores would change.

If, on the other hand, contributions largely have the effect of altering established patterns of congressional voting, we would expect preelection support scores to be better predictors of postelection support on the part of representatives who received little or no money from the interest in question. In other words, if campaign contributions mainly have the effect of changing patterns of support, then the more funds representatives receive from an interest, the more their level of support for the interest should be altered.

Table 4 reports the coefficients obtained from the correlation of representatives' postelection support scores with preelection support scores, controlling for the receipt of campaign contributions. The findings indicate quite strongly that campaign contributions are considerably more important factors for the alteration than for the preservation of established patterns of congressional support. Among representatives who received no contributions from a given

Table 4

**Correlation between pre- and postelection congressional support for interest groups, controlling for receipt of contributions**

| | Representatives who received no contribution | | Representatives who received $0–$500 | | Representatives who received $500 + | |
|---|---|---|---|---|---|---|
| | 1972 | 1974 | 1972 | 1974 | 1972 | 1974 |
| Agriculture | .31 (319)[a] | .30 (263) | .20 (34) | .26 (48) | .09 (32) | .14 (61) |
| Dairy | .36 (296) | .26 (284) | .18 (38) | .17 (381) | .10 (51) | .16 (50) |
| Aerospace | .25 (332) | .24 (324) | .20 (21) | .13 (25) | .11 (18) | .10 (38) |
| Trucking | .19 (346) | .20 (292) | .09 (31) | .15 (425) | .07 (25) | .08 (38) |
| Oil | .16 (300) | .24 (275) | .10 (24) | .09 (51) | .07 (28) | .10 (59) |
| Chemicals | .29 (333) | .30 (314) | .28 (26) | .19 (33) | .12 (30) | .09 (38) |
| Food processing | .33 (329) | .39 (301) | .21 (62) | .20 (441) | .09 (46) | .11 (62) |
| Banking | .36 (277) | .30 (261) | .19 (118) | .17 (52) | .12 (111) | .06 (66) |
| Law | — | .25 (323) | — | .18 (24) | — | .10 (25) |
| Medicine | .31 (156) | .21 (112) | .20 (109) | .13 (119) | .14 (120) | .08 (141) |
| Labor | .22 (124) | .28 (102) | .16 (106) | .12 (110) | .06 (156) | .01 (121) |
| Business | .29 (159) | .21 (141) | .19 (107) | .10 (113) | .13 (119) | .07 (117) |
| Liberals | .39 (304) | .20 (276) | .27 (53) | .21 (49) | .16 (28) | .16 (47) |
| Conservatives | .40 (339) | .21 (314) | .27 (20) | .18 (26) | .20 (26) | .16 (32) |

a. The number of cases is given in parentheses. All coefficients are significant at the .05 level or better.

interest, postelection congressional support is considerably more strongly corre-
lated with preelection support than is the case among representatives who did
receive funds from the interest. Moreover, the more money representatives
received from an interest, the weaker the association between preelection and
postelection roll-call voting behavior. These patterns of associations suggest that
the greater the amount of contributions received from an interest by congression-
al representatives, the more the representatives' roll-call support for that interest
tended to change. Conversely, the less money representatives received from an
interest, the less their support for that interest tended to change.

These findings are based upon very simple comparisons and need to be
buttressed by a much more sophisticated form of analysis than we have used.
Nevertheless, the findings would appear to support the contention that campaign
contributions are much more likely to be important to groups seeking to change
legislative behavior than they are to interests satisfied with the legislative status
quo. It is principally *in the absence* of campaign contributions that patterns of
legislative support for interest groups change least from one Congress to the next.

It is very likely for just this reason that the heaviest contributors to congres-
sional campaigns often tend to be what might be termed ''insurgent interests.''
For example, antiwar groups were among the largest contributors to congression-
al campaigns in 1972.[15] Similarly, among the PACs associated with business
firms in 1972 and 1974, the forty that contributed the largest total amounts to
congressional races represented relatively small firms attempting to enter new
markets or seeking larger shares of existing markets against the opposition of
well-entrenched rivals and, sometimes, the constellation of legislative and bu-
reaucratic forces supporting those rivals.[16]

The case of one particular insurgent economic interest group is revealing.
In 1972, dairy interests contributed approximately seventeen times as much
money to congressional campaigns as all other agricultural interest groups com-
bined. Through the 1950s, dairy farmers had simply been a part of the general
farm lobby, which formed one point of a well-known ''iron triangle'' between an
interest group, a congressional committee, and a bureaucratic agency. In the
1960s, however, disputes concerning agricultural price supports led dairy farm-
ers to break with the farm lobby. Essentially, increased price supports for the
commodities fed to cattle raised dairy farmers' costs, but other members of the
farm lobby refused to back compensatory increases in milk prices. The problem
that dairy farmers faced in attempting to mount an independent lobbying effort
was that their legislative goals were now thwarted by precisely the agricultural
''iron triangle'' of which they had previously been part. The response of the dairy
farmers was to spend heavily, sometimes illegally—it was dairy money that was
found in Maurice Stans's safe—in political campaigns to attempt to alter patterns
of political support in the agricultural sector. Though the spending practices of
the dairy cooperatives may indeed have been reprehensible, this tactic was one of
the few avenues open to them to break the stranglehold of rival farm interests on
national agricultural policy.[17]

## Electoral Reform

"Special interests," Senator Edward Kennedy has asserted, "are doing their best to buy every senator, every representative and every issue in sight. . . . [The Senate and House are] awash in a sea of special interest campaign contributions and special interest lobbying."[18]

Kennedy's assertion is not at all inconsistent with the facts of American political life. Special interests do contribute large amounts of money to congressional candidates. And our findings indicate that these campaign contributions do influence the roll-call voting behavior of congressional representatives. Members of Congress strongly committed or firmly opposed to an interest group appear unlikely to be swayed by monetary rewards. But, those representatives who lack any particular predisposition toward a given interest appear susceptible to its influence via campaign contributions.

Even if all representatives cannot be influenced by money all of the time, the capacity of special interests to change the behavior of some representatives some of the time through contributions to their electoral campaigns is still incompatible with democratic ideals. In particular, the impact of private campaign contributions undermines the fundamental principle of the vote as a mechanism through which each individual can exercise an equal measure of influence upon the political process. Unlike the right to vote, the capacity to make large contributions to candidates for office is surely unequally distributed.

Yet, ironically, reforms aimed at diminishing the influence of private campaign contributors and thus reinforcing the electoral ideal of equal opportunity could very well lead to unequal results. First, as a number of analysts have noted, reforms eliminating private contributions from congressional campaigns might have the effect of diminishing the electoral chances of congressional challengers, though perhaps the problems of challengers could be eased through compensatory public subsidies.[19]

The problem to which our findings point, however, is not so easily resolved. Stringent ceilings upon or the total elimination of private campaign contributions would be more damaging to the prospects of groups seeking to change legislative behavior than to groups content with the status quo. Interests that already benefit from congressional support need spend little or no money for its maintenance. The elimination of private campaign contributions would likely add to the advantage that accommodated groups enjoy, by removing a potent weapon from the arsenals of potential rivals. It is certainly true that political change is not intrinsically more desirable than preservation of an existing state of affairs; nevertheless, American policymaking processes are already so heavily weighted in favor of those who wish to keep matters as they are that additional assistance hardly seems necessary.

It is certainly true that not all groups seeking to change legislative processes have the capacity to contribute millions or even thousands of dollars to congressional candidates. Possibly, elimination of the political role of private funds would enhance the prospects of such groups. Unfortunately, however, there is no guarantee that the alternative sources of influence whose role might be enhanced by restrictions on the use of money would themselves be equally distributed. And there is by no means a guarantee that the removal of one potential source of change in the legislative process would, in and of itself, open the way for others. Electoral reforms leading to elimination of the political impact of private dollars might remove one barrier to political equality, but, as Tocqueville argued long ago, political equality can mean equality of political impotence.

One avenue of reform may exist that would diminish the capacity of special interests to influence the legislative process without, at the same time, producing conservative electoral and legislative effects. Reforms that channeled a larger share of private and public campaign funds through the national parties could conceivably substitute the legislative influence of broadly based party organizations for that of narrowly defined special interests. However, for reasons that are too well known to require discussion here, it is not likely that congressional approval could be obtained for reforms that made parties the principal beneficiaries of campaign contributions.

## Notes

1. A brief but excellent discussion is presented in Walter Dean Burnham, *Critical Elections and the Mainsprings of American Electoral Politics* (New York: W. W. Norton, 1970), ch. 4.

2. Among the volumes dealing with this subject are Michael J. Malbin, ed., *Money and Politics in the United States* (Chatham, N.J.: Chatham House, 1984); Herbert P. Alexander, *Financing Politics*, 3d ed. (Washington, D.C.: Congressional Quarterly Press, 1984); and Alexander Heard, *The Costs of Democracy* (Garden City: Doubleday, 1962).

3. Gary C. Jacobson, "The Effects of Campaign Spending in Congressional Elections," *American Political Science Review* 72, 2 (June 1978):469–91.

4. Common Cause, *1972 Congressional Campaign Finances* and *1974 Congressional Finances* (Washington, D.C., 1972, 1974).

5. Under federal statute, political action committees are also required to file reports of campaign contributions. The Common Cause volumes, however, contain only the reports of PACs that contributed more than $5,000 in the given election. Therefore, we calculated all PAC contributions from the candidate reports.

6. We were greatly assisted in this review of interest-group materials by the participation of some twenty students from Cornell University's Undergraduate Research Program.

7. Warren E. Miller and Donald E. Stokes, "Constituency Influence in Congress," in *Elections and the Political Order*, ed. Angus Campbell, Philip E. Converse, Warren E. Miller, and Donald E. Stokes (New York: Wiley, 1967), presents what continues to be the best statement of this model.

8. The correspondence between electoral and monetary pathways is not perfect. Constituencies elect representatives. Campaign contributions, at best, only facilitate their election.

9. Estimation of the impact of any interest group's contributions on the composition of the Congress depends on the development of a "vote function" for the translation of dollars contributed into votes received by a candidate under stated conditions. This is by no means a trivial problem.

10. Jacobson, "Effects of Campaign Spending."

11. Hypothetically, contributions made to the opponents of successful candidates might also influence representatives' behavior either by inducing them to diminish their support for the interests that opposed them or by covincing them to increase their support for those interests to discourage future opposition. We tested for both these possibilities and found no evidence that either obtained. Unfortunately, in the context of the present analysis we are unable to examine the impact that interest-group opposition to one candidate might have on another. It could be, for example, that interest-group contributions that helped to defeat one representative might persuade others of the wisdom of supporting the interest.

12. An alternative procedure might be to include all representatives present in $C_2$ even when the particular representative was not present in $C_1$, and ask whether interest-group contributions altered the degree of support obtained from congressional seats rather than individual representatives. Unfortunately, this alternative becomes enmeshed in the problem of the impact of campaign contributions on electoral outcomes.

13. Other studies that also find "access buying" include Henry W. Chappel, Jr., "Campaign Contributions and Voting on the Cargo Preference Bill," *Public Choice* 36 (1981), pp. 301–22; W. P. Welch, "Campaign Contributions and Voting: Milk Money and Dairy Price Supports," *Western Political Quarterly* 35 (1982), pp. 478–95; and John Frendeis and Richard Waterman, "PAC Contributions and Legislative Behavior," *Social Science Quarterly* 36 (1985), pp. 401–12.

14. Our empirical tests indicate that representatives exhibit quite high levels of support for interests that are major employers in their districts whether or not they receive campaign contributions from those interests; moreover, they exhibit no changes in roll-call support in response to campaign contributions.

15. In 1972, antiwar groups contributed approximately $104,000 to congressional campaigns.

16. Interestingly, not a single member of the "Fortune 500" was among the major contributors to congressional campaigns in 1972 or 1974. The explosion of PAC activity since 1976 has altered this pattern, though smaller firms still account for most corporate PACs. See Theodore J. Eismeier and Philip H. Pollock III, "Political Action Committees: Varieties of Organization and Strategy," in Malbin, ed., *Money and Politics*, pp. 122–41.

17. For an excellent account of the political activities of the milk producers see James L. Guth, "The Milk Fund Scandal of 1971," *Furman Studies* 25, 1 (June 1978).

18. Quoted in Common Cause, *How Money Talks in Congress* (Washington, D.C.: Common Cause, 1979).

19. Jacobson, "Effects of Campaign Spending."

# Candidate Appeals and the Meaning of Elections

Richard A. Joslyn

## Introduction

Our understanding of the meaning of elections in the United States has come primarily from the analysis of the attitudes and behavior of the American citizenry. An impressive amount of data concerning citizens' electoral behavior has been carefully collected over the past three decades, and a voluminous literature has appeared concerning the attitude formation process and the electoral participation of both individuals and groups.

Focusing exclusively, or even primarily, on the behavior of the citizen or voter, however, risks the development of a limited and misleading view of elections. Voters, after all, do not behave in an environmental vacuum, but respond to and interact with the behavior of other electoral participants. Research that fails to recognize this may incorrectly infer that citizen behaviors observed in one context represent some inherent tendency or capability of citizens, and it may obscure the broader, systemic consequences of elections for democratic systems. As Page has argued, "Electoral politics do not take place entirely inside voters' heads; what choices are made depend largely upon what choices are offered."[1]

In an attempt to contribute to a more complete understanding of American elections, this chapter explores the rhetorical behavior of political candidates during election campaigns. Candidate behavior is clearly significant since candidates contribute much to the meaning of election campaigns and their behavior represents a constraint upon how citizens and other actors, such as journalists, respond. An accurate understanding of elections requires a synthesis of what we

Richard A. Joslyn teaches at Temple University.

know about the behavior of candidates and of the citizens with whom they communicate.

This chapter is limited to one aspect of candidate behavior: verbal appeals made by candidates to potential voters in an attempt to influence their behavior.[2] This approach assumes that one may look at election campaigns as communication events, that candidate communication is important because citizens are exposed to it directly and journalists are constrained by it, that the nature of the communication influences the extent to which elections contribute to political understanding, and that the types of communication candidates engage in reveal much about the meaning of elections more generally. Although candidates do many things, one of the most important is to tell us why we ought to vote for them. When they are telling us that, they are also telling us what the nature of the electoral choice is, and what kind of message can be sent with one's vote. In Converse's terms, we must understand not only the electoral "message-as-sent" and "message-as-received," but also the "message-as-shaped-by-candidates."[3] Although it is common to presume that the meaning of elections is that they provide an opportunity for citizens to control public policy decisions, the communication of candidates may actually deflect the attention of citizens away from such concerns. If so, the meaning of elections would have to lie elsewhere.

## Perspectives on Candidate/Campaign Communication

Before turning to an empirical analysis of the appeals used by candidates, it will be helpful to contrast three different approaches to campaign communication. Although there are few extensive, systematic studies of the communication of candidates, several different perspectives toward candidate communication have appeared. Most scholarly comment on candidate communication has been critical of the quality of campaign rhetoric; that is nothing new. But scholars differ about the types of shortcomings they perceive, the reasons for these shortcomings, and their implications for the meaning of elections.

The brief review of the three perspectives that follows is not meant to be exhaustive, but rather to illustrate the diversity of approaches to campaign communication and to assist in analyzing the significance of that communication. The three perspectives to be contrasted may be labeled the *policy-oriented* approach, the *rhetorical* approach, and the *ritualistic* approach.

### The Policy-Oriented Approach

Most of the post-1960 research on elections and voting behavior has shared a *policy-oriented* approach toward candidate communication. Although very little of this research has focused specifically or systematically on the campaign rhetoric of candidates, the implicit assumptions of the research have been that the policy-related rhetoric of (usually presidential) candidates is potentially important, that the specificity and consistency of this rhetoric vary significantly across candidates and campaigns, that voters respond in meaningful ways to this policy-oriented rhetoric, and that, therefore, the most important question to ask about the meaning of elections is the extent to which they allow for popular control over public policy.

This policy-oriented approach may be seen in a number of different areas of the literature on public opinion and voting behavior. One such area is the post-1964 literature on the belief systems of American citizens. A number of researchers have attempted to demonstrate that the consistency, constraint, and ideological character of mass belief systems have undergone a quantum jump in the last two decades. Although there is considerable debate over the accuracy of these observations, for our purpose the most significant aspect of this line of inquiry is that the increase in ideology is often attributed to a more specific, consistent, and ideological discussion of public policy issues by political candidates in the post-1960 presidential elections. In the 1964 election, for example, the candidates are thought to have provided "sharply contrasting philosophies of government," with Goldwater in particular providing "an ideological stimulus" and a "meaningful test of liberal-conservative sentiment."[4] The 1968 election included the third-party candidacy of George Wallace, whose "candidacy was reacted to by the public as an *issue* candidacy."[5] The 1972 election was one in which candidate "issue positions were unusually sharply defined,"[6] and it marked the endpoint of a twelve-year process during which there was an "upgrading in the quality of political rhetoric and debate" and an "increased articulation of the ideological differences between the parties."[7] Nie, Verba, and Petrocik summarize much of this line of argument in their analysis of public opinion since the 1950s when they argue that candidates have shown an increased willingness to present voters with "meaningful bundles of issues," with positions "on the liberal-conservative continuum that [are] both unambiguous and fairly far from the center," with "issue choices," and with a "coherent set of issue positions."[8]

Some analysts thought that this presumed increase in the distinctiveness, specificity, and ideological quality of campaign rhetoric was so important that it would allow political parties to "stand as 'groups of like-minded men' offering particular stances toward public issues,"[9] that it might mean that subsequent electoral contests would "be fought along lines of deepening policy cleavages" with issues "expected to play an increasingly significant role in future elections," and that it would "permit or force responsible party government into existence."[10]

A second body of literature on candidate communication has argued that candidate policy-oriented rhetoric not only has had an effect on the structure of citizen belief systems, but has also significantly altered the nature of the process by which citizens make a candidate choice and the meaning that may be attached to a particular electoral outcome. The policy-oriented rhetoric of candidates and the increased tendency of citizens to perceive policy-oriented differences between the parties and to have constrained policy positions themselves were thought to permit electoral outcomes to be interpreted as "policy referenda," "policy mandates," and "popular control over public policy." For example, Pomper has argued that party victories in elections "can now reasonably be interpreted as related to the mass choice of one set of issue positions over another," and Boyd has asserted that there are at least some issues on which "the public severely limits the options of leaders at the time policy is made."[11] Though this literature has become concerned more recently with the thorny theoretical and methodological issues associated with precisely measuring the prevalence of "policy" or "issue" voting, the assumption of this modern emphasis is that the rhetoric of candidates has some capacity to allow, if not encourage, citizens to consider public policy controversies when making candidate choices. In fact, one of the most recent and sophisticated contributions to this literature has concluded that in the 1976 presidential election "the policy differences consensually perceived to exist between the candidates, coupled with prior differences in voter positions on these issues, had a noteworthy effect on voters' comparative assessments of the candidates, and through these invidious assessments, the policy terms ultimately left their mark on final voting decisions."[12]

A third body of research that reflects this policy-oriented approach to candidate communication is the developing literature on the effects of campaign communication on citizen perceptions. Much of this research has focused on the ability of campaign communication to increase the accuracy of citizen perceptions of the policy positions of candidates and has studied the policy-related impact of presidential debates and televised spot ads. For example, the Patterson and McClure study of the 1972 spot ads of presidential candidates focused on the ability of ads to alter the policy preferences and perceptions of voters. Although Patterson and McClure found that there are two sides to political advertising—an illusory and symbolic side as well as a substantive and reasonable side—it was the latter that they found to be both more prevalent and more influential. In their judgment "presidential candidates do make heavy use of hard issue information in their advertising appeals" and "people do come to understand better where the candidates stand on election issues from watching televised political commercials."[13] Similarly, Atkin and Heald explored the relationship between radio and television advertising exposure and the accuracy of perceptions about the policy preferences of two congressional candidates in 1974,[14] and others have explored the possibility that exposure to presidential debates leads to more accurate perceptions of candidate policy positions.[15] Two of these authors have stated categorically that "the 1976 presidential debates produced a better informed electorate than would have been the case without them."[16]

Finally, the literature on partisan realignments reflects the policy-oriented perspective on campaign communications. While generalizations are particularly hazardous here, much of this literature relies upon the policy positions taken by parties and candidates to explain partisan realignments, critical elections, changes in group voting behavior, and durable partisan coalitions. For example, Ladd has analyzed the partisan periods of American history in terms of the positions taken by political leaders on the policy issues of each "socioeconomic" period, and Ginsberg has argued that critical elections are characterized by noticeable partisan conflict on policy questions and are followed by periods of policy innovation at the national level.[18] Rusk and Weisberg have predicted that the recent changes in candidate rhetoric and the organization of citizen belief systems could lead to partisan realignment resulting from a "new position issue [that] polarizes the electorate in a manner unrelated to existing partisan divisions."[19]

Despite the variety of research topics and conclusions that this literature represents, it has three distinctive features for the study of campaign communication. First, these studies all share the assumption that the policy-related communication of candidates is important. Candidates are thought to take issue positions and to express them in such a way that they are consequential. Issue voting, attitudinal constraint, partisan realignments, and public awareness are some of the hypothesized consequences of this communication.

Second, the clarity and distinctiveness of policy-related candidate communication is thought to vary, with significant effects. Some candidates are more coherent, less ambiguous, and more ideological than others, and some campaigns contain more issue choice or divergence than others. Furthermore, this variation is thought to be important since voters have the capacity to respond to it. As Pomper has asserted, "When there *are* party positions and differences, the voter can perceive them."[20]

Third, the meaning of elections tends to be found in the ability to inform the electorate about "policy issues" and to provide the electorate with a measure of popular influence or control over public policy. Although these ideals may not have been fully satisfied in recent elections, the goals are assumed to be normatively attractive and at least potentially approachable. Elections tend to be viewed as an arena in which prospective policy choices can be, and at least occasionally are, made.

What has just been described is currently the dominant approach to candidate communication. Although some do not share this perspective, and some of the authors just cited have a more complex view of candidate communication than has been implied thus far, their voices tend to be overwhelmed by the sheer volume of policy-oriented research. However, it is not at all clear that this characterization of candidate communication is accurate. For one thing, few of these researchers have studied candidate communication itself systemically. Their conclusions concerning the policy-related communication of candidates are usually unsystematically arrived at or inferred from citizen behavior. This is ironic, given the assumption that citizen responses depend upon the political stimuli presented them; it is probably more an indication of the ease with which certain kinds of data can be collected than anything else. It also means, however, that this approach to candidate communication may be inaccurate.

## The Rhetorical Approach

A number of observers have offered another view of candidate communication in which the most salient feature of candidate appeals is not their policy content but rather the nonprogrammatic rhetorical devices that are used by candidates to persuade citizens to support them. Much of this argument has been made in popular discussions of campaign rhetoric where the focus has been on assertions that candidate appeals lack substance, utilize symbolic and emotional imagery, and deceive and manupulate the citizenry.[21]

Within the scholarly literature on campaign communication, two studies stand out as providing an alternative to the policy-oriented approach discussed above. At the presidential level, Benjamin Page's *Choices and Echoes in Presidential Elections* offers a different view of candidate communication, while Richard Fenno's *Home Style* does the same at the subpresidential level.[22]

Page begins his analysis of presidential campaign appeals as a policy-oriented researcher would, with a consideration of the policy pronouncements of candidates. He investigates whether these pronouncements agree with public opinion, whether they change during a campaign, and whether the appeals of different candidates differ from each other. After an exhaustive review of candidate rhetoric and public opinion data, Page concludes that the policy agreement between candidates and the public is considerable but imperfect, that candidates differ most on those issues on which the parties have typically disagreed during the New Deal era, and that candidates seldom change their policy positions appreciably during the course of a campaign.

For Page, however, the more significant discovery regarding the policy rhetoric of presidential candidates is not how representative, divergent, or consistent it is, but rather how infrequent, vague, and ambiguous it is. In fact, his conclusion concerning the *policy* rhetoric of candidates is a damning indictment of the whole policy-oriented approach to candidate communication: "The most striking feature of candidates' rhetoric about policy is its extreme vagueness . . . policy stands are infrequent, inconspicuous, and unspecific. Presidential candidates are skilled at appearing to say much while actually saying little."[23] This discovery, he argues, even holds for much of the policy-oriented rhetoric of the post-1964 candidates characterized by other researchers as employing unusually precise, distinctive, and ideological appeals.

Given the dearth of meaningful communication concerning policy positions, Page finds it difficult to believe that elections could have the sort of policy significance asserted by some of the authors discussed previously. Instead, the ambiguity, vagueness, and invisibility of policy pronouncements by presidential candidates thwarts the sort of prospective policy voting or popular influence over public policy that some theorists consider synonymous with democratic elections. Furthermore, the content of campaign rhetoric would also seem to delimit the educational effect that a campaign could have on public understanding of policy-related issues. In fact, in an article written with Richard Brody, Page wonders if the amount of policy voting observed by Boyd and others is not the result of projection and persuasion rather than prospective policy choices.[24]

Given the truncated policy meaning that candidate communication permits elections to have, Page believes that the significance of elections must lie elsewhere. He finds that two other types of candidate communication are prevalent, and that they point toward two different theories of elections.

One frequent type of candidate appeal discusses general political goals and promises and evaluates the past performance of public officials. Page finds this sort of communication to be vague, symbolic, and susceptible to distortion and deception, but he argues that it also permits a "reward and punishment" variety of democratic choice in which voters exercise *retrospective* judgments concerning the global evaluation of how satisfactory life is. When times are good, incumbents are rewarded and retained; when times are bad, incumbents are punished and removed from office. In this way, a measure of democratic control by the populace through elections is preserved, not on the basis of specific public policies, but by creating an incentive among decisionmakers to anticipate the preferences of citizens and accomplish desired ends, through whatever means they select. Page is troubled by relegating popular influence to this truncated process because of the possibility of citizen misperception, the ability of incumbents to engineer short-term, preelection benefits, and the difficulty of assigning responsibilty for policy performance to any one candidate or institution. However, he regards it as a more empirically accurate view of candidate appeals, citizen responses, and the collective message that an electoral outcome represents.

A second prevalent type of candidate communication, Page finds, focuses on the personal characteristics and personality traits of candidates. This communication allows voters ample opportunity to choose candidates on this basis, not only because the cost of information concerning these traits is much lower than for policy-related information, but also because citizens are better equipped to make judgments on this basis. Unfortunately, though, this type of appeal is the most amenable to distorted and misleading "image building" and has only an indirect relationship to public policy decisions.

Fenno's analysis of the "home styles" of members of Congress is also representative of this rhetorical approach. Fenno describes the way in which incumbent congressmen "present themselves" to their constituents and the way in which verbal communication is used to leave "impressions" of the congressman with the populace. He finds that policy-oriented rhetoric is not a prevalent type of appeal, though some congressmen do use issue-related communication to generate personal impressions. So, for example, one congressman (B) focuses almost exclusively on one issue (national defense) about which there is considerable consensus while attempting to convey an impression of popularity, humor, and trustworthiness. Another congressman (C) is conversant on a variety of issues but is more concerned with remaining visible to his constituents and leaving the impression of being concerned about them. Even the most issue-oriented congressman (D) uses his bold, outspoken, rational, policy-focused communication to demonstrate his verbal agility and mental quickness and to attempt to create feelings of empathy between his constituents' cynicism and his ''antipolitician'' criticism of government.

According to Fenno, then, most members of Congress feel that support within their constituency and their prospects for reelection depend more on how they are perceived as a person than on the public policy positions they have taken. They use issue-based rhetoric not to persuade constituents of the rightness of their views, nor to inform the populace concerning public policy alternatives, nor to permit citizens to cast policy-based votes, but rather ''to convey their qualifications, their sense of identification and their sense of empathy'' with their district.[25] Issue-related debates, furthermore, are not used to permit citizens to exert some measures of influence over policy decisions, but rather are used by competing candidates to convey their ''trustworthiness'' to ''prospective constituents.''

The approach to candidate communication represented by the work of Page and Fenno differs from the policy-oriented approach in at least three significant ways. First, neither Page nor Fenno thinks that taking positions on public policy questions is the most significant or prevalent type of candidate campaign appeal. At the presidential level, Page finds little evidence in candidate rhetoric for ''issue candidacies,'' ''meaningful policy alternatives,'' ''coherent bundles of policy preferences,'' or ''issue-oriented party realignments.'' Instead, policy-related appeals are more notable for their ambiguity, vagueness, and invisibility. At the congressional level, Fenno finds considerable issue-related rhetoric, but much of it focuses on consensually held values and is used to depict the personal qualities of the incumbent.

How is it possible for Page's assessment of policy-related appeals to differ so from that of the policy-oriented researchers? One answer is simply that Page's analysis is more systematic and comprehensive and hence more accurate. In addition, our impressions of the policy content of candidate appeals are shaped not only (and perhaps not even primarily) by candidate rhetoric, but rather by the previous behavior of candidates and the candidate's bases of support. Hence, Page argues, even the campaign rhetoric of such ''insurgent'' candidates as Goldwater in 1964 and McGovern in 1972 was not unusually specific, visible, or distinctive, yet many of us perceived more meaningful policy communication because of previous actions or the types of citizens who were supporting each candidate.

A second way in which this rhetorical approach differs from the policy-oriented approach is in the amount and type of learning that is apt to take place during an election campaign. Given the paucity, ambiguity, and intent of policy appeals at both the presidential and congressional levels, it is difficult to see how candidate rhetoric could contribute very much to the policy-related understanding of citizens. Instead, both Page and Fenno think that the learning that is apt to occur concerns a global evaluation of the incumbent's job performance and the personal characteristics (such as competence, empathy, and leadership qualities) of the candidates. Policy-related learning may result from exposure to other information sources but is not apt to result, according to this view, from candidate rhetoric.

Finally, the rhetorical approach differs from the policy-oriented approach in that the primary meaning of elections is something other than the popular-control-over-public-policy model posited by policy-oriented researchers. Instead, Page argues, presidential elections at most provide the voter with the opportunity to reward or punish incumbents for general policy performance and to select candidates with more attractive personal characteristics. These meanings represent a much more indirect avenue for popular influence over public policy, so much so that Page is uncomfortable with treating them as democratic phenomena. He concludes that "the workings of electoral reward and punishment can, at best, ensure only a rather limited sort of democratic control" while the " 'selection of a benevolent leader' offers only an attenuated kind of control over government action, but in combination with other processes it can make a significant contribution to popular sovereignty."[26]

At the congressional level, Fenno argues that the implication of incumbent rhetoric is that our notion of representation must be altered to allow for behavior other than achieving congruence between the policy preferences of constituents and the policy decisions of legislators. Constituents may want things other than policy agreement from their representatives—such as assurances of access and trustworthiness—and incumbent rhetoric reflects this understanding. Although Fenno is not as distressed as Page is that elections and representation may not be as policy-oriented as some maintain, it is clear that his approach represents a significant alteration in the policy-oriented approach.[27]

## The Ritualistic Approach

A third perspective on candidate communication, one which also represents a minority view among political scientists, maintains that elections have nowhere near the policy significance found by either the policy-oriented or rhetorical researchers. In fact, the ritualists, represented best by Murray Edelman and W. Lance Bennett, find the significance of candidate communication and the meaning of elections to be of a vastly different nature.

The ritualists hold that the most significant features of candidate communication are its irrationality, symbolism, and articulation of cultural values. In this view, public opinion responds to elite communication, which consists largely of myths and cultural ideals (such as "free enterprise, honesty, industry, bravery, tolerance, perseverance, and individualism") and lacks substance concerning public policies.[28] These myths strike a responsive, but noncognitive, chord in the mass citizenry and are capable of stimulating political controversy as individuals differ over which myth to apply to which circumstance. Communication containing these myths tends to be dramatic and filled with imagery or symbols, and its imprecision permits multiple interpretations on the part of the citizenry. The myths themselves are selected from a rigid cultural consensus concerning the limits of acceptable debate and rhetoric, and they stimulate recognition and response from the deepest levels of our consciousness.[29]

Election campaigns, in this view, are a ritual in which mythical representations are transmitted to and reinforced among the populace. "Rituals use dramatic themes and actions to attract attention, simplify problems, emphasize particular principles, and structure the responses of participants."[30] The meaning of elections, then, is not to be found in the populace controlling policy decisions except in the most trivial of senses. The populace might reject the policy proposals of a candidate (e.g., George McGovern's guaranteed minimum income plan) due to the confusion stimulated by the unfamiliar mythical context in which it is placed rather than out of a cognitive understanding of what the policy entails. Elections, then, serve mainly to establish the dominance of authorities and perpetuate the submissiveness of the powerless, and to act as a conserving and stabilizing force. As Edelman has observed, "most campaign speeches consist of the exchange of cliches among people who agree with each other. The talk, therefore, serves to dull the critical faculties rather than to arouse them."[31]

Political observers have criticized the emptiness of candidate communication for some time. The ritualists, however, see this emptiness to be a fundamental aspect of candidate communication and hence not reformable. Bennett, in particular, is critical of researchers (usually policy-oriented ones) who criticize candidate communication and then suggest ways in which elections could be reformed to increase the substance, rationality, or clarity of these appeals. These reformist sentiments, according to Bennett, ignore the inevitability of the political communication of any ritual and, ironically, reflect and contribute to the mythical view of the policy-making capabilities of elections by suggesting that they could be reformed. Instead, he says, one ought to recognize the limited policy-making meaning of elections and realize that their significance is to be found in their ability to "limit the possibilities for political change, broad interest representation, or effective political action . . . while organizing support for the government and reinforcing particular images of policy and society."[32]

To the ritualist, then, it is not the policy-oriented communication of candidates per se that is significant, or even the discussions of past performances or personal qualities. Rather it is the articulation of certain culturally agreed upon values or "world-views." Furthermore, the ritualist considers the variations in candidate appeals that are typically studied to be epiphenomena. Instead, it is the similarity of the myths and symbols used by all candidates that is of most consequence.

The ritualist also does not consider election campaigns to be opportunities for public education or enlightenment. Instead, they "dull the critical faculties" and serve to reinforce prevailing world-views and general principles.

Finally, elections, to the ritualist, do not represent opportunities for popular control or even popular influence, for that is only a part of the mythology of elections. Instead, it is primarily elites who benefit from elections through the legitimation of their positions and the delimiting of popular influence. Nonelites benefit primarily only from the symbolic reassurance that elections provide: "In short, the standard view of elections as policy processes ignores the functions of campaign practices in the context of the election ritual. As a result, it is easy to overlook the possibility that the public opinion expressed in response to campaign issues has less to do with making policy than with reducing social tensions and reinforcing enduring images of the political order."[33]

## The Content of Candidate Appeals

These three perspectives on candidate communication see the content, use, and consequences of candidate appeals differently. Since there have been very few systematic and comprehensive analyses of candidate communication (Page's work being the most notable exception), it is difficult to choose among these approaches on empirical grounds. In the remainder of this chapter, an empirical analysis of candidate appeals in two different formats will be presented in the hope of shedding some much-needed light on this debate.

In the paragraphs that follow, candidate appeals made in a sample of televised spot ads and in the televised presidential general election debates of 1960, 1976, and 1980 are analyzed. Since these are two forms of campaign communication through which candidates may make unfiltered appeals and to which a large proportion of the citizenry is exposed, appeals made there should be especially important for the definition of the meaning of an election and for citizen responses to that definition. The appeals made by candidates have been divided into four categories which match up with prevailing approaches to voting behavior and which will correspond imperfectly to the three approaches to candidate communication discussed above. After the content of the appeals made in these formats is analyzed, an evaluation of the three approaches and of the meaning of elections will be more possible.

One type of appeal a candidate might make is a *partisan* appeal. This might involve mentioning a candidate's partisan identification, mentioning other members of the same party, or describing the similarity between a candidate's characteristics and those of other party representatives. Communicating such information assumes that voters are motivated by partisan loyalties and that the voter

Figure 1    **Partisan appeal**

Partisan Ad

Narrator:    A Wisconsin political quiz. You have sixty seconds to answer the following questions:

In the last six years, which party has twice raised taxes after promising no tax increases? The Republicans.

Which party was responsible for eliminating $322,000 in funds for campus security? The Republicans.

Which party refuses to enforce antipollution laws against Wisconsin's big industries? The Republicans.

Which party claimed a 3 million dollar surplus in 1968 and a 29 million dollar debt sixty days later? The Republicans.

Which candidate for governor led the fight to raise the sales tax to 4 percent? Olsen.

Which candidate best promises a real change for Wisconsin? Lucey. November 3rd.

Partisan Debate Content (1976)

Carter:    Mr. Ford takes the same attitude that the Republicans always take. In the last three months before an election, they are always for the programs that they fight the other three and a half years.

would find it useful to know that a candidate is a "good Republican" or a "loyal Democrat." Figure 1 shows an example of a television spot ad that is primarily partisan in content, and a partisan appeal from the first presidential debate in 1976, in which Jimmy Carter links Gerald Ford with the Republican party.

A second type of candidate appeal communicates the *personal attributes* of the candidate. This type of appeal attempts to convince the voter that the candidate possesses qualities such as leadership, experience, honesty, and intelligence or that the opponent does not. The use of this appeal assumes that the voter is motivated by perceptions of such qualities, and that some qualities, characteristics, or traits are valued in the American political context. Figure 2 shows an example of a television spot ad that emphasizes the leadership, responsibility, and respect of a candidate and excerpts from the 1976 presidential debate in which Gerald Ford claims to be experienced and Jimmy Carter questions Ford's leadership qualities.

A third type of candidate appeal transmits information regarding the *demo-*

---

Figure 2  **Personal attribute appeal**

### Personal Attribute Ad

Narrator:    There are times in our nation's history when leadership, responsibility, and respect are measured not by age, but by ability. This is the time and this is the place. Kennedy, of Massachusetts.

### Personal Attribute Debate Content (1976)

Ford:    For the last two years, I've been President, and I have found from experience that it's much more difficult to make those decisions than it is to second-guess them.

Carter:    This kind of confusion and absence of leadership has let us drift now for two years with the constantly increasing threat of atomic weapons throughout the world.

---

graphic group identities of the citizenry. This type of appeal usually portrays the candidate as understanding and sympathizing with the problems, goals, needs, or outlook of certain groups in American society. This appeal need not necessarily involve any verbal communication, since the visual presentation of a candidate with a member of a readily identifiable group may be sufficient to make the point, and it assumes that an important factor in voting behavior is group interest or group identification. Figure 3 shows an example of a television spot ad that contains an appeal expressing the candidate's concern for the working man and an excerpt from a 1976 presidential debate in which Jimmy Carter expresses his concern for the problems of the young.

The fourth type of appeal that candidates may use concerns *issues* or matters of *public policy*. This type of information is more complex than the other three since there are a number of different ways in which candidates can discuss policy questions.

One type of policy-related appeal deals with the candidate's policy concerns. This is simply an expression by the candidate that he cares about some issue or that the issue is salient to him. This type of communication need not necessarily include any indication of what the candidate would propose to do about the issue.

The second type of policy-related appeal does reveal a policy position or preference of the candidate, but only in the most vague, ambiguous, or symbolic way. A candidate, for example, may be opposed to inflation or in favor of adequate medical care (who isn't?). Issues of this type have been called ''valence issues,'' and the positions candidates take are usually not particularly illuminating about the legislative or bureaucratic steps the candidate would propose or support.

Figure 3  **Demographic group appeal**

## Demographic Group Ad

Goldberg:  So this fellow gets this letter: You have reached retirement age. We enclose a check for 20 cents and wish you well on your retirement.

Narrator:  There is no man in or out of public life who has devoted more time or has been more successful in protecting the rights of the man who works. Goldberg, leadership for a change.

## Demographic Group–Related Debate Content

Carter:  We could also help our youth with some of the proposals that would give to young people an opportunity to work and learn at the same time, just as we give money to young people who are going to college.

The third type of policy-related appeal involves the articulation of more specific policy proposals or recommendations. What separates this type from the previous one is that it is possible to imagine or anticipate a fairly precise legislative or bureaucratic action consistent with the communication.

Figure 4 displays some examples of issue-related campaign appeals. The first television spot ad indicates that the candidate cares about medical care, and the first debate excerpt indicates that Carter is concerned about crime, without any subsequent indication in either case of what the candidate would propose doing about it. The second ad contains a series of vague promises regarding policies dealing with the elderly, and the second debate excerpt contains vague goals concerning our educational system, governmental secrecy, personal privacy, and the rights of union members, none of which would help a citizen anticipate the policies apt to be supported by the candidate. The third ad contains a fairly specific description of a piece of legislation supported by that candidate, and the third debate excerpt contains Carter's fairly definite position concerning a pardon for draft evaders and Ford's recommendation concerning the personal income tax exemption.[34]

In terms of the three approaches to candidate communication discussed above, each approach would expect to find a somewhat different mix of candidate appeals. Although none of the approaches would expect to find that only one kind of candidate appeal is used, the approaches clearly differ in their expectations concerning the prevalence of different types of appeals. The policy-oriented researchers would expect to find a significant amount of specific policy appeals. The rhetorical researchers would expect to encounter numerous demographic group appeals (to demonstrate empathy and identification), personal qualities appeals, and policy salience appeals, but fewer specific policy appeals. The

---

Figure 4  **Policy-related appeal**

### Issue Salience Ad

Hart:       You don't have to be a young revolutionary to say something's wrong. We think that we're the healthiest people in the world—best medical system. Truth is, we're 18th among 23 of all the developed nations. We can do better than that.

Narrator:   Phil Hart, the senior Senator from Michigan.

### Issue Salience Debate Content (1976)

Carter:     But I think that now is the time to heal our country after the Vietnam War, and I think that what the people are concerned about is not the pardon or the amnesty of those who evaded the draft, but whether or not our crime system is fair. . . . And the whole subject of crime is one that concerns our people very much. . . .

### Vague Issue Ad

(Church shown with a group of old people)

Narrator:   For them, his unequaled accomplishments on behalf of the elderly are more than statistics, for them they are life itself.

Church:     They're proud people and they ought to be entitled as a matter of right to a decent retirement income and adequate medical care. That's a pretty modest program for a country as rich as ours.

Old Man:    Boy, I guess that's correct.

Narrator:   Frank Church, Idaho's man.

### Vague Issue Debate Content (1976)

Carter:     Our education system can be improved. Secrecy ought to be stripped away from government, and a maximum of personal privacy ought to be maintained.

Ford:       The member of a labor union must have his rights strengthened and broadened, and our children in their education should have an opportunity to improve themselves, based on their talents and their abilities.

### Specific Issue Position Ad

(Mondale talking to workers. They tell him of their contributions to the pension fund of a local industry which is now moving out of town)

Mondale:    What's happening to you guys here is not just a scandal, it's a national scandal. No one, no employers should ever be able to get away with this. Here's what we want to do in our plan. First of all, we want the plan to vest—after you've been a certain number of years you got a legal right to that money.

Worker:    That's correct.

Mondale:    Secondly, it should be portable—that fifteen years oughta be added. . . .

Worker:    You would be able to take it with you.

Mondale:    Yes, it should be a right you carry with you. And then we need some rules to govern these pension funds because some of these funds are being raided: they're being used by the company to make money for themselves when the money's supposed to go back into that fund to make it secure for the people that are there. So we need control over these funds so they're run for the workers and not for somebody else.

Narrator:    Mondale, of Minnesota.

### Specific Issue Debate Content (1976)

Carter:    Well, I think it is very difficult for President Ford to explain the difference between the pardon of President Nixon and his attitude toward those who violated the draft laws. As a matter of fact, now, I don't advocate amnesty, I advocate pardon. There is a difference, in my opinion and in accordance with the ruling of the Supreme Court and, of course, the definition in the dictionary. Amnesty means that what you did was right. Pardon means that what you did—whether right or wrong—you are forgiven for it. And I do advocate a pardon for draft evaders.

Ford:    In my tax reduction program for middle-income taxpayers, I recommended that the Congress increase personal exemptions from $750 per person to $1000 per person. . . .

---

ritualists would expect the most prevalent use of vague policy, policy salience, and personal qualities appeals.[35]

## Candidate Appeals in Spot Advertisements

When the appeals made by candidates in a sample of spot ads are categorized into the four types described above, the distribution shown in Table 1 results.[36] The breakdown of the policy-related appeals shows that many ads contain no policy-

Table 1

**Content of televised political spot advertisements**

(N = 156)

| | |
|---|---|
| Partisanship | |
| Overt | 9.6% |
| Marginal | 15.4% |
| Nonpartisan | 71.2% |
| Bipartisan, crosspartisan | 3.8% |
| | 100.0% |
| Issue position | |
| Specific | 19.9% |
| Vague | 37.8% |
| Salience | 19.2% |
| None | 42.3% |
| | 119.2%[a] |
| Candidate qualities | |
| Yes | 47.4% |
| No | 52.6% |
| | 100.0% |
| Groups | |
| Yes | 39.7% |
| No | 60.3% |
| | 100.0% |

a. This category sums to more than 100% since more than one type of policy appeal may appear in each ad.

related appeal at all, and of those that do touch on policy matters, most of the appeals are vague. One-fifth of the ads contain a policy salience appeal, usually involving the criticism of the incumbent administration for failing to achieve some performance goal, and one-fifth of the ads contain some type of specific policy position. Although it is unclear whether this distribution seriously undercuts the policy-oriented approach since those researchers usually only claim to find some undefined minimum of specific policy pronouncements, it is clear that a specific policy position is one of the least prevalent of candidate appeals.[37]

The single most prevalent type of appeal found in spot ads is the type that focuses attention on the personal attributes of the candidate. Almost half of these ads contained such an appeal, an underestimate of the prevalence of such appeals in all likelihood since only the *verbal* component of the ad is taken into account. These are the kinds of appeals consistent with Page's theory of the selection of the benevolent leader and with Bennett's argument concerning the way in which popular concerns are dramatized.

The second most prevalent type of appeal in spot ads involves the presentation of demographic group–related messages. Most of these appeals are devoid of specific content and portray a candidate so as to display identification, empathy, responsiveness, and concern. Fenno has found this to be a prevalent component of a congressman's interaction with the constituency.

In summary, then, the content of candidate appeals made in televised spot ads seems to be more consistent with rhetorical and ritualist perspectives on 7 elections than with the assumptions of the policy-oriented approach. [38]

## Candidate Appeals in Televised Presidential Debates

It is commonplace to suppose that the appeals made by candidates during debates are much more policy-oriented than they are in spot ads. After all, virtually all of the questions that candidates respond to in debates are about policy, and most responses at least involve policy-related matters. One analysis of the 1960 debates found that the majority of candidate statements contained specific policy positions, the reasoning behind the policy positions, or the use of evidence to support the policy positions taken by candidates, and an analysis of the 1976 debates found that the interrogating reporters spent 92 percent of their time on "issues," and that candidates responded with issue-related comments about 80 percent of the time. [39]

To provide a comparison between the appeals made by candidates in debates and in spot ads, the content of the nine presidential debates held during the general elections of 1960, 1976, and 1980 has been categorized using the same categories of information used to analyze the spot ads (Table 2).

In general, all the presidential debates have included more policy-related appeals than are encountered in spot ads. Roughly two-thirds of each debate analyzed contained policy-related appeals. Although presidential debates have been primarily concerned with discussions of public policies, however, the specificity of these discussions has not been overwhelming. The vague policy appeal was the most prevalent appeal used in every one of the nine debates, indicating that most of what passes for policy discussions includes the statement of general, vague, and often consensual goals, such as full employment, economic growth, an equitable tax system, elimination of governmental waste, and development of a strong military capability. A smaller portion of the policy-related discussion involves the raising of issues without any subsequent discussion of what policies might be recommended to meet them or the assertion that some issues ought not to be considered particularly serious.

Nonetheless, a significant portion of debate content has included a fairly specific revelation of policy preferences by the presidential candidates (it was the second most prevalent appeal in six of the nine debates). In 1960, for example, John Kennedy and Richard Nixon discussed with a fair degree of specificity the

Table 2

## Content of 1960, 1976, and 1980 presidential debates

| 1960 | Partisan | Group | Personal attributes | Policy salience | Policy vague | Policy specific | Unclas-sified |
|---|---|---|---|---|---|---|---|
| First (Domestic) | 27.1 | 13.8 | 9.8 | 11.3 | 40.6 | 12.7 | 5.3 |
| Second (Open) | 16.8 | 2.5 | 15.0 | 14.3 | 32.3 | 27.6 | 7.4 |
| Third (Open) | 9.0 | 2.0 | 16.4 | 8.7 | 43.4 | 22.9 | 6.1 |
| Fourth (Foreign) | 16.6 | 0.0 | 19.6 | 20.6 | 30.5 | 18.9 | 7.0 |
| **1976** | | | | | | | |
| First (Domestic) | 7.4 | 7.3 | 10.9 | 8.0 | 31.5 | 30.8 | 4.0 |
| Second (Foreign) | 3.2 | 6.1 | 17.1 | 8.4 | 42.6 | 24.9 | 2.5 |
| Third (Open) | 1.7 | 7.6 | 22.8 | 10.1 | 23.1 | 21.1 | 11.5 |
| **1980** | | | | | | | |
| First (Reagan-Anderson) | 0.0 | 0.5 | 6.9 | 16.5 | 36.2 | 32.9 | 6.8 |
| Second (Reagan-Carter) | 4.8 | 6.1 | 12.9 | 12.7 | 33.8 | 28.3 | 6.4 |
| **Spot Ads** | | | | | | | |
| 1960–1968 | 37.7 | 25.9 | 48.1 | 14.8 | 37.0 | 27.8 | — |
| 1970–1979 | 19.6 | 47.1 | 47.1 | 21.6 | 38.2 | 15.7 | — |

defense of Formosa, federal aid to education, medical care for the aged, presidential powers to deal with strikes, relations with Cuba, the oil depletion allowance, foreign aid, and nuclear testing, among other things. In 1976 Gerald Ford and Jimmy Carter debated policy concerning tax reductions, defense spending, gun-control legislation, foreign relations with a number of countries, energy policy, revenue sharing, the Federal Reserve Board, arms reduction, abortion, and other topics. And in the truncated debates of 1980, Ronald Reagan and John Anderson debated tax policy, energy conservation and production, reinstatement of the draft, military weaponry, and abortion; Ronald Reagan and Jimmy Carter debated tax policy, defense spending, minimum wage legislation, nuclear arms reduction, energy production, social security, women's rights, and air pollution legislation.

Next to the policy-related appeals of debates, none of the other appeals has occurred with anywhere near the same frequency. Partisan appeals were quite noticeable in 1960 but have virtually disappeared since then, demographic group appeals have never been frequently used, and even personal attribute appeals have seldom been explicitly and verbally made. It seems, then, that the predominance of vague policy appeals coupled with the personal qualities appeals in debates is the most consistent with the ritualist approach to candidate communication, with the rhetorical and policy-oriented approaches receiving some but much less substantiation as well.[40]

## Conclusion

This look at the appeals made by candidates in two of the most visible campaign formats has found that these appeals are most consistent with the ritualistic approach to elections and least consistent with the policy-oriented approach. Vague policy and personal qualities appeals predominate in both forms, whereas specific policy appeals are rare in spot ads and only slightly more frequent in debates. The appeals of the rhetorical approach—demographic group, personal qualities, and policy salience—are as frequent in spot ads as are the ritualist's appeals but are only slightly more frequent than specific policy appeals in debates.

This finding takes on theoretical significance as it forces us to reevaluate the meaning that is commonly attributed to elections and electoral outcomes. I will conclude by discussing three implications of this pattern of candidate communication for the meaning of electoral choices and of elections more generally.

First, candidate appeals generally make unlikely the kind of intended, prospective policy choices that the policy-oriented researchers have in mind. Candidates make it difficult for voters to know what their future intentions are beyond the support for consensually held values and policy goals. This does not mean, however, that elections can never have this kind of prospective policy choice meaning. There may be certain circumstances—"critical election" periods and whenever there is an "insurgent" candidate—where more specific, future-oriented policy positions of candidates become known to the citizenry and are used to guide electoral choices. In these circumstances, though, this awareness is more likely the result of information originating from places other than the candidate's campaign appeals. During critical election periods, the policy debate presumably takes place between parties over an extended period of time and the rhetoric of individual candidates is relatively consequential. In the case of "insurgent" candidates, perceptions of policy positions are probably more likely formed, as Page has argued, from our memory of previous candidate behavior and from journalistic commentary about the origins of a candidate's support and the strategic decisions a candidate makes to mobilize a supportive coalition. In neither case is there any reason to expect that it is candidate rhetoric that communicates policy positions or gives elections what little intended, prospective policy meaning they have.

Second, this lack of intended, prospective policy meaning does not mean that elections have no other policy significance. In fact, a number of other policy-related meanings to elections that are more plausible in light of candidate communication are possible.[41] As a number of theorists have concluded, elections may have intended but *retrospective* policy meaning. In this view candidate appeals help voters decide whether or not to "toss the rascals out" based on a global evaluation of policy satisfaction. The phenomenon may create in officeholders a greater incentive for virtuous behavior, but it is also a much more blunt, indirect, and problematical method of influencing the contours of public policy. Elections might also have an indirect policy significance in that citizens choose leaders with certain attributes (fairness, compassion, vigor) which in turn have a bearing on subsequent policy choices. The relationship between these attributes and policy decisions is so tenuous, however, that there would seem to be very little consistent, dependable popular influence over policy choices left in this view. Finally, it is entirely possible that electoral choices may have prospective but *unintended* policy consequences. That is, we may select a public official for nonpolicy reasons and in the process also get an officeholder who holds certain (to us previously unknown) policy preferences quite different from his opponent's. If electoral winners (mis)interpret thier victory as a "mandate" for their policies (as victors are wont to do) they may even be encouraged to be more assertive about those same policy preferences. Candidate rhetoric encourages this type of result by deflecting the attention of the citizenry away from these hidden policy positions. Though this possibility preserves a policy significance for elections, it is some considerable distance from the intended popular influence or control over public policy with which we began this discussion.

Third, though we may be tempted to bemoan the possibility that elections usually do not (and perhaps cannot) have a direct, intended, prospective policy consequence, and that what policy significance there is to elections is more likely to be indirect, retrospective, and unintended, this does not begin to exhaust the range of other interesting possibilities. Apart from their policy meanings, elections may also help shape the political agenda, reinforce cultural myths and values, insulate officeholders from accountability (leaving them free to govern), channel popular participation away from more violent and disruptive forms, and allow for the construction of the modern liberal state. In fact, as one of the editors of this volume has argued elsewhere, it may be that the fact that elections are held is more important than their immediate outcomes.

> What voters decide is not at all the most significant aspect of the electoral process. Voters' decisions can sometimes be important. But in many respects, what voters decide, and thus how they come to vote as they do, is far less consequential for government and politics than the simple fact of voting itself. . . . The fact of mass electoral participation is generally far more significant

for the state than what or how citizens decide once they participate. It is the institution of the election rather than any particular pattern of voting that is critical, even for those regimes that can sometimes be affected by what voters decide.[42]

If this is true, candidate appeals would still be important since, presumably, for elections to have these other consequences, citizens would still have to be convinced that electoral choices have some significance.

We need to think more carefully, then, about the difference that having elections makes, and to construct a view of elections that takes account of the behavior not only of citizens and voters, but of candidates and other relevant actors as well. Candidate rhetoric does not provide a fertile basis for analyzing elections in the prospective policy choice manner with which much of the voting behavior literature is concerned. Yet candidate rhetoric is real, patterned, and important. A complete and accurate view of elections must synthesize this behavior with the behavior of voters and take account of how it is that candidates spend their time and money to persuade us that we ought to behave in a particular manner. It is hoped that this analysis has made a contribution toward this shift in focus and toward the development of a more plausible and comprehensive theory of elections.

## Notes

1. Benjamin Page, *Choices and Echoes in Presidential Elections* (Chicago: University of Chicago Press, 1978), p. 4. V. O. Key, Jr. has made a similar point: "Voters respond to what they see and hear; the nature of their response depends upon what they see and hear (which, in turn, is conditioned by what is in their heads to begin with). Points of political leadership and of communication of political intelligence, by influencing what people see and hear, fix the range of voter response (within the limits of the situation as shaped by the irrepressible flow of events) as they transmit information to the electorate." *The Responsible Electorate: Rationality in Presidential Voting, 1936–1960* (Cambridge, MA.: Harvard University Press, 1966), pp. 110–11.

2. Verbal communication is not, of course, the only way in which candidates communicate with citizens. Masters has argued that the nonverbal gestures of candidates are also a revealing aspect of elite-nonelite interaction. Roger D. Masters, "The Impact of Ethology on Political Science," paper presented at the International Political Science Association Colloquium on Biopolitics, Paris, 1975.

3. Philip E. Converse, "Public Opinion and Voting Behavior," in *Handbook of Political Science*, vol. 4, *Nongovernmental Politics*, ed. Fred I. Greenstein and Nelson W. Polsby (Reading, Mass.: Addison-Wesley, 1975).

4. John Osgood Field and Ronald E. Anderson, "Ideology in the Public's Conceptualization of the 1964 Presidential Election," *Public Opinion Quarterly* 33 (1969):380, and John C. Pierce, "Party Identification and the Changing Role of Ideology in American Politics," *Midwest Journal of Political Science* 14 (1979):33.

5. Philip E. Converse, Warren E. Miller, Jerrold G. Rusk, Arthur C. Wolfe, "Continuity and Change in American Politics: Parties and Issues in the 1968 Election,"

*American Political Science Review* 63 (1969):1097.

6. James A. Stimson, "Belief Systems: Constraint, Complexity, and the 1972 Election," *American Journal of Political Science* 19 (1975):141.

7. Arthur H. Miller, Warren E. Miller, Alden S. Raine, and Thad A. Brown, "A Majority in Disarray: Policy Polarization in the 1972 Election," *American Political Science Review* 70 (1976):754.

8. Norman H. Nie, Sidney Verba, John R. Petrocik, *The Changing American Voter* (Cambridge: Harvard University Press, 1976). The quotations are on pp. 151, 163, 173, and 192.

9. Gerald M. Pomper, "From Confusion to Clarity: Issues and American Voters, 1956–1968," *American Political Science Review* 66 (June 1972):426.

10. Miller et al., "A Majority Party in Disarray," pp. 771, 754.

11. Pomper, "From Confusion to Clarity," p. 426, and Richard W. Boyd, "Popular Control of Public Policy: A Normal Vote Analysis of the 1968 Election," *American Political Science Review* 66 (June 1972):429.

12. Gregory B. Markus and Philip E. Converse, "A Dynamic Simultaneous Equation Model of Electoral Choice," *American Political Science Review* 73 (December 1979):1068.

13. Thomas E. Patterson and Robert D. McClure, *The Unseeing Eye* (New York: Putnam, 1976), p. 23.

14. Charles Atkin and Garry Heald, "Effects of Political Advertising," *Public Opinion Quarterly* 40 (1976):216–28.

15. George F. Bishop, Robert W. Oldendick, and Alfred J. Tuchfarber, "The Presidential Debates as a Device for Increasing the 'Rationality' of Electoral Behavior," in *The Presidential Debates*, ed. George F. Bishop, Robert G. Meadow, and Marilyn Jackson-Beeck (New York: Praeger, 1978), and Arthur H. Miller and Michael Mackuen, "Learning about the Candidates: The 1976 Presidential Debates," *Public Opinion Quarterly* 43 (Fall 1979):326–46.

16. Miller and Mackuen, "Learning about the Candidates," p. 344.

17. Everett C. Ladd, *American Political Parties: Social Change and Political Response* (New York: Norton, 1970).

18. Benjamin Ginsberg, "Critical Elections and the Substance of Party Conflict: 1844 to 1968," *Midwest Journal of Political Science* 16 (November 1972):603–25, and "Elections and Public Policy," *American Political Science Review* 70 (March 1976):41–49.

19. Jerrold G. Rusk and Herbert F. Weisberg, "Perceptions of Presidential Candidates: Implications for Electoral Change," *Midwest Journal of Political Science* 16 (1972), p. 407.

20. Pomper, "From Confusion to Clarity," p. 427.

21. Robert MacNeil, *The People Machine* (New York: Harper and Row, 1968); Dan Nimmo, *The Political Persuaders* (Englewood Cliffs, N.J.: Prentice-Hall, 1970); Gene Wykoff, *The Image Candidates* (New York: Macmillan, 1968); Joe McGinniss, *The Selling of the President, 1968* (New York: Trident, 1969).

22. Page, *Choices and Echoes*; Richard F. Fenno, Jr., *Home Style: House Members in Their Districts* (Boston: Little, Brown, 1978).

23. Page, *Choices and Echoes*, pp. 152–53.

24. Benjamin I. Page and Richard A. Brody, "Policy Voting and the Electoral Process," *American Political Science Review* 66 (1972):979–95.

25.  Fenno, *Home Style*, p. 134.

26.  Page, *Choices and Echoes*, pp. 231, 233.

27.  V. O. Key is difficult to place in this categorization. In *The Responsible Elector-ate*, Key is clearly intent on making the point that "the voter [is] a person who appraises the actions of government, who has policy preferences, and who relates his vote to those appraisals and preferences" (pp. 58–59). In this respect he is like the other policy-oriented researchers discussed earlier. However, he also observes that the meaning of voter choices is more likely to be of the retrospective than the prospective type: "The patterns of flow of the major streams of shifting voters graphically reflect the electorate in its great, and perhaps principal, role as an appraiser of past events, past performance, and past actions. It judges retrospectively; it commands prospectively only insofar as it expresses either approval or disapproval of that which has happened before" (p. 61). He recognizes that the nature of voter responses and decisions depends, in part, on the nature of candidate communication and the way in which electoral choices are framed. Hence, the 1960 election, according to Key, involved two candidates who were ambiguous and in "agree-ment on many basic propositions," who had no record of past performance on which to campaign, and who devised a campaign "composed chiefly of fluffy and foggy political stimuli," thus limiting the ability of voters to make policy-related choices. Here Key is more like Page.

Another example of this rhetorical approach to candidate communication is the work of Nimmo and Savage. Their analysis concentrates on the "images" citizens have of candi-dates, and what the origins and consequences of these images are. Though their definition of an image is simply how one is perceived by another and includes perceptions of the policy preferences of candidates, the bulk of their research focuses on the personal qualities (such as "strong leader," "man of integrity," and "empathetic person") that candidates are perceived to possess, and the origins and impact of these perceptions. Unlike Page, however, Nimmo and Savage fail to draw any conclusions from their research about the consequences of these "images" for the meaning of elections more generally. Dan Nimmo and Robert L. Savage, *Candidates and Their Images* (Pacific Palisades, Calif.: Goodyear, 1976).

28.  W. Lance Bennett, "Culture, Communication and Political Control," paper pre-sented to the American Political Science Association, Washington, D.C., 1980, p. 3.

29.  Another example of this perspective may be found in Nimmo and Combs. They argue that candidate communication is primarily mythical in nature, filled with images, illusions, fantasies, and "pseudo-realities." They conclude that what they call "campaign flackdom" has become remarkably sophisticated in the exploitation of myths:

> Many of the messages constructed are directed at people's emotions, tugging at deeply held myths about their country, political values, and prejudices. Flacks also create fantasy worlds for people, allowing potential voters to be transported into the drama presented. Many social critics have thus argued that contemporary cam-paigns are a massive exercise in human gullibility consisting of voters repeatedly believing the myth that a particular candidate can change things for good or ill if elected. In any case, it is likely that campaign myth-making will continue.

Dan Nimmo and James E. Combs, *Subliminal Politics: Myths and Mythmakers in America* (Englewood Cliffs, N.J.: Prentice-Hall, 1980).

30.  W. Lance Bennett, *Public Opinion in American Politics* (New York: Harcourt,

Brace, Jovanovich, 1980), p. 386.

31. Murray Edelman, *The Symbolic Uses of Politics* (Urbana: University of Illinois Press, 1964), pp. 17–18.

32. Bennett, "Culture, Communication and Political Control."

33. Bennett, *Public Opinion in American Politics*, p. 390.

34. In reality, most spot ads and many debate excerpts contain more than one type of appeal. Carter's statement in Figure 2, for example, which is an example of a personal attribute appeal, was also coded as containing a policy salience (atomic weapons) appeal, and Golberg's ad in Figure 3, which was coded as a demographic group appeal, also contains a personal attribute (leadership) appeal. Both ads and debate excerpts (phrases, sentences, or paragraphs) were coded as containing more than one type of appeal where such was the case.

35. Bennett, *Public Opinion in American Politics*, pp. 383–90.

36. Some 156 spot ads were viewed, transcribed, and coded according to the content categories discussed above. Although no such thing as a representative sample of spot ads could possibly be constructed, these 156 ads do represent a variety electoral situations.

37. This raises the possibility that Patterson and McClure happened to pick an unusually policy-oriented series of spot ads for their analysis. The paucity of specific policy appeals in spot ads is corroborated in Sabato's study. He viewed more than 1,100 spot ads and reports that American spot ads contain few specific policy appeals, much fewer than ads shown in Great Britain. Larry J. Sabato, *The Rise of the Political Consultants* (New York: Basic Books, 1981), p. 129.

38. A more detailed analysis reveals that there is no relationship between the partisan identity of the candidates and the appeals made. Richard A. Joslyn, "The Content of Political Spot Ads," *Journalism Quarterly* 57, 1 (Spring 1980):92–98.

39. John W. Ellsworth, "Rationality and Campaigning: A Content Analysis of the 1960 Presidential Campaign Debates," *Western Political Quarterly* 18 (December 1965):794–802, and David O. Sears and Steven H. Chaffee, "Uses and Effects of the 1976 Debates: An Overview of Empirical Studies," in *The Great Debates, 1976: Ford v. Carter*, ed. Sidney Kraus (Bloomington: Indiana University Press, 1979).

40. In general, there is little relationship between the particular candidate and the appeals used in the debates. Jimmy Carter was slightly more apt to use partisan, demographic group, and personal attribute appeals in 1976 and 1980, and John Anderson did make a noticeably greater use of specific policy and policy salience appeals in 1980, as did Gerald Ford in 1976. The one more general pattern that emerges, however, is that challengers are consistently and significantly more apt to use policy salience appeals than incumbents are. This reflects the tendency of challengers to concentrate on the performance of the incumbents and to promote the kind of retrospective judgment of which Page speaks.

41. Robert Weissberg, *Public Opinion and Popular Government* (Englewood Cliffs, N.J.: Prentice-Hall, 1976), pp. 22–24.

42. Benjamin Ginsberg, *The Consequences of Consent* (Reading, Mass.: Addison-Wesley, 1982), p. 5.

## 2.3

# Primary Elections and the Evanescence of Third Party Activity in the United States

## Peter F. Galderisi and Benjamin Ginsberg

Opposition to party was the basis for a number of the institutional reforms of the American political process promulgated during the Progressive era. Many Progressive reformers were undoubtedly motivated by a sincere desire to rid politics of corruption and to improve the quality and efficiency of government in the United States. But, simultaneously, from the perspective of middle and upper class Progressives and the financial, commercial, and industrial elites with whom they were often associated, the weakening or elimination of party organization would also serve a number of other important political functions. The enervation of party would mean that power could more readily be acquired and retained by the "best men," that is, those with wealth, position, and education. The elimination of party organization, moreover, would have the effect of denying access to power to reformers' political opponents who, indeed, relied on party organization. Not coincidentally, Progressive reform was aimed particularly at the destruction of the powerful urban political machines built by the representatives of lower class, ethnic voters.[1]

The list of antiparty reforms of the Progressive era is a familiar one. The Australian ballot took away the parties' privilege of printing and distributing ballots. The introduction of nonpartisan local elections eroded the parties' control at the local level. The extension of "merit systems" for administrative appointments stripped party organizations of their critically important access to patronage. And, of course, the introduction of the direct primary substantially

Peter F. Galderisi teaches at Utah State University. Benjamin Ginsberg teaches at Cornell University.

reduced party leaders' capacity to control candidate nominations.

Of all these reforms, the direct primary is in many respects the most interesting. The primary can be seen as an antiparty reform on three separate counts. First, by weakening party leaders' capacity to control nominating processes, primary elections undermine the organizational coherence of established parties. Second, primaries tend to direct the attention of voters and political activists toward the nominating contests of the party most likely to win the general election, and away from the interparty race. Over time, primary elections have probably helped to erode two-party competition in at least some states.[2]

Last, and most interesting, primary elections have the effect of inhibiting the formation of new parties. Third party activity, an important phenomenon in nineteenth-century American politics, not only at the national but also at the state and local levels, has ebbed considerably over the past half century. During the past twenty-five years, for example, only one successful candidate for the U.S. House of Representatives has been affiliated with a minor party. At the turn of the century, by contrast, approximately twenty representatives typically claimed to represent third parties or to be independent of any party tie. The introduction of the primary election, beginning around the turn of the century, is probably one of the major factors behind this phenomenon. The existence of the primary allows dissident groups and individuals an opportunity to contend for office within, rather than in opposition to, the established parties. Perhaps the most politically doctrinaire or socially exotic splinter group, interested in presenting ideas rather than winning office, would be unwilling to risk losing its identity on the ballot. But for most aspirants to office the possibility of obtaining a major party's nomination offers a strong inducement to forgo the uncertainties of independence. At the same time, the existence of the primary diminishes the ability of established party leaders to reject dissidents and outsiders. The primary formally awards the party's nomination to the winner of an electoral plurality. These two factors taken together mean that the established parties will very likely internalize forces that might otherwise result in independent, factional, and third party candidacies on the general election ballot.[3]

Our empirical analysis in this chapter explores the relationship between primary elections and party formation in the United States. We first examine the historical relationship between the introduction of the direct primary and candidacy for office in several American states. Second, employing data from recent senatorial, gubernatorial, and congressional elections in all fifty states, we analyze the effect of state primary and general election law upon minor party, factional, and independent candidacy in general elections. Finally, we consider the political significance of primary elections and the decline of third parties in American politics.

## The Advent of the Direct Primary

A number of discussions of the origin and history of the direct primary are available elsewhere.[4] Though the motives of some reformers were profoundly antidemocratic, some of the early supporters of the primary system were interested simply in broader popular control of the governmental process, particularly in those states where a single party's nomination was tantamount to election.[5] In other instances, demands for the introduction of the primary were in part an outgrowth of intraparty rivalries, with one or another party faction perceiving the possibility of a direct appeal to voters to be to its own advantage.[6] Interestingly enough, at least some early advocates of reform in both the South and the North appear to have conceived the primary to be a means of encouraging dissidents to remain within their own parties.[7]

Laws requiring nomination through primary elections were enacted by most states between 1903 and 1920. A handful of states, such as Connecticut, did not establish a mandatory primary until many years later. The precise legal form of the primary varied widely from state to state and, within each state, was subject to many modifications over time. For the moment, however, we shall ignore such variations and simply consider the impact of the primary's introduction.

To begin to assess the effect of the adoption of the primary, we constructed a set of ''before and after'' pictures of candidacy for office in two states. This involved a rather simple though time-consuming procedure. For each state we calculated the average number of congressional candidates per district on the general election ballot during each election year between 1870 and 1974.[8] We selected congressional races for this procedure simply because the relatively large number of candidates per state provides a smoother time series than would any statewide office. The congressional data for two states are presented graphically in figures 1–4.

We will not offer a detailed analysis of the ebbs and flows of candidacy for office during this hundred-year period. An adequate explanation of the events in any state would obviously require close examination of each state's politics, history, legal system, and so on. Several observations, however, are in order. First, the level of general election activity within each state varies considerably over time and in many instances appears to have an obvious relationship with national political and economic conflicts. In Ohio, for example, campaigns by the Greenback party, the Populist party, and the like account for an increased incidence of candidacy for office during the 1880s and 1890s. Similarly, an upsurge of campaign activity after 1908 is largely a product of Progressive politics, with the national Progressive party and several other Progressive groups mounting campaigns in a number of congressional districts.

Second, at any point, the absolute number of candidates in the general election varies considerably from state to state. For example, though the flow of candidacy in Indiana coincides to some extent with that in Ohio, the relationship is by no means perfect. The most obvious discrepancy is caused by the very active Indiana Prohibition party during the 1940s and 1950s. Whatever the specific causes, let us merely observe the obvious: Factors peculiar to each state's political or social climate have an impact on the state's level of campaign activity,

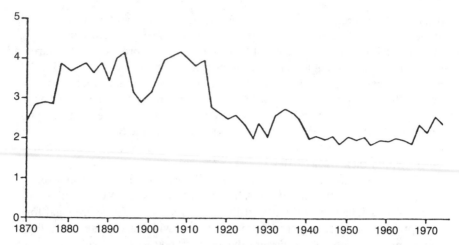

Figure 1  **Average number of general election candidates per congressional district, 1870–1974—Ohio**

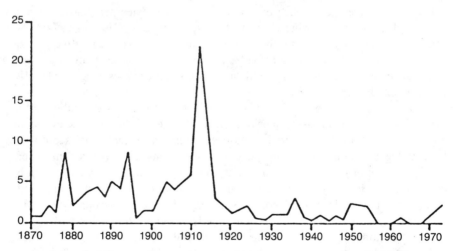

Figure 2  **Proportion of popular congressional vote received by third parties, 1870–1974—Ohio**

either as independent causal agents or as mediators of national events.

Third, and most important for our purposes, in both these states as well as a number of others we examined, the introduction of the direct primary was more or less quickly followed by a marked and persisting diminution of third party and independent efforts in the general election. For the most part, the third parties that do appear after the advent of the primary tend to be either very doctrinaire or

Figure 3 **Average number of general election candidates per congressional district, 1870–1974—Indiana**

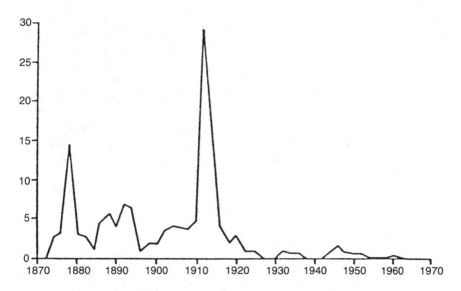

Figure 4 **Proportion of popular congressional vote received by third parties, 1870–1974—Indiana**

relatively exotic and attract no popular interest or support. Ohio provides one of the most clear-cut cases. A mandatory primary for all congressional races was introduced in Ohio in 1911.[9] Within three elections following the advent of the primary, third party activity had ceased and, possibly more important, was never again a significant factor in Ohio politics. With the exception of Progressive campaigns in the races immediately following the primary's introduction, only occasional Communist and Socialist Labor candidates challenged major party nominees in Ohio congressional elections after 1911. These third parties seldom presented any particular threat to the Republicans and Democrats. After the advent of the primary, Ohio voters were not again offered an even remotely attractive third party alternative.

A similar pattern is evident in Indiana. The introduction of a mandatory primary for congressional elections in 1915 was followed by a decline in the number of general election candidates, though not so marked or persistent a decline as we observed in Ohio.[10] Yet, as was the case in Ohio, only the most politically or socially exotic groups entered Indiana's general elections after the introduction of the primary. Few attractive third parties of independents presented themselves in Indiana congressional races after 1915.

The advent of the primary and the ensuing diminution of third party and independent activity in these states may, of course, be nothing more than historical coincidence. There were a great many changes in the shape of American politics at the turn of the century that could conceivably account for the decline of such candidacies.[11] Indeed, examination of the data for Connecticut, a state which did not introduce the primary until 1955, indicates a lessening of third party activity after 1920, a sharp upturn during the 1930s, and only limited activity after 1940. Though in the twentieth century third parties and independents were more active in Connecticut than in Ohio or Indiana, they were not markedly more active than in Pennsylvania, for example, a state which introduced the primary in 1906.

Though intriguing and suggestive, the historical evidence is far from conclusive. Let us turn, therefore, to a more precise statistical analysis of the relationship between the availability of the primary and the incidence of minor party and independent candidacy in general elections.

## The Primary Election in Contemporary Politics

Our historical overview did not take account of two important pieces of information. First, legal variations exist, both across states and over time within states, in the ease of candidate access to the primary ballot. At the time of the primary's introduction, a candidate for office in Ohio could obtain a place on the primary ballot with little or no trouble. In some other states, achieving a place on the ballot was, as a matter of law, quite difficult. Second, changes in the incidence of *primary* election candidacy occur over time, and these we did not examine because of the difficulty in obtaining reliable historical data. Without the information we cannot be certain that declines in third party and independent general election activity actually resulted from the channeling of candidacies into the primary. It might instead be the case, for example, that the incidence of such candidacy was depressed by some other factor which happened merely to be historically synchronous with the advent of the direct primary. We therefore use data from several recent years to define precisely the legal availability of the primary and the relative extent to which candidacy for office occurs in the primary or general electoral arenas.

## The Legal Availability of the Primary

In a number of states, obtaining a place on the primary ballot is a rather simple matter. A candidate need only file a declaration of candidacy endorsed by a handful of supporters and pay a nominal filing fee. Other states, though, have shown a great deal of ingenuity in restricting candidate access to the primary ballot. The central legal restriction is the nominating petition. More than twenty states require petitions signed by some proportion of the state's registered voters. In the case of a candidate for statewide office in New York, for example, this would come to approximately 20,000 signatures to be collected within a relatively short period of time.

Though the nominating petition is the central restriction on candidate access to the primary ballot, most states have adopted additional forms of regulation as well. One is the signature distribution requirement. Several states stipulate that a certain number of petition signatures be drawn from each of some defined set of subdivisions of the state, thus complicating the task of signature collection. Another is the requirement that candidates for a party's nomination obtain signatures only from among the party's registered voters, thus decreasing the potential pool of petition signers.

Most ingenious is what might be called the "mini-max" rule. Every state specifies a number of conditions of acceptability for nominating petitions.[12] New York, for example, requires that voters' signatures appear on the petition in precisely the same form as their signatures on the voter registration rolls. For example, if a voter who registered under the name Mary Adams Smith used the name Mary A. Smith to sign a nominating petition, the signature could be ruled invalid if challenged. New York petitions must also be a specified color and be signed with the proper color ink. In one amusing but not atypical case, Peter Peyser, a candidate for the 1976 Republican senatorial nomination, found that several thousand of the more than 27,000 signatures he had collected were signed on the wrong color paper—white rather than pink—and that a number of signatures, including his own, were subject to challenge on the ground of either illegibility or failure to coincide precisely with the name found on the voter registration lists. To deal with the problem of possibly invalid signatures, most candidates attempt to collect more than the required minumum number of signatures. This is where the mini-max rule becomes important. Several states specify not only a minimum but also a maximum number of signatures that may be submitted in a candidate's behalf, thus limiting the extent to which candidates can protect themselves from the risk of invalid signatures.

To measure variations in the legal availability of the primary, we collected and coded each of the fifty states' requirements for nominating-petition signatures, the presence or absence of a distribution requirement, the presence or absence of a mini-max rule, and whether or not only party registrants were eligible to sign petitions.[13] Because collection of these data was extremely time-consuming, particularly given the fact that most states insist upon amending their election laws each year, we obtained only the statutes relevant to the congressional, senatorial, and gubernatorial primary elections for the years 1968 through 1976. It should be noted that for purposes of analysis the relevant unit becomes the artificial legal entity defined by a set of election laws rather than the state *per se*. For example, Colorado 1972 and Colorado 1974 are for our purposes different "states" because of changes in election law between those two years.

## The Incidence of Candidacy: A "Quantum" Theory

A second shortcoming of our historical overview is that we were able to examine only changes in the number of general election candidates over time. But, to establish a relationship between the availability of the primary election and the incidence of third party and independent activity requires that we also take into account the extent of political activity in the primary arena. Activity in both arenas, after all, may be declining at the same time. We therefore obtained the number of candidates for congressional, senatorial, and gubernatorial office in every state's primary and general elections between 1968 and 1976.[14]

When we examined the historical data, we asked whether the introduction of the primary appeared synchronous with absolute declines in levels of general election campaign activity. Data drawn from a relatively short period, however, must be viewed from a slightly different perspective. It would be unreasonable to assume that the availability of the primary necessarily has much impact upon the absolute level of campaign activity in either the primary or general election arenas at any single point. At best, the availability of the primary is only one of a number of factors affecting absolute levels of candidacy.

Let us assume, instead, that the total amount of campaign activity, in both the primary and general election arenas, in any state at a given point is a complex function of the state's social structure, the state's political climate, the impact of national events, and a variety of other factors about which we can only conjecture. Though we cannot specify all of the causes that increase or decrease the absolute number of candidates, we can describe the relevant effect at any time: the total amount or "quantum" of campaign activity at that time.

If the availability of the primary election has any effect at a particular time, this effect should be manifested not so much in the size of the total quantum of campaign activity at that time as in the amount of campaign activity that occurs in the general election arena relative to the total amount of campaign activity in the given state. One convenient way to express this relationship is $\frac{G}{P + G}$, where $P$ stands for the number of candidates in the primary election and $G$ for the number of candidates in the general election.[15]

Our expectation is that the more available the primary election becomes across states, the greater will be the incidence of primary election candidacy, and the lesser will be the incidence of general election activity, *in relation* to the total quantum of activity within each state. Again, we are not attempting to establish an association between the legal availability of the primary and the absolute amount of activity in either the general or primary arenas. We assume the absolute number of candidates to be the result of a very large number of factors. Our question is, instead, whether the primary channels this activity away from the general election.

There are several possible ways to assess the association between the ease of candidate access to the primary ballot and the relative incidence of candidacy in the general election arena. Our approach was designed to be consistent with the logical relationships among the four types of state legal requirements. The central statutory requirement is the number of nominating petition signatures required by the state. In addition, states may or may not impose conditions for the collection of signatures, such as a signature distribution requirement. Therefore, our procedure was first to examine the simple association between the number of signatures required and the relative importance of the general arena. Then we reexamined this association in the presence of each of the conditions for signature collection.

In addition to regression analysis (included for those more comfortable with this procedure), the method of paired comparison was used. Paired comparison permits tests of the ordinal relationship between two variables across all possible pairs of cases in a data set. A set containing 'n' cases will, therefore, produce $\frac{n(n - 1)}{2}$ comparisons. This process allows counts of the percentage of comparisons that are compatible with a hypothesis. Let us say that the investigator wishes to test the hypothesis that "the more of x, the less of y" (the form of our own major hypothesis, "As primaries become easier to enter, the relative importance of the general election arena declines"). Paired comparisons will yield every possible combination of pairs between cases on the independent (x) and dependent (y) variables. The coding would be as follows:

a = those pairs for which the independent variable is equal and the dependent variable is equal;

b = those pairs for which the independent variable is equal and the dependent variable in unequal;

c = those pairs for which the independent and dependent variables are unequal in the same direction;

d = those pairs for which the independent and dependent variables are unequal in the opposite directions;

e = those pairs for which the independent variable is unequal and the dependent variable is equal.

The stated hypothesis deals only with inequality on x (our independent measure). Thus, counts c, d, and e serve as the universe of comparison; the proper percentage is therefore represented as $\dfrac{c}{c + d + e}$.[16]

Our first comparison is between the number of signatures required for access to the primary ballot and the relative importance of the general election arena across all states. Examination of the findings, reported in Table 1, clearly indicates that the posited relationship systematically obtains. At all three electoral levels, the relative importance of the general election arena declines as the primary petition signature requirement is eased. This relationship obtains in over two-thirds of the possible paired instances.

The data reported in Table 1 do not distinguish between those states that do and those that do not impose restrictions in addition to the signature requirement. To obtain a better idea of the precise importance of each type of legal restriction, we have isolated all of the available "pure" types of legal conditions and examined the association between each and the relative importance of arenas. Our findings are reported in Table 2. Only House races provided enough cases to isolate "pure" types.

These findings indicate, first, that among those states that have *only* a signature requirement, the precise number of signatures required does not appear to be overwhelmingly important.[17] As additional legal conditions are introduced, however, the number of signatures required becomes considerably more significant. Thus, for example, in those states that permit signatures to be collected from party registrants only, the relative incidence of general election activity decreases with drops in the signature requirement in 57 percent of all paired instances. Where all legal requirements were in effect, the hypothesized relationship holds in nearly 70 percent of all paired instances.

Taken together, the findings reported in tables 1 and 2 would appear quite clearly to indicate a strong association between the availability of the primary and the relative importance of the two electoral arenas. One remaining question, however, is the importance of laws governing candidate access to the general election ballot. The very same types of legal requirements used by states to regulate access to the primary also are used in the case of the general election. It is certainly plausible to presume that ease of access to the general election ballot might have some impact on candidacy for office either in and of itself or in conjunction with primary election law.

To assess this possibility we collected and coded the laws of all fifty states

Table 1

**Proportion of paired instances in which relative importance of general election is inversely related to ease of candidate access to primary**

| House races | Senate races | Gubernatorial races |
|---|---|---|
| 67.0% | 68.3% | 70.4% |
| (235)[a] | (153) | (123) |

| | Pearson r | |
|---|---|---|
| −.32 | −.46 | −.52 |

a. The number of cases is given in parentheses. The number of comparisons would be n (n−1)/2 where 'n' is the number of cases. For example, 235 House races allowed 27,495 comparisons.

Table 2

**Proportion of paired instances in which relative importance of general election is inversely related to ease of candidate access to primary under specified legal conditions (House races only)**

| | | r |
|---|---|---|
| Signature requirement only | 31.9% | .327 |
| | (16)[a] | |
| Petition + party signatures only | 56.7% | −.455 |
| | (49) | |
| Petition + party + distribution | 53.6% | −.371 |
| | (12) | |
| Petition + party + mini-max | 57.4% | −.143 |
| | (24) | |
| Petition + party + distribution + mini-max | 66.7% | −.758 |
| | (5) | |

a. See note to Table 1.

governing access to the general election ballot for the congressional, senatorial, and gubernatorial elections of 1968 through 1976.[18] We then compared the role of primary election law and general election law as determinants of the relative importance of the general election arena. Our findings, reported in Table 3, indicate that the availability of the *primary election* is a far more important factor in explaining campaign activity than the rules governing the general election.[19]

Table 3

**Proportion of paired instances in which relative importance of general election is inversely related to ease of candidate access to primary and directly related to ease of candidate access to general election**

|  | Paired comparison | | |
| --- | --- | --- | --- |
|  | House races (235)" | Senate races (153) | Gubernatorial races (123) |
| Primary election signatures | 67.0% | 68.3% | 70.4% |
| General election signatures | 53.0% | 51.0% | 53.7% |
|  | Pearson r | | |
|  | House races (235) | Senate races (153) | Gubernatorial races (123) |
| Primary election signatures | −.32 | −.46 | −.52 |
| General election signatures | .09 | .27 | .21 |

a. See note to Table 1.

Quite probably, determined groups and individuals are not easily deterred by direct legal restriction of access to the general election ballot. The primary election, however, appears effectively to channel candidates away from the general electoral arena. The very marked effect of the primary is to inhibit third party and independent campaigns in the general election by inducing aspirants to office and power to vie for a major party's nomination.

Though we do not have a data base with which to study the impact of presidential primaries, there is every reason to believe that the same effects obtain. The very open 1976 Democratic processes of delegate selection, for example, appeared to generate a large and ideologically diverse group of contenders, permitted a political outsider to win, and, perhaps most telling, encouraged George Wallace to reject the possibility of a third party campaign. In short, the party's very open presidential nominating processes may well have allowed it to internalize potentially centrifugal forces. The availability of presidential primaries—even coupled with federal campaign finance laws, state ballot access laws, and party rules that make third party bids much less attractive than primary races—certainly does not prohibit or preclude the emergence of new parties (witness John Anderson's candidacy in 1980). The availability of the primary does, however, increase the likelihood that groups that might have undertaken to organize the new parties will instead devote their energies and attentions to factional politics within one of the major party groupings.

## Primary Elections and Changes in the Party System

Both longitudinal and cross-sectional analysis suggest that the availability of the direct primary discourages aspirants to political office from entering the general election in competition with major party nominees. Instead, the more readily available the primary, the more likely political campaigns are to be channeled into the primary arena. Groups that might in the nineteenth century have emerged as third parties are in the twentieth century more likely to be internalized by one of the major parties.[20]

In the United States, the vast majority of new parties have been politically inconsequential. But American political history suggests nonetheless that, even when short-lived, third party challenges can have considerable impact. First, though their own electoral support may be limited, new parties can alter the balance of power between the more established partisan forces. Second, challenges to the established parties can sharply redefine the focus of political debate and electoral choice. In a number of conspicuous instances in American political history, third parties have precipitated conflicts that theretofore had been partially suppressed by the established party system. The formation of the Republicans and later of the Populists are well-known cases in point. Redefinition of the focus of political debate by new parties has typically been an important precipitating factor in sequences of critical electoral realignment in the United States. Indeed, during realigning sequences new parties have helped to change the agenda of political issues as well as to shake voters from their traditional partisan moorings and normal patterns of political participation. Finally, new parties are of particular importance in the United States because of the dependence of the presidency, as we have known it, on a two-party system. If, for example, the 1968 Wallace candidacy had succeeded in forcing the presidential choice into the House of Representatives, it might well have upset the existing institutional relationship between Congress and the Executive.

Clearly, the emergence of new parties is not the only route to change in party systems. Change can also result from the penetration of established parties by new groups. Quite probably the primary facilitates this type of change, permitting new groups to displace established party leaders via direct appeals to the electorate. The difference between the two routes, however, is important.

When social or economic change produces new groups and forces, one of the most significant questions for any government is whether new demands, aspirations, and conflicts can be channeled into and expressed through existing institutional mechanisms. When new groups seek to assert demands, the availability of the suffrage, for example, can be crucial. In the absence of routine channels of participation, the emergence of new groups may lead to violence, disruption, and disorder.

Similarly, the capacity of the existing party system to absorb and respond to new groups and forces can have important implications. To take an obvious example, whether the emerging working classes were able to enter existing parties or were compelled to create their own had significant consequences for the subsequent political life of every Western nation.[21] In the United States, the ability of urban ethnic and working class leaders to achieve a measure of power through the Democratic party quite likely prevented much more divisive conflicts and far-reaching changes than those that actually occurred at the time of the New Deal.[22]

The addition of new factions to established party coalitions is generally far less disruptive to the agenda of issues and alternatives than independent political activity by those same groups. It is for precisely this reason that some doctrinaire and exotic parties resist the lure of the primary election. Factions campaigning in a primary, as Key pointed out long ago, have little visibility, little identity, and make little permanent impression on the electorate.[23]

At the same time that they inhibit the emergence of new parties, primary elections also diminish the organizational coherence and competitiveness of existing partisan groupings. The extensive use of primary elections in the contemporary United States helps to preserve the general outlines of the established two-party system by discouraging the formation of parties to challenge the Democrats and Republicans. But the Democratic and Republican parties *as organizations* have hardly been helped by this result. The two-party system preserved by the primary might be characterized as almost a party system without parties—the term "two-party system" having come to refer more to the process whereby the number of candidates per office is typically reduced to only two than to a politics characterized by competition between two organized entities. It almost goes without saying that the present-day party system without parties hardly offers a favorable environment for the political aspirations of subordinate social and economic groups—a result that would surely have pleased many of the Progressive reformers of the nineteenth century.

## Notes

1. Walter Dean Burnham, *Critical Elections and the Mainsprings of American Electoral Politics* (New York: Norton, 1970), ch. 4.

2. V. O. Key, *American State Politics* (New York: Knopf, 1956), chs. 4–6.

3. The primary offers every party faction an opportunity to take its case to the people without renouncing its partisan affiliations. Factions defeated in the primary are likely to have some difficulty raising funds for an additional campaign. But, possibly more important in the context of American political norms, losing factions may be more likely to abide by and accept the legitimacy of an electorate's decision than they would the decision of party "bosses." The importance for party unity of a nominating process that conforms to

democratic norms is discussed in Robert A. Dahl, *Who Governs?* (New Haven: Yale University Press, 1961), pp. 112–14. Data analyzed by Johnson and Gibson and by Comer suggest that even a very divisive primary does not tend to disrupt coalitions of party activists permanently. Donald B. Johnson and James R. Gibson, "The Divisive Primary Revisited: Party Activists in Iowa," *American Political Science Review* 68 (March 1974); John Comer, "Another Look at the Effect of the Divisive Primary: A Research Note," *American Political Quarterly* 7 (January 1976). A number of news accounts following the 1976 presidential campaign suggested that the perceived openness of the nominating process helped to persuade many Reagan workers to campaign actively for Ford in the general election.

4. The most thorough is Charles Merriam and Louise Overacker, *Primary Elections* (Chicago: University of Chicago Press, 1928).

5. Key, *American State Politics*, ch. 4.

6. Robert LaFollette, for example, was not completely unaware of the potential advantages of the primary system. Allen Lovejoy, *LaFollette and the Establishment of the Direct Primary in Wisconsin* (New Haven: Yale University Press, 1941), ch. 3.

7. J. Morgan Kousser, *The Shaping of Southern Politics* (New Haven: Yale University Press, 1974), ch. 3. New York Republicans also seemed cognizant of the benefits of primary reform for internalizing opposition. See Richard L. McCormick, *From Realignment to Reform* (Ithaca: Cornell University Press, 1981), ch. 4. Also see Howard Scarrow, "Have Primary Elections Caused Party Decline? The Evidence from New York State," presented at the MPSA meetings, Chicago, April 12–14, 1984.

8. Data were drawn from the historical archives of the Inter-University Consortium for Political and Social Research.

9. An earlier primary law, enacted in 1906, applied only to four congressional districts.

10. The portion of the Indiana law applying to statewide offices was repealed in 1929. Only congressmen were nominated via the primary election during the entire period 1915–1974.

11. The general question of political change at the turn of the century has been the subject of considerable debate. See, for example, Walter Dean Burnham, "The Changing Shape of the American Political Universe," *American Political Science Review* 54 (March 1965). Also, Philip E. Converse, "Change in the American Electorate," in *The Human Meaning of Social Change*, ed. Angus Campbell and Philip E. Converse (New York: Russell Sage, 1972). Of particular interest is the interchange between Burnham, Converse, and Rusk. Walter Dean Burnham, Philip Converse, Jerrold Rusk, and Jesse F. Marquiette, "Political Change in America," *American Political Science Review* 68 (September 1974).

12. There are also other legal provisions. Most states impose a filing fee, for example. Although in the recent past filing fees could range to five thousand dollars, during the time period we considered, fees were minimal in every state. We nevertheless tested for the possible impact of filing fees and found no discernible effect. We also ran tests to determine whether laws relating to voting in primaries, that is, whether the primary was open or closed, had any effect upon candidacy; again, we found none. Most interesting was the problem of run-off primaries in several southern states. According to Key and others, a second ballot run-off has the effect of inflating the number of candidates competing on the first ballot. This could obviously have the potential of confounding the effects of the legal arrangements on which our analysis focuses. We, therefore, tested for the effects

of run-off primaries, but found no systematic evidence of an inflationary effect of the sort suggested by Key. The number of primary candidates in run-off states was no greater than in non-runoff states with similar statutory access to the primary ballot.

13. Data were obtained from the statutes of the fifty states. Information for three states—Connecticut, Delaware, and Utah—was eliminated since most nominations in these states are obtained through convention procedures.

14. Data were obtained from Richard A. Scammon, *America Votes* (Washington, D.C.: Elections Research Center, 1968–1976).

15. Other plausible ways of expressing this relationship include $\frac{P - G}{\min (P, G)}$. We repeated all our tests using several formulations of the relationship without noting any significant effect on the results.

16. A detailed discussion can be found in E. W. Kelley, "The Methodology of Hypothesis Testing," unpublished manuscript, Cornell University, 1975. Counting ties on the dependent variable (e) totally against us actually produces a somewhat conservative measure of support for our hypothesis.

17. To maintain compatibility throughout this table, states with no signature requirement at all (i.e., signature = 0) were excluded. In such states the relative importance of the general election arena tends to be quite low. Thus the percentages in Table 2 are lower than expected from our overall analysis in Table 1.

18. Again, data were drawn from the statutes of the fifty states. Controlling for the ease of access to the general election ballot still produces a Beta coefficient of -.310 between primary access and general election importance. A Beta coefficient of .051 is produced for the alternate control.

19. General election rules can, to a limited extent, reinforce primary rules. For example, where access to the primary ballot is relatively simple, candidates may be given some additional incentive to enter the primary by general election regulations that make it difficult to mount an independent or third party general election bid. See Peter F. Galderisi, "The Direct Primary and Party Maintenance," Ph.D. dissertation, Cornell University, 1981.

20. One of the more interesting historical cases is that of the Non-Partisan League (NPL), a nascent third party that discovered the virtues of the primary. The NPL is discussed in Samuel Huntington, "The Electoral Tactics of the Non-Partisan League," *Mississippi Valley Historical Review* 36 (1950).

21. There are, of course, any number of analyses of the impact of the way in which conflicts are organized. For example, see S. M. Lipset and Stein Rokkan, "Cleavage Structures, Party Systems, and Voter Alignments" in *Party Systems and Voter Alignments*, ed. S. M. Lipset and Stein Rokkan (New York: Free Press, 1967). The case of the birth of the British Labour Party is discussed in Henry Pelling, *The Origins of the Labour Party* (London: Macmillan, 1954), esp. ch. 4. According to Pelling, one of the factors precipitating the formation of the Labour Party was the inhospitability of the Liberals to new groups.

22. Lubell's discussion is still among the most interesting. Samuel Lubell, *The Future of American Politics* (New York: Doubleday, 1955), esp. ch. 9. For a more general analysis, J. David Greenstone, *Labor in American Politics* (New York: Knopf, 1969).

23. This is one of Key's major points. V. O. Key, *Southern Politics* (New York: Vintage, 1949), esp. ch. 14.

# 3. CONTEMPORARY POLITICAL FORCES AND THE MEANING OF ELECTIONS

A number of significant social and political movements have emerged or re-emerged during the past two decades, involving consumers, environmentalists, women, religious fundamentalists, neoconservatives, business political activists, and so on. Much of the impetus for these movements derives from the explosive politicizing effects of the vast economic and social programs of modern governments. The activities of organized groups are generally viewed in terms of their effects upon governmental action. But interest-group activity is often more a consequence than an antecedent of the state's programs. Even when national policies are initially responses to the appeals of pressure groups and the like, government involvement in a given area is a powerful stimulus for political organization and action, or increases in political action, by those whose interests are affected. During the 1970s, expanded federal regulation of the automobile, oil, gas, education, and health-care industries impelled each of these interests substantially to increase its efforts to influence the government's behavior. These efforts, in turn, spurred the organization of other groups to augment or oppose the activities of the first. One political action committee (PAC) director observed: "It was not the Federal Election Campaign Act and the Federal Election Commission that promoted the Pac Movement: it was every other law and every other regulatory body that began intruding into the business of business." A clear pattern emerges when reviewing who does and does not have a PAC—the more regulated an industry and the more obvious an industry is as a congressional target, the more likely it is to have a political action committee.

Similarly, federal social programs have often sparked political organization and action on the part of clientele groups seeking to influence the distribution of beneftis and, in turn, the organization of groups opposed to the character of the benefits or cost of the programs in question. One example of a pressure group "caused" by a federal program is the National Welfare Rights Organization (NWRO), whose formation during the 1960s was a response to federal and local welfare policies. Substantially increased political organization and activity by fundamentalist religious groups in recent years obviously came in response to federal legislative programs and judicial actions relating to such matters as abortion.

At the same time that political party leaders and formal organizations have declined in importance, these groups have become more active and important participants in the political process. In recent years, a host of single-issue groups organized around matters ranging from abortion to trade regulation have subjected Congress to enormous pressures and cross-pressures on behalf of their various causes. These groups often threaten severe reprisals against their congressional opponents. For example, the National Conservative Political Action Committee (NCPAC) has spent millions of dollars to attempt to unseat opponents of its stands on gun control and abortion. NCPAC funds came to play important roles in the defeat of liberal Democrats such as Frank Church in the 1980 Senate races. A particular target of conservative political action groups was George McGovern, who was also defeated in his 1980 senatorial reelection bid. Groups opposing McGovern included the National Right-to-Life Committee, Life Amendment Political Action Committee, Committee for the Survival of a Free Congress, National Conservative Caucus, the American Conservative Union, Fund for a Conservative Majority, Young Americans for Freedom, John Birch Society, Citizens for the Republic, National Right to Work Committee, Eagle Forum, Citizens' Committee for the Right to Keep and Bear Arms, Gun Owners of America, Tax Limitation Committee, Committee to Defeat the Union Bosses, and Committee to Save the Panama Canal.

Are the new groups and forces of the 1970s and 1980s simply the latest chapters in the pluralist history of the United States, or do they represent a new pattern in American politics? What effects will these new political forces have upon American government and policymaking processes? Two chapters in this section examine important political movements of the 1980s—the feminist movement on the left and the religious right—which have clashed in the forum of elections on such issues as abortion.

Taken together, the essays by Laura Vertz and by Loch Johnson and Charles Bullock raise another important issue. Why have such social issues as abortion and school prayer, once located in the realm of interest-group politics, moved into the realm of electoral politics? One reason, certainly, is that the leadership of a movement sees greater opportunities in electoral rather than interest-group politics. As both chapters make clear, the new religious right and the feminists see the opportunity to mobilize large numbers of adherents and to direct their votes toward and against particular candidates. Yet as Johnson and Bullock emphasize, the voting patterns of both targeted and favored legislators do not necessarily respond to the conspicuous demands of such groups.

The answer may lie in Thomas Ferguson's contention that the public policy behavior of elected officials is more closely linked with the demands and interests of the major investors in them. Ferguson identifies such major investors as predominantly business blocs and urges that they, much more than social movements, have historically been largely responsible for major changes in policy direction. The issue is clearly a critical and open one. Yet it is not clear that the underlying purposes of free elections are well served by the undue influence of either investors or highly mobilized social and political movements, both of which may hold views widely variant from those of most voters.

## 3.1

# The New Feminist Politics

## Laura L. Vertz

Until recently, most studies of elections have concluded that few differences exist between women and men in voting behavior.[1] In the 1980 election, however, clear differences were observed to exist between the political preferences of women and men, and these attitudinal differences appeared to be translated into aggregate differences in voting.[2] The 1982 midterm election results suggest that the differences seen in the 1980 election were not random phenomena; instead, similar patterns emerged, with women's votes actually providing the winning margin in some contests.[3] As a result, scholarly and popular attention has been refocused toward the role of women in the electorate and, more particularly, toward the phenomenon popularly referred to as the "gender gap."

With more attention focused on women in the 1984 presidential campaign than in other recent contests, a question arises: What role has the women's movement played in developing and maintaining the emergent differences between women and men in the electorate? In analyzing the impact of the women's movement on 1984 election-year politics, this chapter addresses three specific points: first, the impact of the women's movement on the development of mass attitudes toward women's rights issues and the link between these attitudes and the vote; second, the impact of the women's movement on the development and maintenance of the differences between women and men on the gender gap issues and the link between these attitudes and the vote; and third, the contextual factors that affect the linkage between the women's movement and the vote.[4] The analysis will confront the question of whether or not elections matter for women and the women's movement.

Laura L. Vertz teaches at North Texas State University.

## The Women's Movement and Mass Attitudes
## toward Women's Rights Issues

Obviously, the women's movement exists to affect the status that women, as a group, hold in society. Sapiro has described the essential elements of the women's movement as (1) a belief that women's opportunities and the quality of their lives are limited in part simply because they are women; (2) a desire to release the constraints imposed by patriarchy and sexism; and (3) a belief not simply in individual action, but also in group action to improve the conditions of women.[5]

The latter point suggests that one important goal of the women's movement is to impress upon women the need to support and promote women's equality in all spheres of life and also to engage in *behaviors* to insure that this equality is achieved. The attitudes that the women's movement is striving to affect are commonly referred to as ''women's rights issues.'' The women's movement is concerned with insuring that women receive equal pay for equal work, establishing the comparable worth of jobs, working for the passage of the Equal Rights Amendment (ERA), promoting prochoice laws and practices, securing more child care support, seeking equal opportunity in education and employment, fighting discrimination, harassment, and violent crimes against women, recruiting more women to high-level positions in government and industry, and searching for equity in insurance, retirement, and divorce laws and customs.

To what extent are attitudes on women's rights issues related to the behavioral differences observed between women and men in the 1980 election? The answer to such a question is important, for if a relationship exists between opinions on these issues and voting behavior, then the women's movement can be directly credited with the recently aroused interest in women in the electorate. However, if attitudes toward women's rights do not account for these behavioral differences, then another set of attitudes, not directly affected by the women's movement, may be of greater explanatory importance.

For the women's movement to be responsible for the power recently achieved by women in the electorate, several conditions must hold. First, women must be more supportive of women's rights issues than men, if these attitudes have *directly* resulted in behavioral differences. Second, a link must actually exist between these attitudes and behavior. Third, an explanation must be possible as to why the differences are emerging at this time on these attitudes and behaviors.

How successful has the women's movement been in attracting a following among women in the mass public? Has the women's movement been able to gain political power from changes in voting behavior based upon its impact on mass political attitudes? These questions can be addressed by reviewing previous studies of the impact of the women's movement, analyzing some recent poll data pertaining to women's rights issues, and drawing conclusions regarding the impact of the women's movement on electoral politics in 1984.

Most research on women's rights has shown that women and men tend to have similar beliefs in this area. Using data from the General Social Survey, Shaffer found that on abortion, women's role in society, teenage birth control, and the Equal Rights Amendment (ERA) few differences exist between men and women. In addition, his research suggests that most people support women's rights, with abortion being one possible exception.[6]

Welch and Sigelmen studied the issue of willingness to support women candidates for public office. They found that there currently exists similar support among women and men on this question. These authors traced the level of support for women candidates back to 1972 and discovered that in the earlier period men were more supportive than women. Over time, however, women have changed, and now both sexes are willing to support women candidates for public office.[7]

Ferree also examined the issue of willingness to support qualified women candidates. She looked at data beginning in 1958 and found that for the 1958–1969 period, men were more supportive of women candidates than women in the mass public were. The level of support began to merge in the 1970s and is currently equal.[8] Howell-Martinez reported that women for the first time are very slightly more willing than men to support women candidates for office.[9]

Howell-Martinez has also shown that on the general issue of the status of women in society, the public is supportive of increased equality for women. In 1970, 40 percent of women compared with 44 percent of men supported an increased and equal role for women in society. By the 1980s the percentage had increased to over 60 percent, and the differences earlier observed between women and men had disappeared. Both sexes are now equally supportive of equal statuses for women and men in American society.

In sum, most authors agree that (1) men supported women's rights issues before women did; (2) on most women's rights issues there is substantial support in the mass public; (3) women and men now have very similar levels of support for these issues, and this level of agreement extends back to the 1970s; and (4) there are a few issues in the area of women's rights that continue to be a source of major public controversy.

Abortion, for example, continues to be a controversial issue. In addition, support for the ERA is waning among the mass public where it was once overwhelming.[10] In general, controversy over specific issues within the area of women's rights stems from two sources. First, if an issue is perceived to be a threat to women in traditional roles, then it is likely to receive less support.[11] Second, if the issue is perceived solely as a symbol of the movement itself, less support is also likely.[12] While there exists majority support on specific issues that can be categorized as women's rights issues, the women's movement often conjures up hostility and may be perceived as a threat to the traditional family.[13]

Recent poll data provide further evidence of the ongoing nature of the similarities between women and men on women's rights issues. Men and women are similar in their approval (in the abstract) of women candidates for public

Table 1

**Recent poll results for women's rights issues**

Question: If your party nominated a woman to run for _____ , would you vote for her if she were qualified for the job?

| Office | % approval for men | % approval for women |
| --- | --- | --- |
| Mayor | 92 | 89 |
| Governor | 89 | 86 |
| Congress | 92 | 91 |
| President | 78 | 78 |

*Source*: *Gallup Reports*, no. 228 and 229.

office. Table 1 gives the current level of approval for the offices of mayor, governor, Congress, and president. As can be seen in the table, there is a high degree of approval for qualified women candidates, especially for mayor, governor, and Congress. The level of approval for the presidency is somewhat lower, although still high at around 78 percent indicating acceptance. The differences between women and men on these items are slight; no greater than a 3 percent disparity is found.

The results obtained from previous research and those shown in Table 1 suggest that there exists strong and consistent support among members of the mass public on women's rights issues. In addition, they indicate that men were slightly more supportive than women of many aspects of women's rights at an earlier time; it now appears, however, that the sexes are equally supportive. Logically, these results suggest that the differences in the vote between women and men for Carter and Reagan in the 1980 election were not a direct function of individuals' attitudes on women's rights issues. Since these are the specific issues that the women's movement is, by definition, most interested in addressing, the conclusion to be drawn is that the women's movement cannot claim *direct* credit for the increased attention and power obtained by women in the electorate due to the male-female voting differences with men. The implications for the 1984 election are obvious: If voting differences are once again seen between women and men, they are not likely to have been due to the direct impact of women's rights issues on their votes.

## The Women's Movement and the Gender Gap

Since the 1980 election, pollsters have consistently found aggregate-level differences between women and men in attitudes toward the use of violence, defense spending, nuclear war and power, social welfare programs, environmental issues, President Reagan and his handling of the economy, and issues pertaining to an

Table 2

## Poll results for gender gap issues

| Issue | Question |
|---|---|
| Satisfaction with U.S. | In general, are you satisfied or dissatisfied with the way things are going in the U.S. at this time? |
| | Men: 55% satisfied.   Women: 45% satisfied |
| Approval of president | Do you approve or disapprove of the way Ronald Reagan is handling his job as president? |
| | Men: 60% approve.   Women: 51% approve |
| President's handling of . . . | Now let me ask you about some specific problems. As I read each problem, would you tell me whether you approve or disapprove of the way President Reagan is handling that problem? |
| the economy | Men: 56% approve.   Women: 45% approve |
| unemployment | Men: 46% approve.   Women: 38% approve |
| foreign policy | Men: 45% approve.   Women: 34% approve |
| relations with Soviets | Men: 51% approve.   Women: 36% approve |
| situation in Lebanon | Men: 31% approve.   Women: 25% approve |
| situation in Central America | Men: 37% approve.   Women: 22% approve |
| Keeping country prosperous | Now which man would do a better job of keeping the country prosperous, Ronald Reagan or Walter Mondale? |
| | Men: 57% Reagan.   Women: 45% Reagan |
| | Men: 32% Mondale.   Women: 35% Mondale |

individual's economic well-being. This set of attitudes has been popularly referred to as the gender gap. The observance of these attitudinal differences has been credited with causing the aggregate-level voting differences between women and men that surfaced in the 1980 election.[14]

It is, however, the behavioral (i.e., voting) differences that have directed scholarly and popular attention toward the gender gap, not the gender gap itself. The primary evidence in support of this assertion is the ongoing nature of the gender gap phenomenon. The gender gap did not suddenly develop just prior to 1980; instead, public opinion polls have shown that differences between women and men on the gender gap issues have existed for quite some time. For example, Smith has demonstrated that differences between women and men on attitudes toward the use of violence are long standing. Citing data obtained from public

| Issue | Question |
|---|---|
| Keeping U.S. from war | Which man, if elected in November, do you think would be more likely to keep the U.S. out of World War III, Ronald Reagan or Walter Mondale? <br><br> Men: 39% Reagan.  Women: 31% Reagan <br> Men: 45% Mondale.  Women: 43% Mondale |
| Safer world | Do you think we live in a safer world now than we did three years ago, or not? <br><br> Men: 64% no.  Women: 73% no |
| Money for food | Have there been times during the last year when you did not have enough money to buy food your family needed? <br><br> Men: 18% yes.  Women: 22% yes |
| for clothing | Men: 22% yes.  Women: 30% yes |
| for health care | Men: 22% yes.  Women: 27% yes |
| Party out of war | Which political party do you think would be more likely to keep the United States out of World War III—the Republican party or the Democratic Party? <br><br> Men: 31% Republican.  Women: 21% Republican <br> Men: 33% Democratic.  Women: 45% Democratic |
| Party for prosperity | Which political party do you think will do a better job of keeping the country prosperous? <br><br> Men: 38% Republican.  Women: 29% Republican <br> Men: 38% Democratic.  Women: 42% Democratic |

*Source*: *Gallup Reports*, no. 217, 220, and 221.

opinion polls that extend back to the 1930s, he examines 285 data points and finds that men are more favorably disposed toward the use of violence in foreign affairs, social combat, law enforcement, and interpersonal relations in 87 percent of the data points observed.[15] Other scholars, including Baer and Jackson and Pomper, have also observed these long-standing differences.[16]

The most recent available evidence also supports the assertion that the gender gap is an ongoing phenomenon in public opinion. Table 2 contains recent Gallup poll results indicative of the gender gap phenomenon. As can be seen, differences between women and men on these issues are found consistently. The gender gap appears to be a well-established characteristic of public opinion in the United States.

Because the gender gap is not a novel occurrence, it follows logically that it alone is not responsible for the recent interest in women in the electorate. As noted above, the most apparent explanation for the attention being paid to women in the electorate is the behavioral differences between women and men that emerged in the 1980 election. The hypothesized link between the gender gap and the behavioral differences seen in 1980 and 1982 accounts for the recent interest in the gender gap. Several political analysts have suggested that the gender gap's linkage with voting caused the margin of difference in several contests in 1982.[17] It was also speculated that the gender gap might affect the outcome of the 1984 presidential election.

This point has not gone unnoticed by the women's movement. In her discussion of the gender gap, Smeal stated:

1. Women can and do vote differently than men. This gender gap in voting appears among all subgroupings of men and women, and transcends differences in age, race, income, education, and party preference.
2. The gender gap is making the women's vote visible by providing a means of measuring it.
3. The gender gap is increasing the political clout of women, their viewpoints and values.
4. Women represent enough votes to be the margin of difference—and provide the victory—for state legislative and congressional candidates, and will elect the next president of the United States.[18]

The women's movement, noting the potential power to be gained from being identified with the gender gap, has successfully laid claim to it by taking credit for the attitudinal differences between women and men contained within the gender gap and by placing women's rights issues squarely within discussions and analyses of the gender gap. Clearly, however, there are only a few specific issues wherein the gender gap and women's rights issues overlap. Figure 1 describes the relationship between these two sets of issues.

Issues pertaining to the employment status of women are contained within both the gender gap and women's rights issues. However, the interpretation given to employment issues differs between the two sets. From the perspective of women's rights, the primary emphasis is on insuring that equal employment opportunities exist for women, working to eliminate institutional and legal barriers that constrain women's employment opportunities, and concentrating upon all aspects of employment as they relate to women's equality. Within the gender gap, employment issues are more directly related to the feminization of poverty, the ability of women to provide their families with the necessities of life, and general humanitarian considerations.[19]

Those issues that are not found within both sets, however, are treated by the women's movement as though they were in fact contained within the same set. In addition, the popular press as well as many political elites treat both women's rights issues and gender gap issues as properly contained within the same subset. The evidence, however, suggests that these two types of issues are not conceptual-

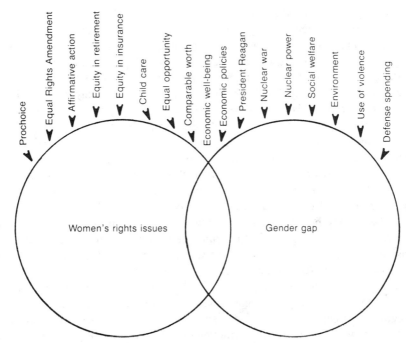

Figure 1  **The relationship between women's rights issues and the gender gap**

ly the same. On women's rights issues, men and women (in the aggregate) do not differ; on the gender gap issues, differences between women and men emerge. Furthermore, there is little evidence to suggest that the women's movement has had an impact on attitudes toward those issues categorized as gender gap issues. In his analysis of attitudes toward the use of violence, Smith made note of this fact: "Overall, the evidence fails to show any impact of feminist ideology on the gender differences on violence. Differences have not appreciably changed since the women's movement was organized in the late sixties, and the gap is the same among profeminist men and women as it is among antifeminists of both sexes, nor do these differences vary by either age or education."[20]

The women's movement has, however, had a direct impact on another factor that has led to the *importance* of the gender gap, that is, the increasing role that women are taking in public (as opposed to private) sphere activities. Since the 1950s women's participation in the labor force has been increasing. Women and men now vote at approximately the same rate, and women are currently registered to vote in greater numbers than men.[21] In other political activities, such as running for office, women still lag behind men. Voting, however, is one of the key contextual factors that have set the stage for the recent attention that women in the electorate have received. The women's movement can legitimately claim at least partial credit for the evolutionary process that has led to the increase in public-sphere activities by women.

The women's movement developed, therefore, an interesting and potentially effective strategy for affecting the outcome of the 1984 presidential election and the ability of women to gain political power. By aligning itself with the gender gap, the women's movement could take advantage of and also help to use effectively any decisive differences between women and men in the mass public. Greater elite influence for the women's movement was also possible, particularly if the gender gap actually did affect election outcomes. Certainly, more political clout is possible with this strategy than with one based solely upon women's rights issues. After all, even female political elites are, from the perspective of the women's movement, at best only "closet feminists," acknowledging that they cannot win political office solely on the basis of women's rights issues.[22] Evidence of the effectiveness of this gender gap strategy existed in the 1984 election: it was the first election in which women were seriously considered for the position of vice-presidential nominee of a major party.

The strategy, however, could fail in two ways. First, if Reagan were reelected, the attempt to affect the election outcome would likely result in even more decisions detrimental to the goals of the women's movement in the Administration's second term. Second, politicians of both parties might see the distinction between women's rights issues and the gender gap. They might make appeals designed to attract the gender gap voters, thereby gaining possible electoral strength, but doing so without addressing women's rights issues or otherwise extending rewards to the women's movement. The task of the women's movement in the 1984 election, therefore, was to work to insure that women's rights issues and the gender gap remained linked as part of the same political agenda in the minds of political elites.

## Conclusion: The Women's Movement, Attitudes, and the Vote

A model summarizing the impact of the women's movement on presidential elections can be developed from this analysis of the women's movement and the 1984 presidential election. Figure 2 contains a diagram of this model.

The model contains two contextual factors and an interactive variable that mediate the direct relationship between attitudes on women's rights and gender gap issues with voting behavior. The importance of contextual factor I (greater public-sphere participation) has already been discussed. Briefly, the increased number of women in employment and politics has resulted in the increased importance of the behavior of women in the electorate. Any model that is used to describe voting behavior must, therefore, include this as a contextual variable. In other words, the discussion of the importance of women in the electorate assumes their participation at current or increasing levels. If this condition does not hold, then the importance of women's behavior is lessened.

The second contextual factor is the election itself. The model suggests that certain contests are more likely to elicit responses based upon gender gap and women's rights issues. The candidates in the 1980 election provided a stimulus

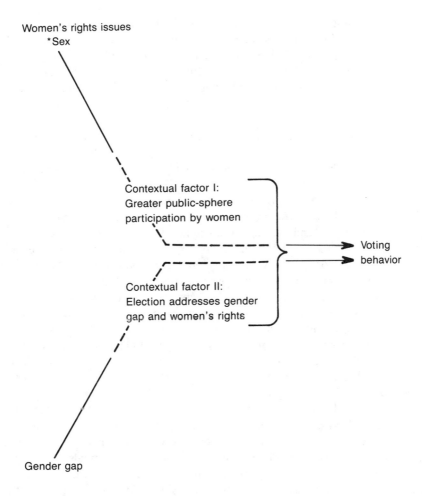

Figure 2  **A model of the impact of the women's movement on presidential elections**

for behavior consistent with attitudes on these issues. Smeal has generally described this factor as follows:

> As long as women view public issues in a substantially different way than do men; as long as significant numbers of women are underpaid and discriminated against economically; as long as there continue to be more and more women who are economically independent of men—or, more important, believe they might be in the future; as long as more women live alone, or are responsible for their children economically; as long as such key

feminist issues as abortion and the ERA, affirmative action in jobs and education, discrimination in insurance and in pay equity persist in the country without resolution—the *potential* for the gender gap will persist. Whether it occurs depends on the circumstances and issues of a particular campaign. This is why the gender gap appears to "blink on and off," to be present sometimes and disappear at others.[23]

This factor is similar to that described for the importance of ideology in the 1964 election. Pierce has argued that ideology was important in the 1964 election because the candidates expressed themselves in ideological terms and because the issues in the election were expressed ideologically.[24] Contextual factor II states an analogous idea for women's rights issues and the gender gap. Particular campaigns are more likely than others to provide a context that sparks behavior based upon women's rights and gender gap attitudes. In fact, it is possible that the context for women's rights and the gender gap is developing into a general ideological dimension. Not only do women and men tend to differ on the gender gap issues, they also differ on ideology and support for political parties, women being more liberal and Democratic.[25] The gender gap may simply be an expression of ideology that is relevant to contemporary politics in the United States.

The model in Figure 2 suggests that these two contextual factors must be operative if the women's movement is to play an important role in a presidential election. First, women must continue to participate in politics and the labor force. Second, the election contest must directly address the cleavages in the gender gap and women's rights issues.

If these conditions hold, then gender gap and women's rights issues should affect voting behavior. The relationship between individuals' attitudes toward the gender gap issues and their voting behavior is described as direct. For women's rights issues, however, the relationship is somewhat more complex. As noted above, attitudinal differences between women and men do not exist on these issues. Therefore, the relationship cannot be a simple, direct one. Instead, it is suggested that attitudes toward women's rights will interact with sex to result in voting behavior. In other words, among women, attitudes toward women's rights issues are expected to have an effect on voting, but for men little impact will be seen. This is because women's right issues are likely to have greater salience for women than for men. The relationship between individuals' attitudes toward women's rights issues and voting is therefore described as interacting with the sex of the individual. Since these issues have greater salience for women, they will have a greater impact on their behavior.

The model indicates that the women's movement will indirectly affect voting behavior through the variables contained in this model. The women's movement can take at least partial credit for the increased public-sphere behaviors of women. Thus far, the movement has had little control over the electoral context, but as more women serve as candidates for public office and in major party roles, their influence on the context may change. The women's movement has an important impact on attitudes toward the women's movement; however, the model suggests that these attitudes affect behavior only for women. Finally, the women's movement has had little impact specifically on attitudes toward the majority of the gender gap issues. Yet, the role of the women's movement has been to attempt to manage the gender gap, thereby increasing its impact on voting and elite behavior.

## Postscript: Did the 1984 Election Matter for Women and the Women's Movement?

In retrospect, the strategy adopted by the women's movement of aligning itself with the gender gap resulted in what has been referred to as *ad nauseum* as an historic victory: the Democratic party's nomination of a woman candidate, Geraldine Ferraro, for the vice-presidency. While the Mondale-Ferraro ticket did not fare well in the November election, the Ferraro candidacy served to open yet another door for women in politics.

The results of the presidential contest showed that the gender gap did predict aggregate-level election outcomes in a consistent, albeit undecisive, fashion. As with the 1980 presidential contest, an 8 to 10 percent difference was seen between women and men in their support for Reagan. Men were more supportive of Reagan than women by this margin;[26] however, a majority of both women and men supported the Reagan–Bush ticket.

In addition to the presidential contest, women had an important impact on several state and local races. Women had a decisive impact on the Harkin, Perry, and Kerry races for the U.S. Senate. Ten additional women were elected to the U.S. House of Representatives over the previous high of fifty-five in 1982. Women made gains in gubernatorial contests and other important statewide offices.[27]

Thus, from the perspective of the women's movement, the impact of the 1984 election must be regarded as of mixed importance. The gender gap was found to be truly decisive in only a few races. The representatives elected by women can, however, be expected to pay special attention to the gender gap and women's rights issues during their terms of office. On the other hand, while operative, the gender gap was not at all decisive in the presidential election. The women's movement may find itself faced with a relatively unsupportive administration for the next four years. Early indications are that Reagan will actively work against the women's movement. His overt support of the prolife movement on the anniversary of *Roe v. Wade* is an example of his willingness to take stands in opposition to the women's movement.

In the final analysis, the answer to the question of whether elections matter matter will have to await a response. Geraldine Ferraro's candidacy does, indeed, have important symbolic meanings attached to it. However, one candidacy should not be assumed to result in a political system with no constraints on the political activity of women. Until a woman actually is elected to the presidency, the movement continues to have much work to do.

## Notes

1. Angus Campbell, Philip E. Converse, Warren E. Miller, and Donald E. Stokes, *The American Voter* (New York: Wiley, 1960); Susan Welch, "Women as Political Animals?" *American Journal of Political Science* 21 (1977):711–30; Goldie Shabad and Kristi Andersen, "Candidate Evaluations by Men and Women," *Public Opinion Quarterly* 48 (1979):18–35; and Stephen D. Shaffer, "Exploring Gender Differences on Political Issues," paper presented at annual meeting of the Southern Political Science Association, Birmingham, November 3–5, 1983.

2. Sandra Baxter and Marjorie Lansing, *Women and Politics: The Invisible Majority* (Ann Arbor: University of Michigan Press, 1980); Denise L. Baer and John S. Jackson, III, "The Gender Gap, Policy Preferences, and Ideology of Party Elites and Followers," paper presented an annual meeting of the Midwest Political Science Association, Chicago, April 19–21, 1984.

3. For example, League of Women Voters Education Fund, *The Women's Vote: Beyond the Nineteenth Amendment* (1983); Eleanor Smeal, *Why and How Women Will Elect the Next President* (New York: Harper and Row, 1984).

4. This chapter focuses on how the women's movement can affect elections and specifically how it related to the 1984 presidential election. Very little attention is be paid to how much elections affect the women's movement. In addition, the wide range of behaviors that the women's movement engages in to affect politics are not discussed; instead, the analysis pertains only to electoral politics. It is thus not a comprehensive treatment of the relationship between the women's movement and politics in the United States.

5. Virginia Sapiro, "When Are Interests Interesting? The Problem of Political Representation of Women," *American Political Science Review* 75 (1981):701–16.

6. Shaffer, "Exploring Gender Differences."

7. Susan Welch and Lee Sigelman, "Changes in Public Attitudes Toward Women in Politics," *Social Science Quarterly* 63 (1982):312–22.

8. Myra Max Ferree, "A Woman for President? Changing Responses: 1958–1972," *Public Opinion Quarterly* (Fall 1974):390–99.

9. Vicky Howell-Martinez, "Women's Changing Political Behavior: The Invisible Majority Becomes a Minority," paper presented at annual meeting of the Southwest Social Science Association, San Antonio, March 17–20, 1982.

10. Glenn Spitze and Joan Huber, "Effects of Anticipated Consequences on ERA Opinion," *Social Science Quarterly* 63 (1982):323–31; Val Burres, "Who Opposed the ERA? The Social Bases of Antifeminism," *Social Science Quarterly* 64 (1983):305–17.

11. Burres, "Who Opposed the ERA?"

12. Susan Welch, "Support among Women for the Issues of the Women's Movement," *The Sociological Quarterly* 16 (1975):216–27.

13. Ibid.; Burres, "Who Opposed the ERA?"

14. Kathleen A. Frankovic, "Sex and Politics—New Alignments, Old Issues," *PS* 15 (1982):439–48.

15. Tom W. Smith, "The Polls: Gender and Attitudes toward Violence," *Public Opinion Quarterly* 48 (1984):384-96.

16. Baer and Jackson, "The Gender Gap"; Gerald Pomper, *Voter's Choice: Varieties of American Electoral Behavior* (New York: Dodd, Mead, 1975).

17. For example, League of Women Voters Education Fund, *The Women's Vote*.

18. Smeal defines the gender gap in terms of voting behavior, women's rights issues, and the issues that I have defined as gender gap issues. Her definition thus confuses the link between attitudes and voting behavior. For the purposes of social scientific analysis and this essay, it is essential that concepts be used in a theoretically and empirically consistent and concise fashion. One concept cannot be used to refer to both attitudes and behavior; therefore, my use of the concept gender gap to refer precisely to a specific subset of political attitudes serves the purpose of separating attitudes and behavior. However, regardless of her imprecision in concept definition, Smeal's quotation is useful for illustrating how the women's movement is attempting to use the gender gap to its advantage. *Why and How*; quotation is from p. 8.

19. See Baer and Jackson, "The Gender Gap."

20. Smith, "The Polls," p. 386.

21. Barbara S. Deckard, *The Women's Movement: Political, Socioeconomic, and Psychological Issues* (New York: Harper and Row, 1979); Baer and Jackson, "The Gender Gap"; Welch, "Women as Political Animals?"; and Smeal, *Why and How*.

22. Susan Carroll, "Women Candidates and Support for Women's Issues: Closet Feminists," paper presented at annual meeting of the Midwest Political Science Association, Chicago, April 19-21, 1979; Jerry Perkins and Diane L. Fowlkes, "Opinion Representation vs. Social Representation," *American Political Science Review* 75 (1980):92-103.

23. Smeal, *Why and How*, p. 13.

24. John C. Pierce, "Party Identification and the Changing Role of Ideology in American Politics," *Midwest Journal of Political Science* 14 (1970):25-42.

25. Ben J. Wattenberg, "The Democrats' Duel," *Public Opinion* 61 (1983):11-12.

26. Lisa Lederer, "Reagan's Reelection: Style over Substance," *National NOW Times* 17, 2 (1984):1.

27. See *National NOW Times* 17, 2 (1984).

# 3.2

# The New Religious Right and the 1980 Congressional Elections

## Loch Johnson and Charles S. Bullock III

### Introduction

Politics and religion have become an all but unavoidable focus for analysts of contemporary American society. In the 1980 elections, they came together with an emotional and organizational force unseen in the United States since the anti-Communist "Christian Crusades" of Carl McIntire, Dr. Billy James Hargis, and Dr. Fred C. Schwarz in the 1950s and early 1960s.[1]

In terms of sheer numbers of followers, the New Religious Right (NRR) may well be unprecedented as a political-religious movement in this country. Upwards of 65 million evangelical Christians live in the United States, and NRR leaders claim to reach most of them regularly through an elaborate radio and television network—the so-called electronic church.[2] One NRR group alone, the Moral Majority, reports a membership of 75,000 religious leaders across the land,[3] who in turn claim a combined national constituency of 50 million Protestant evangelicals, 30 million "morally conservative" Catholics, and a few million Mormons and Orthodox Jews.[4] Even lesser known groups in the movement point to a sizable band of loyalists. The Christian Voice, for example, is reported to have a membership roster of 210,000 individuals.[5]

The goals of NRR affiliates are no less ambitious than their membership claims. Their primary objective (in coalition with the broader New Right) is, in the words of proponent Paul Weyrich, "to overturn the present power struc-

Loch Johnson and Charles S. Bullock III teach at the University of Georgia. They gratefully acknowledge the research assistance of Bill Mattox, Brooks Tennyson, and Susan Duffin.

ture in this country . . . we're talking about Christianizing America."[6] Reverend Jerry Falwell, president of the Moral Majority, puts it this way: "Moral Americans will no longer permit the minority of treacherous individuals to destroy our country with their Godless liberal philosophies."[7] In a word, a new religious movement is underway—one with distinct political objectives, a broad following, and a leadership far more skillful, well-connected, and visible than its forebearers McIntire, Hargis, and Schwarz.[8]

The purposes of this study are, first, to examine the structure, origins, and *raison d'être* of the New Religious Right, as well as its bases of support; and, second, to explore its electoral techniques and influence (if any) on the 1980 elections and on policymaking in the U.S. House of Representatives.

## Form and Function

### Structure

The organizations within the New Religious Right are overlapping and interlocking, as indeed are their relationships with nonreligious groups comprising the broader New Right coalition. Most well-known of NRR components is doubtless the Moral Majority (see Figure 1). Founded in 1978, the Moral Majority now boasts of chapters in every state,[9] though the most elaborate organizations have sprouted in the Deep South.[10] It claims over two million active donors and an ability to raise 40 to 70 million dollars a year through radio, television, and newsletter solicitations.[11]

Whereas the Moral Majority relies upon a national network of fundamentalist pastors for organizational leadership and is 90 percent Baptist, Christian Voice recruits lay people from around the country to head state organizations and has a membership said to represent forty-five denominations. "Pastors are too busy to lead political groups; we prefer lay people," states Christian Voice's Washington, D.C., director.[12] Founded in 1978, Christian Voice is an amalgam of antigay (American Christian Cause), antipornography (Citizens for Decency Through Law), and antiabortion (Pro-Family Coalition) groups. Christian Voice had an estimated combined budget in 1980 of 3 to 4 million dollars and has sixteen members of Congress on its advisory board.[13]

Robert Billings, Moral Majority cofounder and a Christian Voice policy member, also established the National Christian Action Coalition (NCAC). Intended originally as a lobbying front for Christian schools, the NCAC has evolved into a Washington-based religious think-tank (the Christian Education and Research Foundation, CERF), as well as an umbrella sheltering several NRR state groups (such as Georgia's Concerned Citizens for Good Government).

Last among the NRR "Big Four" is the Religious Roundtable. Essentially a training academy for would-be NRR leaders, Roundtable operates on an annual budget of approximately $1 million.

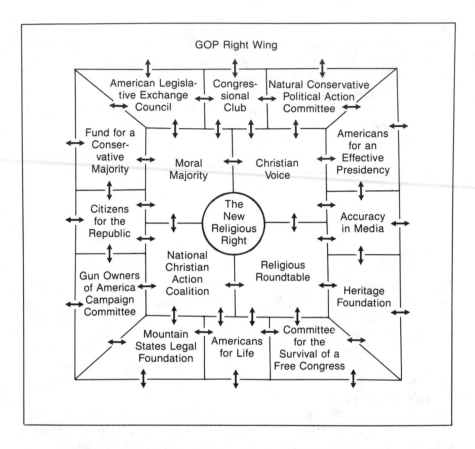

Figure 1 **Schematic depiction of key elements in the right-wing coalition affiliated with the Republican party. (Arrows indicate flow of ideas, personnel, and other resources.)**

Around these core organizations revolve satellite groupings. One Moral Majority board member, for instance, heads a Christian family lobby in Washington called Family America; NCAC Director William Billings also leads the Washington-based Conservative Leadership Youth Foundation; Christian Voice board member Senator James McClure (Republican, Idaho) chairs the "Steering Committee," a New Right caucus on Capitol Hill. The list of interconnections could go on, including ties to various nonreligious organizations across the right end of the political spectrum such as the prominent think-tank, Heritage Foundation (see Figure 1).

As an empirical test of NRR cohesion, we correlated Christian Voice and NCAC legislative ratings for House members.[14] The result was a strong positive

Table 1

**Candidate targeting as measure of cohesion between New Religious Right and New Right**

| Christian Voice targets and endorsees[b] | NCPAC targets[a] | |
|---|---|---|
| | Yes | No |
| First-priority targets | 57.5% | 00.0% |
| | (27)[c] | (0) |
| Second-priority targets | 12.8% | 45.5% |
| | (6) | (5) |
| Endorsees | 29.8% | 54.5% |
| | (14) | (6) |

a. National Conservative Political Action Committee. This targeting information is from *Congressional Quarterly Weekly Report* (1980), pp. 3300–34.
b. Source: Christian Voice (1980).
c. Number of cases in parentheses.

association (r = .92), indicating almost total agreement on policy orientation between these organizations (and with the Moral Majority, which endorses NCAC ratings. NRR components identify essentially the same "friends" and "enemies" in the House of Representatives.

To explore the cohesion between the NRR and other New Right organizations, we compared the 1980 House candidates "targeted" for defeat by the Christian Voice and by the National Conservative Political Action Committee. NCPAC is the best known and richest of the right-wing political action committees. The fundamental agreement between Christian Voice and NCPAC over House "good guys" and "bad guys" is evident in Table 1. NCPAC targeted all of Christian Voice's first-priority targets. Their agreement fell short of complete, however, as NCPAC opposed only six of eleven second-priority Christian Voice targets. NCPAC also refused to endorse six candidates, including three Republicans, anointed by Christian Voice.

Another way to appraise NRR–New Right congruence is to compare Christian Voice/NCAC legislative ratings of House members against the list of NCPAC targets. NCPAC targets were about twice as apt to include Christian Voice "devils" (low ratings) as "angels" (high); whereas the figures for NCAC were less lopsided, NCAC "devils" were still predominant among NCPAC targets. Significantly, though, 32 and 42 percent of the NCPAC targets were Christian Voice or NCAC "angels" respectively. In short, cohesion between the

NRR and the New Right is reasonably strong, as one might expect, but weaker than the bonds of agreement within the NRR itself.

So, to say that groups within the NRR and the New Right are closely associated is not to say that they speak with a single tongue or represent a monolithic unity (let alone a conspiracy). While organizational memberships overlap and boards of directors often interlock, distinct leaders head each group and they tend to be fiercely independent in Biblical interpretation, in funding, and in guarding their religious constituencies from rival interlopers. To some extent they are in competition for the allegiance of a common pool of evangelical worshippers; this competition can produce bruised egoes, resentment, and some internecine conflict.[15] To put this another way, viewed from the outside the NRR looks extraordinarily cohesive; viewed from within, though, divisions are apparent, just as many black groups in American share a common perspective yet sometimes feud among themselves over issues and goals.

## Beliefs

A concern for ''morality'' is an essential glue that holds together these groups on the right. They seek to reverse what they perceive to be a decline in the moral standards of the United States which, in a kind of religious domino-theory, they believe will lead next to the fall of our internal freedoms and—fatally—a lowered resistance to assault from ''godless Communists'' abroad. The cause of this decline, from the NRR perspective, is a nefarious ''secular humanism'' that has swept the nation, bringing in its tide the evils of gay rights, drugs, abortion, the Equal Rights Amendment (ERA), pornography and promiscuity, naive arms agreements with the Soviets, sex education, a weakened defense, and a host of other calamities.[16] Their objective is to restore virtue to the home and to the nation—''to reinstate Norman Rockwell's America.''[17]

Fighting initially in this century to ban the sale of liquor (Prohibition), the teaching of evolution (the Scopes trial), and social dancing, the fundamentalist movement focused its energies in the fifties on a struggle against Communism—a worldwide conspiracy led by Satan himself (so preached McIntire, Hargis, Schwarz, and the most popular evangelical minister of all, Reverend Billy Graham).[18] On this new battlefield, the chief villains were the Soviet leaders; a close second, however, were liberals in the United States. ''I'm a radio preacher, fighting liberalism and Communism,'' declared Hargis in 1962.[19]

If in the 1950s and 1960s it was Soviet armies that members of Religious Right feared most, by 1978 their focus had come to rest more on domestic liberals. As FitzGerald writes, ''the feminists, the pornographers, and the militant homosexuals were destroying the American family [argue Falwell et al.], and its destruction would (in Confucian sequence) lead to the destruction of the nation by Communist armies.''[20] Drunkards, evolutionists, foxtrotters, Communists, and liberals—the battle lines were drawn. The function of the Religious Right is to join the war against these forces—with greater numbers, more money, and sharper electoral skills than ever before.

## Bases of Support

Whereas we have highlighted the concern with morality expressed by the New (and the old) Religious Right, the disaffections propelling this movement are probably broader. Extensive research by Lipset, Bell, and Lipset and Raab, among others, documents the importance of "status anxiety" as a source of support for the political right. As Bell writes: "What the right wing is fighting, in the shadow of Communism, is essentially 'modernity'—that complex of attitudes that might be defined most simply as the belief in rational assessment, rather than established custom, for the evolution of social change—and what it seeks to defend is its fading dominance, exercised once through the institutions of small-town American, over the control of social change." Viewed from the perspective of one's status in society, a working hypothesis on the NRR becomes: The social groups most threatened by changes in society (especially economic changes) are the most apt to support right-wing movements. More specifically, the ample empirical evidence on right-wing politics from Father Coughlin to Joe McCarthy points to these core centers of support: rural residents, low wage earners, the aged, the poorly educated, nativists, conservatives, and Republicans.[21] We tested this hypothesis against recent data on the NRR.

To examine the affinity between NRR support for legislators and the population characteristics listed above, we established a profile of all U.S. House districts. If the earlier scholarship on rightist movements remains valid for today's Christian right, we expected legislators from rural, poor, Republican, and conservative districts with low percentage of "foreign stock" (that is, immigrant classes) and low median-age population to score high on NRR voting evaluations. As measures of NRR policy preferences, we used Christian Voice and NCAC legislative vote-ratings, which range from 100 percent (good Christians) to 0 (the bedeviled).[22]

In Table 2, we report the association between the indices of right-wing support established by previous scholarship and NRR ratings. In most instances, the expected relationship was strongly borne out; as in earlier incarnations, the NRR demonstrated a decided preference for conservatives from rural and Republican districts with native stock (that is, few foreign born).

The three other characteristics—advanced age, low income, and low education—were, however, only weakly associated with NRR legislative ratings (see Table 2). While NRR legislative "angels" tended to represent districts with demographic profiles closely matching reported bases of support for right-wing movements in the past (namely, conservative, rural, nativist Republicans), these weak correlations with age, income, and education suggest that the NRR has cast a wider net than did its historical antecedents. NRR "angels" were just as apt to

Table 2

**Relationship between 1980 Religious Right ratings for U.S. house members and selected independent variables**

| | | Ratings | |
| | | CV[a] | NCAC[b] |
| --- | --- | --- | --- |
| Rurality | Percent urban population in district[c] | −.32[d] | −.34 |
| Income | Median income of total population in district[c] | −.15 | −.21 |
| Party | Democratic party membership of member[e] | −.63 | −.58 |
| | District support for Democratic candidate[e] | −.63 | −.35 |
| Ideology | Liberal orientation of member[f] | −.86 | −.86 |
| Nativism | Percent foreign-born in district[c] | −.32 | −.37 |
| Age | Median age of total population in district[c] | .03 | .04 |
| Education | Median age of total population in district[c] | .02 | .08 |

a. Christian Voice.
b. National Christian Action Coalition.
c. 1970 census.
d. The entries are Pearson's r.
e. In 1980.
f. Measured by 1979 Americans for Democratic Action (ADA) Index.

come from districts with a youngish, affluent, well-educated constituency as one predominantly elderly, poor, and undereducated.

## The NRR and Elections

### Electoral Techniques

Probably one of the main reasons why the NRR has enjoyed wider support nationally than earlier movements is its extensive use of the media. Particularly favored by its leaders is the electronic church. Today some thirty religious-oriented television stations are operating, along with more than a thousand religious radio stations and four religious networks.

This saturation of the ether with electronic transmissions is complemented by a neighborhood network of more direct, personal ties. "The church organization is a political dream," observes a Christian Voice leader. "It allows us to tap into the best precinct organization in the country: the churches. We don't have to build new organizations across the country; we just recruit a minister, or a layman, in an existing congregation."[23] The combination of national-media and local-grassroots contact with constituents provides an impressive set of channels for distributing the political views of NRR leaders.

These two means of mobilization are only the beginning. "We generate media attention, alert our church leaders, then follow up with a mass mailing," explains the chief Christian Voice issues director.[24] With direct-mail pioneer Viguerie as an ally, the NRR has honed this powerful political tool, filling the mailbags of America with NRR communications specifically targeted to likely adherents. These letters are designed to raise funds, as well as to carry "report cards" on legislative apostates, voting records of congressional members on key "family issues," and questionnaires (often simplistic, such as "Do you want more taxes or less taxes?").

The NRR has also used such common political techniques as telephone banks, fundraising through political action committees, sloganeering ("John Culver deserves your prayers, but not your votes"), candidate endorsements (usually implicit), legislative lobbying, volunteerism, voter registration, and mass rallies. (A Religious Roundtable "National Affairs Briefing" drew 15,000 people in Dallas during August 1980, including presidential aspirant Ronald Reagan.)

Through its CERF arm, NCAC also produces and distributes political films. Its first film, "Politics: A Christian Viewpoint," consists of interviews with Weyrich and conservative politicians. The film's lead-in features a protest parade of lesbians and homosexuals, followed by a montage of pornographic theaters. Then, with the song "America" in the background, the host begins the interviews with archconservative Senator Jesse Helms (Republican, North Carolina). One conclusion drawn in the film: the most important goal short of attaining eternal salvation is to register the 20,000 "Bible-believing Americans" in each congressional district who remain unregistered. (The Christian Voice, among other religious groups, launched a major Christian voter registration drive on behalf of presidential candidate Reagan in 1980.[25])

At the December 1981 Democratic National Committee "Training Academy," held in Washington, D.C. for party activists, a workshop on "Combatting the New Right" attempted to sum up the approaches to elections used by the NRR and other right groups. The strategy of the right, according to this interpretation, is to (1) select a "clean-cut, all-American family person" as a candidate; (2) attack the government office sought ("Legislators have too much staff"); (3) discredit the incumbent by picking an issue on which he or she may be vulnerable ("He's introduced bills for [criminals, homosexuals, Communists, New York City, giving away the Panama Canal, etc.]"); (4) use targeted mailing and phone banks (to mobilize single-issue groups like antiabortionists); and (5) tap PACs, especially oil corporations.

## NRR Candidate Targeting

From the long list of techniques, old and new, used by the NRR, what interested us most was their selection of incumbents for defeat. This targeting is likely the most important decision made in NRR political campaigns. Targets are established about eighteen months before the elections based on three criteria: the incumbent's voting record ("antifamily/moral"), his or her vulnerability, and the availability of a "quality" opponent.[26] We examined these criteria by comparing the list of House candidates targeted by Christian Voice in 1980 with, first, Christian Voice legislative ratings and, second, the incumbent's vulnerability, as gauged by his or her margin of electoral success in the previous election—55 percent of the vote or more being the standard usually accepted as a "safe seat."

All but three of thirty-nine targeted incumbents were in the lower half of the Christian Voice scale on legislative performance—with more than half of the targets siding with Christian Voice on legislative votes less than 25 percent of the time. However, 161 House members who scored below 50 on the Christian Voice scale escaped targeting; their voting record qualified them for electoral elimination, but Christian Voice apparently found them insufficiently vulnerable or lacked a qualified opponent.

When we explored the relationship between vulnerability and Christian Voice targeting, we found that Christian Voice had been bold in its targeting, choosing to go after twenty-three Democrats who had won by sizable margins in 1978. Looking at the other side of the coin, though, Christian Voice failed to target almost two-thirds of the Democrats who were narrowly elected in 1978. Evidently, Christian Voice suffered from a dearth of "quality" challengers, resources to support them, or perhaps both.[27] Overall, then, Christian Voice targeted only 9 percent of House Democratic incumbents with "very low" Christian Voice legislative ratings and 35 percent of House Democratic incumbents narrowly elected in 1978. In choosing its targets, Christian Voice apparently has been concerned less with low Christian Voice ratings than with indications of opponent vulnerability.

## Influence of the NRR

### Elections

So far we have examined the organization, purpose, and practice of the NRR. Now we address the vital question of whether the Christian right exercised influence on the 1980 House elections and subsequent policymaking in that chamber. We begin with a look at its electoral success.

Elections, of course, are complicated human events and, despite years of careful analysis, political scientists are unable to explain (let alone predict) outcomes with certitude. We are certainly in no position to declare that the presence of the NRR was, or was not, the deciding factor in any given House election. The personality of Ronald Reagan and the efforts of the national Republican party were no doubt influential factors in the 1980 election, too. We can, nevertheless, state a series of empirical findings about the NRR and these elections. First, of Christian Voice's twenty-eight first-priority targets, half tri-

Table 3

**Defeat rates in 1980 general election among CV and NCPAC targets compared with other Democratic incumbents, in % (N in parentheses)**

| | Christian Voice | | National Conservative Political Action Committee | |
|---|---|---|---|---|
| | Targets | Nontargets | Targets | Nontargets |
| Marginal Democrats (won 50–55% of 1978 vote) | 37.5 (16) | 13.3 (30) | 31.8 (22) | 12.5 (24) |
| Safe Democrats (won 56–100% of 1978 vote) | 45.5 (22) | 4.4 (183) | 29.2 (48) | 2.5 (157) |

umphed. Despite losing as many contests as it won, Christian Voice's record is impressive, since at least 90 percent of House incumbents are typically reelected. Incumbents on Christian Voice's top-priority list were defeated at a rate six times higher than were House incumbents generally in 1980.

Secondary Christian Voice targets fared considerably better against NRR opposition, winning in eight of eleven contests. When first and second target categories are combined, Christian Voice's success rate is 44 percent. For those candidates who received endorsements from Christian Voice, incumbents lived up to their reputation with all six winning; Christian Voice-backed challengers for open seats also performed impressively, losing only one of twelve contests. All in all, Christian Voice's record in the 1980 elections was remarkable (a 60 percent overall winning percentage), paling even the notable showing of NCPAC (44 percent). The impressive success rate for the NRR found here is consonant with findings presented by Miller and Wattenberg using data from the University of Michigan 1980 National Election Survey.[28]

Some of Christian Voice's victories were hardly surprising: One target was involved in the ABSCAM scandal (John Jenrette, Democrat, South Carolina); another in a sex scandal (Bill Burlison, Democrat, Missouri); a third in a controversy over a drunk-driving record (Thomas Ashley, Democrat, Ohio, whose plight was amply publicized by Christian Voice); and others held shaky seats. Still, several of the targets were stanchions of the House, including Democrats John Brademas (Indiana), Mo Udall (Arizona), Al Ullman (Oregon), and Jim Wright (Texas), two of whom were defeated (Brademas and Ullmann).

The success of Christian Voice—and to a slightly lesser extent NCPAC—appears even more impressive when we consider the comparisons presented in Table 3. Contrasting the frequency of defeats for these two groups' targets with the defeats for similar nontargeted Democrats, it is obvious that incumbents who incurred the ire of the New Religious Right were far less likely to be reelected.

Particularly remarkable is the incidence of defeats among targeted incumbents who won at least 56 percent of the vote in 1978 and would therefore be considered relatively safe. Defeats among targeted "safe" incumbents were ten times greater than for the nontargeted for both Christian Voice and NCPAC. Indeed, Christian Voice targets in the "safe" category were more likely to be defeated than were targets in the marginal category. Among NCPAC targets, defeat rates are approximately equal for safe and marginal Democrats.

## Policy Voting

The purpose of elections is to choose officials, who in turn make public policy choices affecting all of us. Just as the NRR tries to influence electoral outcomes, so would it like to mold public policy within its areas of interest. That is its purpose for contesting elections in the first place. We explored this side of the influence equation by testing whether NRR electoral successes produced new House voting patterns more responsive to cues from the Christian right. To accomplish this, roll calls on six issues central to the NRR's political agenda were analyzed. The votes of House members before the 1980 election are compared with those cast on similar issues during 1981.

The issues selected are from those used by NCAC in scoring all incumbents prior to the 1980 election. We used the roll calls from NCAC rather than Christian Voice's rating list; but choice of one set rather than the other should have little impact, since the correlation between the two scales is .91 (Pearson's r). Four of the roll calls were cast in 1979, while the roll calls on anti-school busing and opposition to homosexual rights were from 1977. Since comparisons are for individual legislators, the use of two 1977 roll calls poses no problems. Legislators who missed a vote are deleted for that comparison.

If the NRR has had an impact on legislators' policy stands, it could show up in several ways. If the Christian Voice strategy of targeting some legislators for defeat has had the anticipated policy payoffs, then when members whom it opposed in 1980 were replaced, the new legislators should vote more conservatively than did their predecessors. Moreover, the behavior of legislators may have been changed as a result of NRR campaign activity. House members opposed by Christian Voice, but who withstood the challenge, may now support NRR policy preferences in the hope that they can avoid being targeted for defeat by Christian Voice in 1982. The voting behavior of victorious Christian Voice-backed challengers and surviving—but possibly intimidated—Christian Voice targets can be compared against that of incumbents whom Christian Voice did not single out for defeat. If Christian Voice's activities have had an effect, the shifts registered by new Christian Voice-oriented incumbents, and perhaps of those who survived its challenge, should be more pronounced than the shifts for those Christian Voice did not target.

Table 4

**Legislators who opposed NRR policy stands before 1980 election but supported them in 1981, in % (N in parentheses)**

|  | Abortion | IRS and private schools | Busing | Homo-sexual rights | School prayers | Balanced budget |
|---|---|---|---|---|---|---|
| Newly elected with CV help" | 69 (13) | 100 (7) | 100 (10) | 91 (11) | 100 (7) | 100 (13) |
| Survived CV opposition | 23 (13) | 0 (0) | 11 (9) | 0 (11) | 42 (12) | 6 (17) |
| Not targeted, reelected | 12 (86) | 16 (50) | 22 (76) | 20 (69) | 54 (74) | 24 (152) |
| Republicans who replaced Democrats, w/o CV support | 78 (9) | 100 (4) | 100 (12) | 57 (7) | 90 (10) | 95 (19) |
| Not targeted, reelected Democrats | 11 (72) | 16 (49) | 19 (67) | 21 (58) | 49 (63) | 14 (132) |

a. In the case of the newly elected legislators backed by Christian Voice (CV), we are comparing new members' voting records with their predecessors.

As the first row in Table 4 shows, when Christian Voice triumphed at the polls the newly elected representatives overwhelmingly voted the NRR line. On four of the issues, all of the new legislators who voted took the NRR position. On abortions and homosexual rights, 69 and 91 percent, respectively, of those who replaced members who had opposed NRR positions voted pro-NRR in 1981. Clearly, then, when Christian Voice targets were defeated, the replacements were far more attuned to NRR objectives than their predecessors had been. There was no backsliding among the newly elected. That is, none of these new representatives opposed the NRR after replacing a legislator who had voted "right" on an issue.

Did Christian Voice targets who survived (row 2) move toward the NRR stand? There was no shift toward the NRR preferred position on the private schools and homosexual rights issues and little shift on budget balancing and busing. On the issue of budget balancing, the modest pro-NRR shift was more than offset by legislators who sided with the NRR in 1979 but opposed its stand in 1981. Only on prayer in the schools were Christian Voice survivors substantially more likely to be converts than backsliders in 1981.

Among incumbents who were not targeted by Christian Voice, conversion rates were 11 to 20 percentage points higher than for Christian Voice survivors, except on the abortion issue. The untargeted were, however, much less likely to adopt NRR positions than were the replacements of members whom Christian Voice opposed. On each issue, there were at least twice as many converts as backsliders.

Using the returning legislators who were not Christian Voice targets as a baseline, we see that when a targeted legislator is defeated it makes quite a difference. However, when a Christian Voice target survives, the legislator is less likely to adopt NRR positions than are returning incumbents.

It may be possible to have better subsets of legislators against whom to compare the Christian Voice targets. Since all of the Christian Voice targets were Democrats, we can compare the voting patterns for new Republicans who defeated non–Christian Voice targets with the pattern for new Republicans who defeated Christian Voice targets. Comparing rows 4 and 1, we see that except on homosexual rights the patterns are similar, and indeed identical for busing and tax exemptions for private schools. Thus, on five of the issue areas dear to the NRR, a strong shift in the direction they prefer occurs by replacing a Democrat with a Republican. There is little evidence that Christian Voice targeting is linked to a change in voting patterns that is distinct from a change in the partisan identity of the incumbent. Sizable shifts in legislative voting patterns resulting from partisan replacements have been frequently noted in the Congress.[29]

As a control group for the survivors of Christian Voice targeting, we can use untargeted Democrats who were reelected in 1980. A comparison of rows 5 and 2 reveals that except on the abortion issue, the survivors were less likely to switch to NRR positions than were the untargeted. The differences were not extreme, being most pronounced on the homosexual issue.

Another way in which to compare the two groups is in terms of the proportion of members who voted for NRR preferred positions before the 1980 election but opposed them in 1981. On four issues, the proportion of backsliders is quite similar for the survivors and the untargeted. On the issue of balancing the budget, backsliders were far more common among survivors than the untargeted, but the number of survivors is so small that we dare not make much of it. On the issue of tax exemption for private schools, however, there is a larger number of cases, and survivors were much more likely to be backsliders (37 percent) than were untargeted Democratic incumbents (11 percent). We conclude that turning back a Christian Voice challenge does not induce representatives to adopt NRR positions with greater frequency than do Democrats whom Christian Voice did not target, but instead may make them more resolute opponents.

Neither Christian Voice successes nor failures thus seem to have an *independent* effect on legislators' policy stands. Christian Voice's important role occurs before the legislative policymaking stage. Although we cannot prove that Christian Voice opposition was the sole element in determining election outcomes, the extraordinarily high incidence of defeats among Christian Voice targets, especially those who had been easily reelected in 1978, suggests that the New Religious Right may have played a significant role in these congressional elections.

## Conclusion

This analysis of the New Religious Right (NRR) indicates that the movement is composed of a cohesive set of organizations with overlapping and interlocking memberships, shared issue perspectives, and common *modi operandi*. Its base of support is similar to earlier right-wing movements, drawing upon a durable core of conservatives from rural, Republican districts with few immigrant classes. The NRR, though, has sought to widen its appeal beyond this core of traditional right-wing supporters. Unlike its historical antecedents, the NRR has demonstrated an affinity toward representatives in Congress from young, affluent, and well-educated constituencies, not only the elderly, the poor, and the undereducated who have sometimes rallied behind the right-wing leaders in the past.

The findings here reveal a high success rate for NRR groups in backing conservative Republican challengers for seats in the House of Representatives. This has led to little independent influence over House voting, though. The Republicans who won election in 1980 without NRR support subsequently voted just as often in accord with NRR positions as the NRR-backed victors in 1980. Democrats targeted by the NRR in 1980 who won reelection regardless failed to be intimidated by the NRR in the subsequent House voting and continued to oppose NRR positions. So while the NRR is effective in siding with triumphant Republican challengers, its influence over voting patterns is far less dramatic.

## Notes

1. On McIntire, see *Time*, May 16, 1949, p. 50. On Hargis and Schwarz, see *New York Times*, May 21, August 6, and October 7, 1961; U.S. Senate, *Report from the Subcommittee on Privileges and Elections* (Washington, D.C.: GPO, 1957); *Christian Science Monitor*, August 5, 1961. For overviews on the subject of politics and religious movements in the United States, see Gerhard Lenski, *The Religious Factor* (New York: Doubleday, 1963); Philip E. Converse, "Religion and Politics: The 1960 Election," in *Elections and the Political Order*, ed. Angus Campbell, Philip E. Converse, Warren E. Miller, and Donald E. Stokes (New York: Wiley, 1966); Harold Quinley, *The Prophetic Clergy: Social Activism among Protestant Ministers* (New York: Wiley, 1974); Irving I. Zaretsky and Mark P. Leone, eds., *Religious Movements in Contemporary America* (Princeton: Princeton University Press, 1974); John Wilson, *Religion in American Society* (Englewood Cliffs, N.J.: Prentice-Hall, 1978); and Thomas Robbins and Dick Anthony, eds., *In God We Trust: New Patterns of Religious Pluralism in America* (New Brunswick: Transaction, 1980). On congressional elections, see Gary Jacobson, "Incumbents' Advantages in the 1978 U.S. Congressional Elections," *Legislative Studies Quarterly* (May 1981): 183–200; Barbarba Hinckley, *Congressional Elections* (Washington, D.C.: Congressional Quarterly, 1981); and Edie N. Goldenberg and Michael W. Thangott, *Campaigning for Congress* (Washington, D.C.: Congressional Quarterly, 1984).

2. On this network, see Frances FitzGerald, "A Reporter at Large," *The New Yorker*, May 18, 1981, pp. 54, 59; Alan Crawford, *Thunder on the Right* (New York: Pantheon, 1980); Jerome L. Himmelstein, "The New Right: An Overview," in *The New*

*Christian Right*, ed. Robert Wuthnow and Robert Liebman (Hawthorne, N.Y.: Aldine, 1983); and Kant Patel, Denny Pilart, and Gary Rose, "Born-Again Christians in the Bible Belt," *American Politics Quarterly* 10 (1982):255–72.

3. Carl Moore, interview, November 19, 1980.

4. FitzGerald, "Reporter at Large," p. 53.

5. Gary Jarmin, interview, November 19, 1980.

6. Weyrich is director of the Committee for the Survival of a Free Congress, a right-wing political action committee (PAC).

7. Richard A. Viguerie, *The New Right: We're Ready to Lead* (Chicago: Caroline House, 1980).

8. Rev. Jerry Falwell's appearance on the covers of national news magazines attests to NRR's national visibility. As for connections, Robert J. Billings, Moral Majority cofounder and religious liaison to the Reagan presidential campaign in 1980, went on to become regional liaison at the Department of Education. President Reagan's Family Policy Advisor Board is headed by Connie Masher, assistant director of Weyrich's Committee for the Survival of a Free Congress (*Washington Star*, November 22, 1980). Justin W. Dart, key fundraiser and confidant of President Reagan, was, in 1961, a leading sponsor of Fred Schwarz's California "Christian Anti-Communism Crusade."

9. Bill Keller, "Evangelist Conservatives Move from Pews to Polls," *Congressional Quarterly Weekly Report*, September 6, 1980, p. 2628.

10. Moore, interview, 1980.

11. Edward E. Plowman, "Is Morality All Right?" *Christianity Today*, November 2, 1979, p. 78; FitzGerald, "Reporter at Large," p. 90; and Koller, "Evangelist Conservatives," p. 2632.

12. Jarmin, interview, 1980.

13. Plowman, "Is Morality All Right?" pp. 76–77.

14. The ten NCAC and seven CV roll-call votes upon which these ratings are based are presented in note 10. These two NRR groups rated legislators by dividing the number of favorable votes by the total number of votes recorded.

15. In our interviews with NRR staffers in Washington, this feeling of competition within the Christian right was apparent—a race to build larger organizations, raise more money, gather in a wider cross-section of adherents. On divisions within the right-tolife segment of the New Right, see the *Washington Post*, February 16, 1982, p. A4. James Q. Wilson, *Political Organizations* (New York: Basic Books, 1973), p. 266, noted how organizations with similar goals try to promote some distinct areas of competence in order to attract a clientele and survive.

16. On the "platform" of the NRR, see FitzGerald, "Reporter at Large," and Plowman, "Is Morality All Right?"

17. Randy Abramson, "Jeremiah Denton: The New Right's Riddle in the Senate," *Los Angeles Times*, December 20, 1981, p. 3.

18. On the Satan-devil theme, the late Congressman Mendel Rivers (Democrat, South Carolina), long-time chairman of the House Armed Services Committee (1965–1971), summed up the cold war simply: It is a battle between "Jesus Christ and the hammer-and-sickle." Charles McCarry, "Ol' Man Rivers," *Esquire* (October 1970):171.

19. Peter Edson, *Washington Daily News*, March 20, 1962.

20. FitzGerald, "Reporter at Large," p. 131.

21. Daniel Bell, "The Dispossessed," in *The Radical Right*, ed. Daniel Bell (New

York: Doubleday, 1962); Seymour M. Lipset, "Three Decades of the Radical Right: Coughlinites, McCarthyites, and Birchers," in *The Radical Right*, ed. Bell; Seymour M. Lipset and Earl Raab, "The Election and the Evangelicals," *Commentary* (march 1981):25–31; and Nelson W. Polsby, "Toward an Explanation of McCarthyism," *Political Studies* (October 1960):250–71.

22. The votes included prayer in school, school busing, IRS and private schools, a balanced budget, abortion, support for Taiwan, and opposition to aid for Nicaragua, as well as eight more domestic issues. See also note 14.

23. Jarmin, interview, 1980.

24. Ibid.

25. Pollster Lou Harris reports that two-thirds of Reagan's 8.5-million-vote margin came from born again Christians who favored Jimmy Carter in 1976 (Viguerie, *Washington Post*, February 16, 1982, p. A4).

26. Even incumbents with Christian Voice ratings in the 70s (on a 100 percent scale) may be earmarked for defeat if a "better Christian candidate" stands waiting in the winds. In 1980 representative David Evans (Democrat, Indiana) had a 79 percent legislative rating, but, as Christian Voice explained in an internal document, "he is known as a Congressman with his 'finger in the wind' who is not always reliable to side [sic] the pro-family/moral position. His opponent, however, David Crane (brother of Reps. Phil and Dan Crane) would no doubt be a 100 percenter" ("Christian Voice Moral Government Fund Targets for 19802 [Washington, D.C.: C. V. Headquarters, 1980], mimeo, p. 2). Evans won despite Christian Voice opposition.

27. According to figures in the reports of the Federal Elections Commission, Christian Voice and other NRR groups gave little cash to 1980 election campaigns—less than $100,000 altogether on the eve of the election. FEC, "FEC Reports on Financial Activity, 1979–80: Interim Report no. 9" (Washington, D.C.: Public Records Office, 1980), pp. C18, C72.

28. Arthur H. Miller and Martin P. Wattenberg, "Politics from the Pulpit: Religiosity and the 1980 Elections," *Public Opinion Quarterly* 48 (1984):301–17.

29. David W. Brady, "Critical Elections, Congressional Parties, and Clusters of Policy Change," *British Journal of Political Science* 8 (1978):79–99; Charles S. Bullock, "Congressional Voting and the Mobilization of a Black Electorate," *Journal of Politics* 43 (1981):662–82; and Morris P. Fiorina, *Representatives, Roll Calls, and Constituencies* (Lexington, Mass.: Lexington Books, 1974).

## 3.3

# Elites and Elections,
## Or What Have They Done To You Lately?

## Thomas Ferguson

Since only correspondence, several lists, and some invitations survive, it is impossible to recapture all of Thomas W. Lamont's reflections as he worked in his office at J. P. Morgan & Co. that last week of October 1932. But it is clear that he was worried. Only a few months earlier Lamont and a huge bloc of allied businessmen had pulled out all the stops, trying to head off Franklin D. Roosevelt's nomination as the Democratic party's candidate for president.

Working through Walter Lippman, Hubert Bayard Swope, and a myriad of less famous journalists, they had laid down a rolling barrage of newspaper stories. Turning loose an army of experienced and well-rewarded delegate hunters, they had blandished, threatened, and cajoled business and professional associates across the United States. With the assistance of Wendell Wilkie (at that time head of Commonwealth and Southern, a huge Morgan-dominated utility), they also had organized a gigantic telegram blitz of the Democratic Convention itself. But their campaign in favor of Cleveland bank attorney Newton D. Baker had fallen barely short. After four tense ballots, Roosevelt had squeaked through.[1]

Having failed to stop Roosevelt in Chicago, Lamont and his allies had involved themselves ever more deeply in the campaign of their preferred candidate, incumbent President Herbert Hoover. Never long out of touch with the White House, they had become virtually a constant presence there since the world financial crisis of June 1931. Transcripts of phone conversations between Lamont

Thomas Ferguson teaches at the University of Texas at Austin.

and Hoover at that time show how completely the big banks dominated the President—to the extent that Hoover began concealing his conversations with the financiers by fabricating entries in a "diary" he left for the edification of later historians.[2]

Subsequently, as Hoover caved in completely to the bankers' demands for a balanced budget, maintenance of the gold standard, higher taxes on the poor and middle classes, and restriction of relief to banks, insurance companies, and railroads, Lamont and his allies virtually took over the President's campaign. They raised funds, prepared campaign releases, and drew up lists of Hoover's "achievements" for the press. As Lamont himself had done in the presidential campaigns of 1920, 1924, and 1928, they wrote all sorts of strategic memoranda for the candidate.

But now, with only a few weeks left before the election, straw polls and informal soundings all over the nation suggested that their attempt to engineer another term for the Great Engineer was in trouble. Unless something were done at once, Hoover appeared headed for defeat.

At this point, almost certainly, flashed the ray of hope that inspired Lamont's latest activities. As the most important partner in the best known bank in the world; as a long time associate of Morgan's allied houses Drexel & Co. in Philadelphia, Morgan Grenfell in London, and Morgan-Harjes in Paris; as a director of too many corporations to enumerate conveniently, including U.S. Steel, International Harvester, Crowell Publishing, Guaranty Trust, International Agricultural Corporation, and the Santa Fe Railroad; as perhaps Wilson's most important adviser at Versailles; as the former owner of the New York *Post* and current owner of the *Saturday Review of Literature*; as an unacknowledged source for many editorials and news stories in the *New York Times* and other leading dailies; and as a trustee of the Council on Foreign Relations and other organizations, Lamont enjoyed immense advantages. One of these was that he knew better than to believe the academic analysts of American politics whose pensions he had long superintended as a trustee of the Carnegie Endowment for the Advancement of Teaching.

For all the energy political scientists, such as Lamont's friend A. Lawrence Lowell (the wealthy president of Harvard, where Lamont was a trustee), invested in their pioneering studies of the influence of voting and public opinion on policy, Lamont's behavior (and occasional guarded remarks) showed that he realized how ludicrously incomplete their views were. Even as he secretly complained to university presidents about faculty who dared to discuss the House of Morgan in class,[3] Lamont recognized that in situations like the one in which he found himself, he and his associates could tap resources beyond the imagination of most critics. Herbert Hoover might be behind, but if anyone or anything were capable of reversing the tide through a last-minute stroke, it was the mighty men of Morgan.

Lamont's efforts to swing the election for Hoover had made the last few days busy ones. Along with his associate of many years, Seward Prosser, of Bankers' Trust, the Morgan banker had begun to orchestrate a gigantic last-minute fundraising effort for Hoover.

> This additional fund will be utilized for two specific and very legitimate purposes. One is for the payment of these radio costs. You realize, I think, that the radio companies charge $25,000 each night that Mr. Hoover speaks, for the use of the radio. But his speeches, of which he is making many more than he had planned, are proving most effective, and it is vitally essential to keep them up. They cannot be kept up, unless these additional funds are raised. The other purpose is to pay for automobiles, etc. in order to get out the votes on election day in the doubtful states. I am told that the Hearst newspaper straw vote indicates that in nineteen pivotal states whose aggregate electoral vote would be sufficient to elect Mr. Hoover there is running a slight margin in Mr. Hoover's favor. This straw vote is, therefore, very encouraging, and Mr. Hoover feels that if the Republicans can only get out their votes in those states it will make all the difference between success and failure.
>    This special committee of which I speak is made up of men like Mr. Prosser and other heads of banking institutions here, together with various well-known industrial leaders of very high character. In order to raise this additional sum, frankly we are being obliged to double up on our contributions and do everything that we can to secure additional ones.[4]

Sometime around October 26, however, Lamont decided that the pace would have to be accelerated. He summoned the heads of most of New York's major corporations and banks to a special meeting at the Morgan offices at 23 Wall Street.

> The special committee of which Steward Prosser is chairman, that is proving very successful in getting additional funds for the Hoover campaign, is very anxious to have various business friends throughout the country realize that this special effort is being made. The committee requests that I should gather a few friends here tomorrow afternoon at 3 o'clock to discuss with them very briefly methods of disseminating this information. This meeting, as you realize, will have nothing to do with soliciting funds, but will be confined simply to a discussion as to how the country could be divided up so as to get this information well distributed. In case you are very much tied up, if one of your close associates could drop in at the time mentioned, we can cover the matter in a very few minutes.[5]

Evidently the discussions among these "industrial leaders of very high character" transcended questions about "how the country could be divided up" to get the word out. A series of notes (some with dollar amounts) on a preliminary memorandum and a final guest list record the reaction of some of the key executives Lamont contacted.

In other essays, I have sought to elucidate the sometimes cryptic remarks entered on the margins of these and many similar documents—to explain in this case, for example, why executives from two large steel companies, Bethlehem and U.S. Steel, at once responded affirmatively; why the handwriting on the page suggests that RCA's David Sarnoff was "engaged" and "hesitates to send anyone else"; how it happened that Standard Oil and Texaco were apparently too preoccupied with other meetings to participate; why no one bothered even to invite General Electric; and, most importantly, why the startled expression "Democrat!" written into the space next to the entry for the Chase National Bank signals incomparably more clearly than any number of voting returns the doom of Lamont's plan and the advent of a true critical realignment.[6] These works also attempt to display how theories of economic behavior, business organization, cultural production, and political analysis can be combined to yield clearly specified, empirically grounded explanations of different stages of American party politics and public policy in the nineteenth and twentieth centuries.

This essay, by contrast, attempts to trace the implications these separate studies have for the study of American politics in general. Originally prepared as the prelude to a much longer study,[7] this chapter analyzes recent research on American party systems. It is particularly concerned with efforts by Key, Burnham, the Michigan School, and other analysts to define voting patterns uniquely characteristic of so-called critical realignments.[8] Following several recent works, notably Clubb, Flanigan, and Zingale's very suggestive *Partisan Realignment*, the essay argues that while these various accounts of critical realignment have undeniable merits, still they have not succeeded in specifying sufficient and conclusive criteria distinguishing "critical" from other types of elections.[9] Quite the contrary, intractable anomalies to critical realignment theory are proliferating, along with apparent exceptions to many of its paradigm cases, and the statistical evidence mustered to support it has become increasingly ambiguous and contradictory.

But while this study thus joins an emerging consensus that realignment theory requires revision, it flatly rejects the recommendation normally proposed by the theory's sympathetic critics, that the way to shore up the theory is to make it even more complicated, more "multidimensional," by supplementing already complex electoral specifications with still more variables. On the contrary, it suggests, the fundamental reason why no social scientists have succeeded in specifying unambiguous *electoral* criteria to identify "partisan realignment" is that there are no such criteria to be found.

As a consequence, the most sensible way to reconstruct the theory is to follow up neglected aspects of work by Burnham and look directly at power blocs that actually control political parties and governments. At a stroke, the multiplying puzzles about dating and definitions disappear and critical realignments can be analyzed for what they really are: the process through which one dominant bloc of major investors—like that headed by Lamont and the Morgan partners in 1932—is succeeded by another.

## Electoral Behavior and Critical Elections: A Reanalysis

It was V. O. Key who first singled out a "critical election" as "an election type in which the depth and intensity of election involvement are high, in which more or less profound readjustments occur in the relations of power within the community, and in which new and durable electoral groupings are formed."[10] In the generation since his essay appeared, an army of distinguished social scientists, including the authors of *The American Voter* as well as Burnham, Pomper, Sundquist, and Kleppner, have attacked the problems it posed. Key's initial formulations have been discussed, amended, amplified, revised, debated, and extended. These inquiries, in turn, have triggered further discussions, including several notable debates over particular episodes in American history, such as the election of 1896.[11]

For all the research and lively controversies it stimulated, Key's general line of argument has, until recently, proven remarkably resilient. Though they often disagreed about statistical measures, the role of particular issues and personalities, or the costs and benefits to American society of certain alignments, most analysts during most of this period implicitly or (more often) explicitly shared an inspired confidence in three propositions clearly rooted in Key's work. First, they agreed with Key that some elections—those in the Jacksonian era, the Civil War, the 1890s, and the Great Depression were most commonly suggested, though others in 1880, 1912, or 1920 were sometimes put forward—were more important than others. Second, they shared Key's belief that durable shifts of the electorate's partisan allegiances and related political behavior (such as turnout and issue orientation) were constitutive and defining of such "critical elections," though other features of the regime, such as the circulation of elites, could also change. Third, like Key, they were persuaded that careful attention to voting statistics would at least eventually permit such elections to be analyzed with almost Cartesian clarity and distinctness.

But in recent years the climate of opinion has changed markedly. A few scholars have actually recommended that critical realignment theory be abandoned.[12] While this remains a minority view, many others—including some who previously subscribed wholeheartedly to the general position—have begun to voice doubts, advance counterexamples, and point to persisting anomalies.[13] Critical realignment theory, they suggest, is becoming almost as amorphous as some of the party systems the theory purports to describe. Though a complete inventory of the various objections would swallow up all available space, the leading counts in the emerging indictment can be summarized as follows.

First, critical realignment theory is evasive about whether one or a handful of concatenated elections constitute realignments. Various authors (sometimes even the same author) slide back and forth, referring alternately to single "critical elections," "realigning eras," or "realigning sequences." Many discussions also clearly conceive of realignments as manifesting "stages." Though at first glance many cases involve nothing more serious than verbal inconsistency, a major theoretical issue does lie just beneath the surface. As discussed in more detail below, critical realignment theorists often explain the changes in long-run partisan balance they believe realignments create in terms of the dramatic effects that high stimulus, issue-oriented campaigns have on voters.[14] Intense, high-stakes elections are comparatively rare, however, so that "realigning sequences" of several dramatic elections are rather difficult to accept.

Second, once a decision is reached about how many elections are relevant, the issue of which elections to count remains open. Put simply, the question is how presidential, congressional, and state (or even local) races should be weighed in deciding whether a particular election qualifies as "critical." Early formulations of critical realignment theory, which highlighted the role of near-nationwide landslides in constituting the phenomenon, suggested that elections at all levels of government should all go the same way. Recent research, however, shows that some parcels of land slide much farther than others during most U.S. landslides.[15] Even in the nineteenth century a substantial number of state and local races seem relatively insulated from national trends. Also, while some realignments, such as those of the 1890s and the New Deal, clearly had drastic effects on party competition within many states, others seem to have produced no clear pattern or indeed, like the Civil War system, witnessed several violent alternations in the status of whole groups of states.[16]

One can, of course, decide to focus only on national outcomes, or, as Burnham's work implicitly suggests, attempt to theorize about the changing links between outcomes at the national, state, and local levels, but at the moment the whole question is largely hanging in the air. Like the first objection, it threatens versions of critical realignment theory that explain the formation and change of deeply held partisan attitudes in terms of the transforming effects of high-intensity elections.

The most serious of the objections leveled against critical realignment theory are those that suggest that the "new and durable electoral groupings" that Key and other analysts believed they saw and expected to find never really existed, or only characterized some realignments. Such conclusions, if true, would of course place critical realignment theorists in the position of geologists without the earth and, accordingly, figure to be objects not only of controversy but of acrimony. Still, as the authors of a work highly sympathetic to the general notion of critical realignments make overwhelmingly clear, the once compelling case for the coincidence of mass electoral realignments with the dates of most commonly accepted political realignments has crumbled.

Clubb, Flanigan, and Zingale show, for example, that very long-run analyses using the most popular method for identifying realignments, calculations of correlations between state (and other governmental unit) votes over successive elections, do not yield results reported by other researchers using data for shorter time spans.[17] In addition they demonstrate that this method is invalid in principle, because it is insensitive to certain critically important types of electoral change.[18] Their own results, obtained with a new and refined technique, show that in general one could plausibly argue that (two-party) voting behavior has hardly changed at all since the early nineteenth century, and that what formerly looked like "critical realignments" were really deviating cases in a stable pattern. Though they do not emphasize the implications of their results, choosing instead to call the evidence "ambiguous," in fact, their research has turned the discussion upside down. Critical realignments now appear the least likely of all occasions for new "durable groupings" to form.[19]

Clubb, Flanigan, and Zingale's analysis does not emphasize the importance of variations in turnout. As a consequence, they could perhaps be partially answered by a reply along the lines of Burnham's famous discussion of turnout in American critical elections. But I doubt it. It takes nothing away from Burnham's penetrating analysis of the significance of voter turnout during various party systems in American history to observe that turnout variations cannot by themselves define American party systems. Burnham's own analysis shows that turnout ran high, with irregular variation, across two different party systems in the nineteenth century.[20] When Clubb, Flanigan, and Zingale use their analysis of variance techniques to analyze turnout, they will undoubtedly discover that the pattern of nonvoting before 1896 was as ragged as the shifts between the parties among those who voted. As a consequence, at least two different party systems will not be distinguished—though those of 1896 and the New Deal certainly will be.[21]

Nor do Burnham's own tests, relying on so-called discontinuity coefficients of the two-party percentage of the vote, provide the urgently needed indicator for distinguishing one party system from another. One can imagine how the "single election vs. realigning era" issue could be adjudicated to make sense of the fact, which Burnham himself observed, that various states lead and lag behind national trends.[22] But his data contain several major anomalies, including indications that 1854, 1874, and 1926 marked realignments.[23] These can, of course, be accounted for—as Burnham does—by appealing to peculiar features of American politics during these periods. But in making these judgments, Burnham relies on his ability to recognize the identity of a party persisting (or disintegrating) through the breaks in his statistical series. His identifications are plausible, and indeed, I am completely persuaded that he is correct, for example, in writing off the 1874 anomaly as an adjustment of the broader Civil War system.[24] But something besides voting patterns has now clearly become the basis for defining the party system.

At least two other doubts can also be entertained about Burnham's results. One arises from the surprising persistence of the New Deal party system. As Burnham himself has emphasized, auxiliary hypotheses are required to account for the absence of a critical realignment sometime in the sixties or seventies. Burnham and, following him, Kleppner suggest that the atrophy of mass political parties (what Burham calls the "onward march of Party decomposition") spells the end of critical realignments as well.[25] Their argument is simple and at first sight appealing. Party realignments require parties; no parties, then no realignments either. But as discussed in more detail below, this argument has less weight than it appears. Almost everyone agrees that Jacksonian America underwent realignment, but it began with a no- (or perhaps a one-) party system. This example suggests that well-organized parties are not essential for major political realignments.

Also, integral to Burnham's statistical procedures for analyzing voting data is a decision to compute moving averages of results from ten elections.[26] Why he selected ten, rather than any other number, and how the results might change if the number of elections analyzed were different are never explored.

Critical realignment theorists, of course, have not ignored the mounting current of dissatisfaction within their field. Reading the same journals and weighing the same data as the skeptics, they have tried to provide additional evidence and to refine their central arguments. But while their replies go some distance toward disarming the most important arguments advanced against the conventional notion of "critical realignment," they do not, I think, really do justice to the mounting case for basic revision of the whole conception. They only postpone the inevitable.

It is interesting to note, for example, that the two most frequent replies to complaints about the diffuse electoral evidence for realignments appeal to an increasingly strong concept of political "system"—but push the argument in almost opposite, indeed contradictory, directions. In places, for example, both Kleppner and Burnham employ the notion of "system" to narrow the scope of the relevant electoral data, so that many of the putative counterexamples become irrelevant. Burnham's published comments on this score, though clear in implication, mostly occur as marginal comments in essays addressed to other problems. In a recent essay, however, Kleppner addresses the issue squarely.

Of course, whether some subpart of the electoral universe (e.g., state, city, country or particular voter group) experienced realignment is of substantive importance. Forests, after all, are composed of individual trees, and sometimes it can be interesting as well as useful to examine them individually. But when we do that, two factors should be kept in mind. First, only macrolevel data are relevant in testing the credibility of propositions bearing on macrolevel behavior. Whether a particular state (or county or voter group), for example, realigned in the mid-1890s reveals nothing that has direct bearing on whether the electoral universe experienced realignment. Only data describing the behavior of the macrolevel universe as such is useful for such tests.[27]

By itself this passage raises misgivings. It is all very well to stress that national-level data must supply the basic reference points about national realignments. And, indeed, several of the cases discussed by Burnham, such as 1896 or the New Deal, can hardly fail to impress by their decisive and far-reaching nature. But other party systems present less clear-cut cases. As suggested earlier, a focus on turnout in the nineteenth century or the changing competitive status of the parties within the Civil War system either fails to discriminate *between* party systems or ends up drawing the crucial distinction *within* them. Also, Kleppner's argument here implicitly concedes the point raised earlier, that substantial elections often display voting patterns markedly at variance with national trends, which again raises questions about critical realignment theory's favorite explanation for partisan change within the electorate.

But the strongest doubt about this passage arises from its use of the term "system." It stands in rather sharp contrast to the emphasis in a closely related context:

[A]nalyses of behavior within a subpart of the electoral universe should not lose sight of the larger whole. The voting behavior of a state or voter group, for example, never occurs, and therefore can never be explained, in isolation. It occurs as an integral part of a larger system of action and can only be analyzed within that framework. Indeed, the most important questions confronting voting behavior analysis are those that bear on the interrelationships between microlevel behaviors and macrolevel contexts.[28]

It is easy to sympathize with Kleppner's point here, but he has just insisted that the only "larger system of action" relevant to the definition of critical realignments is constituted by national voting patterns. Yet, as we have just seen, these are equivocal. If the relevant notion of "system" is now expanded to include not only national, but all other electoral outcomes (which "can only be analyzed within that framework"), then his proposal verges perilously on the suggestion that the obscure be used to illuminate the opaque. What constitutes the identity of the system is murkier than ever. All that one can say in such cases is that if, for some reason or other, one decides that a critical realignment has in fact occurred, then one will be able to describe a complex set of voting patterns associated with it. But the voting patterns themselves are unlikely to persuade the unconvinced or match the characteristics of other realignments.

Other attempts to clarify the notion of critical realignment also place increasing weight on an elongated notion of "system." In contrast to the passage just quoted, however, they expand the range of reference to include nonelectoral forms of political behavior.

In principle, suggestions that studies of American electoral behavior have concentrated excessively on a very narrow range of politically significant action are certainly plausible. Because of this *prima facie* validity it makes perfect sense to examine critical realignments from this standpoint. But several difficulties arise at once.

The first is that all of the various suggestions either over- or underpredict critical realignments. Burnham, Clubb, and Flanigan's suggestion that periods of unified control of the presidency and Congress could help distinguish realignments does both, for example. It overpredicts the 1920s and the 1960–68 period, which most analysts probably would not recognize as critical realignments. Depending on one's interpretation of the Jacksonian period, it might also miss that consensus realignment.[29] Benjamin Ginsberg's painstaking quantitative analyses of issue "differences between the national parties over time" and "total change in policy over time" does exactly the same: Though the former indicator's overpredictions of 1852 and 1856 could, as Ginsberg suggests, be brought into harmony with a broad view of the Civil War realignment, his 1880 date cannot.[30] In addition, his figures for 1860 and 1936, being suspiciously low, are hard to reconcile with the known facts of these elections.[31] While his index of policy change is immensely valuable for its hints about overlooked themes and periods requiring reexamination, it also overpredicts 1881 and misses the Jacksonian period entirely.[32]

A complete time series of another frequently invoked indicator of critical realignments, partisan differences on congressional roll calls, seems not to be currently available. The published long-run analyses, however, are fairly ragged, showing all sorts of trends.[33] They scarcely provide conclusive evidence of anything except that, like other local political outcomes, congressional elections relate differently to presidential-level outcomes at different points in American history.

Nor do proposals that "major" policy departures or political "crises" or even major policy departures during political crises add up to a specification of critical realignments that most writers on the subject would recognize. Tables 1 through 4 chart indicators of policy change and political events that most analysts would probably recognize as potential heralds of such "political crises," including financial crises, (high) cabinet turnover (net of death), abandonment of the gold (or gold exchange) standard, and foreign interventions.[34] Two points are immediately apparent. The first is that some classically recognized critical realignments certainly coincided with some of the peak values in these series. The second is that many more political crises than critical realignments occurred. Indeed, as several authors, including Burnham, have previously noted, crises of

Table 1

## Major U.S. financial crises

| | |
|---|---|
| 1819 | 1907 |
| 1837 | 1920–21 |
| 1857 | 1929 |
| 1873 | 1975–75 |
| 1893 | |

*Source*: Adapted from list in Kindleberger, *Manias, Panics, and Crashes*. (New York: Basic Books, 1978), pp. 253–59.

Table 2

## Foreign interventions by U.S. military forces

| Year | Number | Year | Number | Year | Number | Year | Number |
|---|---|---|---|---|---|---|---|
| 1813 | 1 | 1865 | 1 | 1904 | 2 | 1956 | 6 |
| 1822 | 1 | 1867 | 1 | 1906 | 1 | 1957 | 9 |
| 1823 | 5 | 1868 | 3 | 1907 | 1 | 1958 | 9 |
| 1824 | 1 | 1870 | 1 | 1910 | 1 | 1959 | 11 |
| 1825 | 1 | 1871 | 1 | 1911 | 1 | 1960 | 10 |
| 1827 | 1 | 1873 | 2 | 1912 | 2 | 1961 | 12 |
| 1831 | 1 | 1874 | 1 | 1914 | 3 | 1962 | 11 |
| 1832 | 1 | 1876 | 1 | 1915 | 1 | 1963 | 18 |
| 1839 | 1 | 1882 | 1 | 1916 | 1 | 1964 | 21 |
| 1840 | 1 | 1885 | 2 | 1917 | 1 | 1965 | 13 |
| 1841 | 1 | 1888 | 1 | 1926 | 2 | 1966 | 3 |
| 1853 | 1 | 1891 | 2 | 1946 | 10 | 1967 | 6 |
| 1854 | 2 | 1893 | 1 | 1947 | 6 | 1968 | 4 |
| 1855 | 2 | 1894 | 3 | 1948 | 8 | 1969 | 3 |
| 1856 | 2 | 1895 | 1 | 1950 | 5 | 1970 | 6 |
| 1858 | 2 | 1899 | 2 | 1951 | 1 | 1971 | 6 |
| 1859 | 1 | 1900 | 1 | 1952 | 4 | 1972 | 3 |
| 1860 | 2 | 1901 | 1 | 1953 | 4 | 1973 | 7 |
| 1863 | 1 | 1902 | 2 | 1954 | 7 | 1973 | 5 |
| 1864 | 2 | 1903 | 2 | 1955 | 2 | 1975 | 7 |

*Source*: Figures for landings by U.S. armed forces "on foreign soil" for 1813–1926 from Offut, "Protection of Citizens"; "Use of U.S. armed forces as a political instrument" from Blechman et. al., *Force Without War*. The differing definitions imply that the two series are not directly comparable.

Table 3

**Gold or gold exchange standard suspensions**

1814 (resumed 1817)
1837 (resumed 1838)
1857 (resumed same year)
1861 (resumed de facto 1873, formally, 1879)
1917 (free export of gold prohibited until June 1918)
1933 (dollar devalued in terms of gold; price fixed at $35.00/oz., 1934)
1968 (two-tier gold market for gold established; U.S. de facto off gold)
1971 (U.S. off gold de jure)

Source: David Williams, "Historical Survey, Gold Prices," Cycles 32,7 (September/October 1981).

various sorts are exceedingly common near the midpoints of some party systems.[35]

Similar difficulties affect three other commonly proposed indicators. While Burnham's well-known observations about the association of third parties with critical realignments have a clear point, his data show that years of especially high votes for third parties cannot be used to indicate realignment.[36] Nor does another indicator he suggests, fights over party credentials or (by extension) internal divisions within parties as measured by major platform fights, provide much help.[37] (Table 5.)

Equally ambiguous is the evidence concerning the adoption of new mass political symbols. Burnham, Clubb, and Flanigan, along with numerous others, have observed that some major political realignments involved the rapid diffusion of new imagery and political symbols, and they have suggested that this phenomenon is characteristic of realignments in general.[38] As it stands, however, their observation is tantalizing, but not wholly convincing. Some of the most famous campaign appeals in American history, such as Warren G. Harding's promise to restore "normalcy," Woodrow Wilson's (not to mention Lyndon Johnson's) pledge to "keep us out of war," "Manifest Destiny" of the early 1840s, or the "Rum, Romanism, and Rebellion," and "Ma, Ma, Where's My Pa, Gone to the White House, Ha Ha Ha" of 1884, can be justified as occurring during critical elections only under a definition more Protean than most analysts are likely to stand for. Probably it is prudent to observe the conjunction of symbols with crises and remember that crises are not equivalent to realignments.

Though questions about identification criteria for critical realignments have occupied center stage in recent discussions, they scarcely exhaust critical realignment theory's litany of difficulties. Any number of other anomalies and puzzles exist as well. Consider, for example, the silence with which most critical

Table 4

## Index of cabinet turnover

| President | No. of Turnovers | President | No. of Turnovers |
|---|---|---|---|
| Washington, 1st term | 0. | Cleveland | .29 |
| 2nd term | 1.5 | Harrison | .29 |
| Adams | .6 | Cleveland | .29 |
| Jefferson, 1st term | .2 | McKinley | .86 |
| 2nd term | .2 | T. Roosevelt, 1st term | .75 |
| Madison, 1st term | .4 | 2nd term | 1.13 |
| 2nd term | .8 | Taft | .25 |
| Monroe, 1st term | .4 | Wilson | .33 |
| 2nd term | .2 | Harding | .11 |
| J. Q. Adams | .2 | Coolidge, 1st term | .22 |
| Jackson, 1st term | 1.0 | 2nd term | .56 |
| 2nd term | 1.4 | Hoover | .33 |
| Van Buren | .6 | F. Roosevelt, 1st term | .0 |
| Harrison | .0 | 2nd term | .67 |
| Tyler | 2.4 | 3rd term | .11 |
| Polk | .67 | 4th term | .11 |
| Taylor | .0 | Truman, 1st term | 1.3 |
| Fillmore | .67 | 2nd term | .88 |
| Pierce | .0 | Eisenhower, 1st term | .22 |
| Buchanan | .67 | 2nd term | .89 |
| Lincoln, 1st term | .67 | Kennedy | .22 |
| (1 mo.) | .17 | Johnson, 1st term | .11 |
| Johnson | 1.17 | 2nd term | 1.09 |
| Grant, 1st term | 1.17 | Nixon, 1st term | .73 |
| 2nd term | 1.3 | 2nd term | 1.0 |
| Hayes | .33 | Ford | .90 |
| Garfield | .0 | Carter | .62 |
| Arthur | 1.17 | | |

*Note*: Numbers are rounded; for explanation of calculations, see note 34.

realignment theorists pass over the early years of the United States. Most analysts begin their discussion sometime in the Jacksonian era. While data limitations make this understandable, it inevitably raises misgivings. Is not the neglect of the birth of American political parties begging important questions if it writes off parties during this period as not really parties, or the party system as not really a "Party System"?

Lending urgency to these inquiries are contemporary discussions about the failure of the United States to experience the realignment many analysts expected sometime in the 1960s or 1970s. Burnham, Kleppner, and others have argued that

Table 5

**Notable platform and credentials fights, 1840–1972[a]**

| Platform fights | | Credential fights | |
|---|---|---|---|
| Year | Party | Year | Party |
| 1860 | Democrats | 1848 | Democrats |
| 1896 | Democrats | 1860 | Democrats |
| 1908 | GOP | 1880 | GOP |
| 1924 | Democrats | 1912 | GOP |
| 1932 | GOP | 1932 | Democrats |
| 1948 | Democrats | 1952 | Democrats |
| 1964 | GOP | 1952 | GOP |
| 1968 | Democrats | 1968 | Democrats |
| 1972 | Democrats | 1972 | Democrats |

a. "Notable" as defined by *Congressional Quarterly*; see note 37 for details.

political parties are now so weak that they are hardly plausible vehicles for realignment. With the decline of mass participation and interests increasingly aggregated outside the electoral system, they suggest, critical realignments are anachronistic.

Now this argument may be correct. But one must wonder. If a complete absence of parties (or the total domination of one party) did not preclude realignment in the Jacksonian era, why should the decline of parties explain the absence of realignment after 1960? Or, as Burnham has also recently suggested, if the cold war is now affording the party system that introduced Social Security to America a retirement experience past all historical precedents, how was this most miraculous of modern life-support marvels accomplished? The extraordinary volatility of the American electorate in recent years, which Burnham has analyzed perhaps more profoundly than anyone else, suggests that not all the "present dangers" agitating individual Americans are those that trouble the Committee for the Present Danger. Moreover, as Table 2 suggests, tense international confrontations sometimes spur realignments. Accordingly, whereas Leon Keyserling's cosponsorship (with legions of less famous but more important figures) of both the Wagner Act and NSC-68 may well be no coincidence, the key links in the causal chain binding the New Deal and the cold war probably were not forged in the heat of any electoral campaign.[39]

These questions about the New Deal system's extraordinary persistence acquire additional urgency when they are raised in the context of the "socialization" theory of partisan identification that most critical realignment theorists after Key himself usually built into the foundation of the theory. In this view, which the work done during the 1950s on *The American Voter* appeared to support, only very low levels of issue consciousness and limited attention spans characterized most voters most of the time. Stable party identifications, which most analysts believed formed the backbone of the political system, were believed to be acquired and transmitted chiefly through non- or arational group and family socialization processes, involving a minimum of cognitive orientation.[40]

Applied to critical realignment theory, this approach to partisan identification almost interpreted itself: During critical realignments, brief spurts of high-intensity, issue-salient political processes disrupted normally low-salience patterns of political involvement. Large-scale changes of partisan allegiance occurred, which dramatically altered the balance of power between parties. Adding to this scenario's plausibility was the striking implication for the periodic, cyclical nature of realignments that one could deduce from it: Over time the original population cohorts died out. After a generation or so had passed, they would constitute a minority of the population. The growing numbers of the "nonimmunized" facilitated the rise of new partisan identifications, making the political system ripe for realignment.

To this theory the persistence of the New Deal system is clearly an embarrassment. Though the theory was always somewhat vague about the nature of the transition from low to high issue salience, realignment should probably have occurred by now. If civil rights, inflation, the war in Vietnam, the 1973–74 recession, Watergate, a decade of political assassinations, tax revolts, and a series of revolving-door presidencies were not enough, what does realignment require? But while a few analysts rushed to proclaim a "Reagan realignment" in 1980, most of the evidence suggests that the American political system, from the standpoint of electoral politics, is still *dealigning*.[41]

Nor is this predictive breakdown the only problem the historical facts about American critical realignment create for the generational theory of partisanship. As observed earlier, the ragged correlation of state- and national-level results suggests that even during the high-stimulus nineteenth-century partisan peaks, the electorate often discriminated carefully among parties and candidates. Because this readiness to draw distinctions is difficult to reconcile with the emphasis on arational socialization experiences, these data inevitably raise questions about the whole model of partisan change.

More recent analysts have proposed that the mobilization of new votes could provide the basis for the sharp shifts in partisan control that realignments were thought to provide.[42] The suggestion is ingenious and, for realignments like the New Deal or the Jacksonian era, which began with largely demobilized electorates, has much plausibility (though it probably underestimates the number of actual conversions in both periods).[43] But though Andersen has advanced the argument, it is more difficult to see how this could explain the Civil War realignment,[44] which began from a much higher base of voter turnout; and applied to the system of 1896, the suggestion has no force at all. In that party system voters were *demobilized* in large numbers. Although successive waves of (non-) voters entering a largely stimulus-free environment certainly helped drive down turnout all through the period, no one has yet constructed an argument that explains how one or two high-stimulus elections—such as those in the 1890s—somehow transformed most voters into enthusiastic Republicans (who, after all, became the majority party) at the same moment as they were persuaded to begin pulling out of the electoral system in record numbers.

Even more devastating to the general "generational change" model of realignment are Lichtman's recent results. Using ecological regressions on data from the 1920s, Lichtman identified groups of first-time voters moving into the electorate. Unfortunately, they voted Republican in slightly larger proportions than the population as a whole.[45]

A final set of difficulties for critical realignment theory arises from the mounting evidence against the theory's bedrock claim that party platforms and government policies bear some significant relation to the substantial majorities rolled up during critical elections. This position is so central to all existing versions of critical realignment theory that it is worth taking a moment to elaborate. Electoral analysis as conducted within the United States is customarily associated with conventional "pluralist" views about the efficacy of democratic control of state policy. Among theorists of critical realignment, however, two quite different positions have been defended. What might be called the "strong" (pluralist) thesis of liberal democratic control exemplified by Gerald Pomper or, I think, most of the Michigan School, sees voters as defining at least the rough outlines of public policy during most elections. In sharp contrast, a "weak" version of that argument, defended formally by Brady, Ginsberg, and, it sometimes appears, Burnham, is far more pessimistic about the possibility of democratic control of the policy.[46] In this second, more somber view, party structures, the institutional apparatus of the state, and perhaps business and other elites normally block the formation of effective popular majorities. Critical realignments, however, momentarily break the usual stalemate. At these times, majority control of policymaking does take place. Articulate majorities form and the state responds.

But a careful institutional analysis of some of the best known and most widely recognized critical realignments in American history suggests that voters were only exiguously responsible for the policies actually pursued during the realigning era.

Consider the New Deal, for example. At first glance, critical realignment theory's implicit claim that Franklin D. Roosevelt's policies mirrored an emergent consensus within an electorate driven almost to distraction by the Great Depression is so clearly true that further discussion appears pointless. But examined closely, this impression almost completely dissolves. FDR either was cold toward or actively opposed many of the famous policy measures, such as the Wagner Act, for which the American electorate later hailed him. Offered an easy chance to score points against Herbert Hoover in the 1932 election, Roosevelt refused it. Instead he called for a balanced budget, preached fiscal conservatism, and urged retrenchment. The first set of policies he tried—the so-called First New Deal—not only was completely incognate with the welfare measures that came in the Second New Deal two years later but was tilted sharply in favor of big business and often harshly antilabor.[47]

Nor is the New Deal an isolated exception among American critical realignments. "Electoral control" theories would look more plausible if Teddy Roosevelt had run for president in the 1890s. But his (greatly overblown) Progressivism did not get running room until after 1900, when most of the system of '96 had already taken shape. Instead McKinley, who related to Mark Hanna and the associated manufacturers of America like Charlie McCarthy to Edgar Bergen, became the people's choice. And, if similar stories about Jackson or Lincoln cannot convince everyone, the memory—or rather, the specters—of Grover Cleveland and Herbert Hoover should suggest that the search for enthusiastic popular majorities is often the last thing on the minds of major party leaders.

The impression that majority control of policy is unlikely even during critical realignments can be given precise quantitative expression though the monumental data base Ginsberg collected for his study *The Consequences of Consent*. If one accepts the data, then several very striking results emerge. First, "policy change" as Ginsberg measured it has almost no relationship with the winning party's margin of victory (as a percentage of the vote) in critical and all other kinds of elections (Figure 1). Second, in those cases where one party ousted another (allowing a clear comparison between the old party's policies and the new party platform), the winning party's platform promises bore wildly fluctuating relations to the policies it subsequently enacted (Figure 2).[48]

In this context it is striking to observe the highly variable reaction of political parties to large-scale depression, when large percentages of the population can be shown to have clamored for relief. The Panic of 1819 led to riots and relief demonstrations all over the United States, but no realignment. Neither did the truly gigantic depression of the early 1870s. Whatever the political effects were of the depressions of 1837–1841, 1857 or 1920–1921, large-scale relief for starving voters was not one of them.[49] In most cases the candidates of both major parties favored balanced budgets, while in 1896 the winner did, but not the loser. Recent quantitative studies suggesting variable and uncertain relationships between symbolic appeals in party platforms and economic conditions underscore this general point.[50]

## Conclusion: Realigning the Study of Realignment

Critical realignment theory might eventually surmount all these difficulties. Perhaps, for example, a new and elaborate combination of electoral returns and public policies can be worked up to yield an unambiguous list of "critical elections," along with a highly refined argument to show, for example, that a

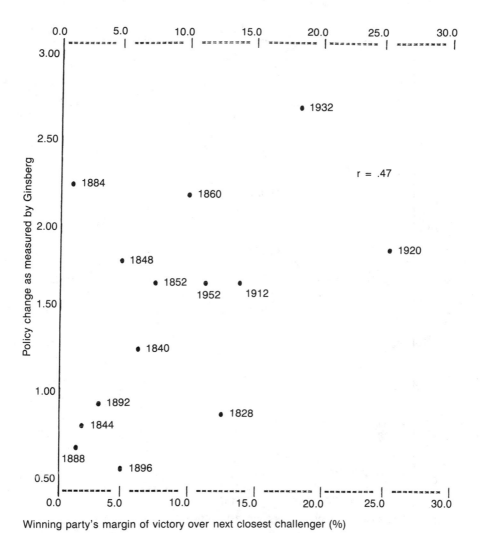

Figure 1  **Policy change is only loosely related to the winning party's victory margin**

majority of voters before the New Deal really did not desire small-farm credit programs, social insurance, the right to join unions, or restrictions on the length of the working day (so that they can then be credited with "choosing" the policies actually pursued).

But a degree of skepticism appears justified. Increasingly sophisticated variations on already baroque themes are likely to generate only rococo variations on the same themes, making the discussions more complicated but no more conclusive. And further research on the actual development of American public

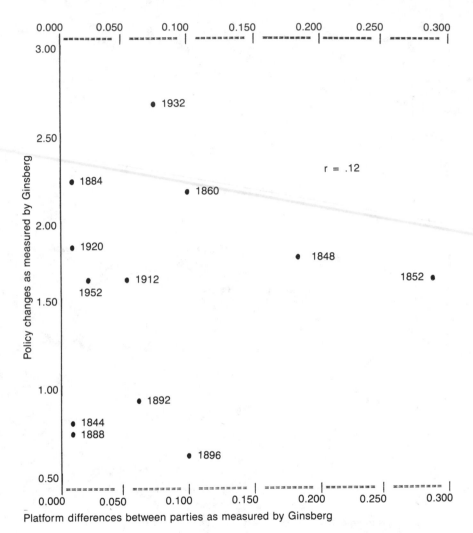

Figure 2  **Policy change is very weakly related to platform differences between parties**

policy during critical realignments, I think, is likely to underscore the tenuousness of the links between those policies and mass political demands.

So ultimately, the alternatives are likely to come down to two: Either critical realignment theory must be revised substantially, or it must be abandoned. While some may prefer the second option, some of the best known work on critical realignments indicates clearly that a different approach might be eminently viable. Though his major work defended a weak version of the electoral control thesis, for example, Walter Dean Burnham's treatment of the System of

'96 and the ensuing withering away of mass political parties almost irresistibly suggests an entirely different interpretation. At the very moment that his account draws attention to the high voting turnout that marked this election, it begins to outline a method for analyzing political systems in which business elites, not voters, play the leading part. It treats mass party structures and voting behavior as dependent variables, explicable in terms of rules for ballot access, issues, and institutional change within the business community.[51]

Though no one, including Burnham himself, has systematically analyzed critical realignment in these terms, this approach is well worth exploring. If a viable methodology could be developed for analyzing coalition formation among major investors, then the definitional puzzles that increasingly beset critical realignment theory might well disappear, as people like Lamont and institutions like the Morgan bank finally receive notice from political science.[52]

## Notes

This essay was originally part of a longer study. The other, longer part of the study, outlining an "investment theory of political parties" as an alternative to conventional "median voter" accounts of elections and party systems, has already been published as "Party Realignment and American Industrial Structure: The Investment Theory of Parties in Historical Perspective," in vol. 6 of *Research in Political Economy*, ed. Paul Zarembka (Greenwich, Conn.: JAI Press, 1983), pp. 1-83.

That paper's conclusions about the primacy of large investors have recently been questioned by two "public choice" analysts. Cf. Richard D. McKelvey and Peter Ordeshook, "Information, Electoral Equilibria and the Democratic Ideal," *Journal of Politics*, forthcoming. Their criticism, however, rests heavily on a notion of "rational expectations" that can, I think, be shown to be generally inappropriate. The argument for this point, however, involves considerations about transactions costs and the "market" for political information that must be left for another paper.

For comments on various drafts of this paper or the larger study I should like to thank Walter Dean Burnham, John Freeman, Benjamin Ginsberg, Anne McCauley, Samuel Popkin, Gail Russell, Martin Shefter, and Alan Stone. I am also grateful to Duane Lockard for much support in the initial stages of work in this area, and to Stanley Kelley for many discussions about the significance of Anthony Downs's work. Thanks also to Gavan Duffy, Lola Klein, and Betty McEuen for other assistance. It should not be necessary to add that readers are not writers of a paper and hence are not to be held responsible for its contents.

My title borrows from Samuel Popkin, John Gorman, Charles Phillips, and Jeffrey Smith, "Comment: What Have You Done for Me Lately—Toward an Investment Theory of Voting," *American Political Science Review* 70 (September 1976). Readers of Popkin's *The Rational Peasant* (Berkeley: University of California Press, 1979) will recognize their article as a case study of peasants at the polls.

1. These and subsequent details of the 1932 Hoover-Roosevelt campaign are all drawn from my *Critical Realignment: The Fall of the House of Morgan and the Origins of the New Deal* (New York: Oxford University Press, forthcoming). Many themes of this work are summarized in my "From 'Normalcy' to New Deal: Industrial Structure, Party

Realignment, and American Public Policy in the Great Depression," *International Organization* 38, 1 (Winter 1984):41–94.

2. The diary has since been used by historians who, lacking access to the telephone transcripts, treated it as a reliable primary source. Cf. the discussion in Ferguson, " 'Normalcy' to New Deal," p. 79 n. 80.

3. Lamont's papers, now at the Baker Library of the Harvard Business School, contain many notes and memoranda that will, in time, probably lead to a sweeping reappraisal of existing views about the development of higher education in America. I hope to discuss some of this material separately in the near future. Among Lowell's many writings, cf. his *Public Opinion and Popular Government* (New York: Longmans, Green, 1913).

4. Lamont to Markle, October 26, 1932, Lamont Papers.

5. Form letter from the file on these meetings, now in the Lamont Papers.

6. Cf. Ferguson, *Critical Realignment* and " 'Normalcy' to New Deal"; "Von Versailles zum New Deal," a catalogue essay to the Neue Gesellschaft für Bildende Kunst's exhibition of American art from 1920 to 1940, *Amerika, Traum und Depression* (Berlin: Neue Gesellschaft für Bildende Kunst, 1980), pp. 436–50; Gerald Epstein and Thomas Ferguson, "Monetary Policy, Loan Liquidation, and Industrial Conflict: The Federal Reserve and the Open Market Operations of 1932," *Journal of Economic History* 44,4 (December 1984):957–83. An amiable critic of an early draft of this paper wondered whether the opening discussion of Hoover and the Morgan bank in 1932 is truly appropriate to this paper's theme. After all, it concerns a case in which some of America's best known investors *lost*. All sorts of replies seem appropriate to this suggestion, but two points are particularly telling. As the text hints (and " 'Normalcy' to New Deal" documents), Lamont and Co. lost to rival investors at Chase and elsewhere and not simply to "voters." Moreover, the example is extremely telling: In any period other than the Depression, such resources would probably have sufficed for a rescue.

7. Ferguson, "Party Realignment and Industrial Structure."

8. See the discussion of specific works by these authors, *infra*.

9. Cf. Jerome Clubb, William Flanigan, and Nancy Zingale, *Partisan Realignment* (Beverly Hills: Sage, 1980).

10. V. O. Key, "A Theory of Critical Elections," *Journal of Politics*, 17 (February 1955):4.

11. The literature on critical realignments is now very large—too large for all the individual contributions to be inventoried here. For a very good bibliography, however, cf. Bruce Campbell and Richard Trilling, eds., *Realignment in American Politics* (Austin: University of Texas Press, 1980), pp. 329–32. Because this work and others like it are readily available, this essay bows to an urgent pressure to conserve space and will hold subsequent references to the minumum essential to precision of argument.

12. Alan J. Lichtman, for example, has strongly criticized all applications of critical realignment theory to twentieth-century American politics. Cf. his "Critical Election Theory and the Reality of American Presidential Politics, 1916–40," *American Historical Review* 81 (April 1976):317–48, especially his remarks on pp. 345ff. J. Morgan Kousser, "History QUASSHED: Quantitative Social Scientific History in Perspective," *American Behavioral Scientist* 23, 6 (July/August 1980):885–904, flatly rejects the theory. Many of their criticisms are discussed below, though space does not permit a detailed discussion of all the points they raise. Lee Benson, Joel Silbey, and Phyllis Field, "Toward

a Theory of Stability and Change in American Voting Patterns: New York State, 1792–1970,'' in *The History of American Electoral Behavior*, ed. Joel Silbey, Allan Bogue, and William Flanigan (Princeton: Princeton University Press, 1978), pp. 80ff. is also skeptical.

Lichtman's very recent "Critical Elections in Historical Perspective,'' California Institute of Technology Social Science Working Paper no. 420, reached me too late to be fully incorporated into this essay. Whereas, for reasons briefly noted in the sketch of the System of '96 presented in my "Party Realignment and American Industrial Structures,'' I disagree with certain aspects of his discussion of the System of '96, the negative results of the tests (for the presence of the stable voting coalitions that are commonly thought to define realignments) that he reports underscore this paper's nihilistic assessment of conventional voting theories of critical realignment.

13. See, for example, Clubb, Flanigan, and Zingale, *Realignment*. The trend runs clearly in this direction.

14. Both Lichtman and Kousser raise questions about the number of elections necessary for realignment. But some of their formulations are so extreme that it is highly doubtful that any scientific theory in any field could ever measure up to their demands. For example, I do not know why any critical realignment theorist has to decide in advance whether two high-stimulus elections over roughly the same issues could not trigger realignment as easily as one by itself, as Kousser seems to expect (cf. "QUASSHED,'' pp. 894–95). As any number of critics of earlier positivist formulations of scientific method have recently stressed, the working procedures in any genuine empirical inquiry are *never* totally defined by a set of rules and definitions and often have to cope with anomalies. See, for example, Imre Lakatos, "Falsification and the Methodology of Scientific Research Programs,'' in *Criticism and the Growth of Knowledge*, ed. I. Lakatos and A. Musgrave (Cambridge: Cambridge University Press, 1970), pp. 91–195. In this paper's inventory of criticism of critical realignment theory, I have, accordingly, sought to connect issues of definition—such as the one, two, or many election questions—with major theoretical questions, such as the sources of partisan change during realignments. Most of the significance of these definitional issues, I think, evaporate if they are considered in isolation.

Kousser's methodological views sometimes admit of peculiar uses. Though he regularly criticizes traditional historiography for any number of unscientific practices, he also concedes that certain traditional historians produce work that is at least potentially scientific. But only a remnant, it appears can be saved. C. Van Woodward, his thesis adviser, can, but Eugene Genovese cannot. Compare Kousser's remarks in his "Quantitative Social Scientific History,'' in *The Past Before Us*, ed. Michael Kammen (Ithaca: Cornell University Press, 1980), p. 447, and in "QUASSHED,'' p. 892. His is certainly an arresting treatment of Genovese; one reviewer, in what might well be thought a less than neutral source, has just hailed a newly published work for presenting evidence that is supposed to *refute* Genovese's thesis. Cf. Eric Foner, "The Slaveholder as Factory Owner,'' *New York Times Book Review*, May 23, 1982, p. 11.

15. See, for example, Clubb, Flanigan, and Zingale, *Realignment*, chs, 2, 3.

16. Ibid., for examples.

17. Ibid., ch. 3.

18. Ibid., esp. pp. 55–74 and 77–83.

19. Ibid., chs. 2, 3.

20. See, for example, Burnham's *Critical Elections and the Mainspring of American Politics* (New York: Norton, 1971), pp. 21ff.

21. Several recent studies have raised various statistical questions about the reality of the turnout decline after the 1890s. For reasons briefly discussed in note 86 of my "Party Realignment and American Industrial Structure," I am very skeptical of the significance of these criticisms. This essay, however, cannot afford to examine the issues. Note that the discussion here refers to turnout. Lichtman's "Critical Elections" discussion of the evidence for distinct voting blocs, I think, devastates claims that 1896 created voting blocs defined along ethnic or religious lines and is ruinous to accounts that see the election of 1896 as pivotal for the formation of distinct blocs in the electorate.

22. Burnham, *Critical Elections*, ch. 3.

23. Ibid., pp. 15ff.

24. Ibid.

25. Cf. ibid., ch. 5, and Paul Kleppner, "Critical Realignments and Electoral Systems," in *The Evolution of American Electoral Systems*, ed. Paul Kleppner *et al.* (Westport, Conn.: Greenwood Press, 1981), pp. 11ff.

26. Burnham, *Critical Elections*, p. 13.

27. Kleppner, "Realignments," p. 11.

28. Ibid.

29. Cf. W. D. Burnham, J. M. Clubb, and W. H. Flanigan, "Partisan Realignment: A Systematic Perspective," in *History of American Electoral Behavior*, ed. Silbey et al., pp. 49ff.

30. Benjamin Ginsberg, *The Consequences of Consent: Elections, Citizens Control and Popular Acquiescence* (Reading, Mass.: Addison-Wesley, 1982), pp. 130ff.

31. Ibid.; see his Table on p. 130. The 1936 election was one of the most bitterly contested in American history.

32. Ibid., pp. 135ff.

33. See the data series presented in Clubb, Flanigan, and Zingale, *Realignment*, ch. 7; and Paul Allen Beck, "The Electoral Cycle and Patterns of American Politics," *British Journal of Political Science* 9 (April 1979):146ff.

34. Because the National Bureau of Economic Research's widely used list of recessions and depressions does not go back far enough, Table 1's list of major financial crises is adapted from Kindleberger's "A Stylized Outline of Financial Crises 1720–95" in his *Manias, Panics, and Crashes* (New York: Basic Books, 1978). Note that his concern is solely with financial crises, which are not quite the same as "economic downturns." One entry for the "1950s, 1960s" has been deleted, since it fits his purposes but not this study's focus on particular events. In Table 2, the data from Milton Offut, *The Protection of Citizens Abroad by the Armed Forces of the United States* (Baltimore: Johns Hopkins Press, 1928) concern only landings abroad by American forces; the data beginning in 1946 from Barry M. Blechman, Stephen Kaplan *et al.*, *Force Without War* (Washington, D.C.: Brookings, 1978), cover the slightly wider notion of the use of "armed forces as a political instrument," which includes naval displays. Table 4's index of cabinet turnover is figured as follows. First a list of all cabinet members excluding the postmaster general was produced. (This was slightly less obvious than it might appear. Treatment of interim appointees, brief holdover officials, and cabinet members who resigned after a president won reelection but who then stayed on for a month or so make standard lists differ very slightly in regard to both personnel and dates. I collated standard almanacs with various

histories, trying to make judgments about the comparatively few holdovers and "interim placeholders," who were eliminated if they could be identified.) Under the theory that political factors were largely irrelevant in their cases, officials who died in office were also deleted from the totals. Counting officials who changed positions within an administration as new appointments, the total number of appointments was then summed and divided by the number of cabinet slots. It should be added that the assumption behind all these tables is that the various peaks of each series mark likely "crises." Also, it is perfectly obvious that two other "crisis" situations—major wars and peak years of strikes (such as 1919, the late 1930s, or the late 1940s)—cannot be used to indicate critical realignment, though (like many events counted in other tables) certain such incidents played roles in particular realignments.

35. Burham, *Critical Elections*, pp. 28–29.

36. Ibid., ch. 1.

37. Ibid., for Burnham's discussion. The list of "Notable Credentials Fights, 1848–1972" comes from *Congressional Quarterly, Guide to U.S. Elections* (Washington: Congressional Quarterly, 1975), p. 5; for the "Platform Fights," cf. p. 12. Beck, "Electoral Cycle," presents a graph of the highly irregular pattern of convention ballots required to nominate major party candidates for the presidency. See p. 142.

38. Burnham, Clubb, and Flanigan, "Systemic Perspective," pp. 71ff.

39. The famous Clark Clifford memoranda in the 1948 election, I think, reflected a larger process rather than created it.

For Burnham's proposal, cf. *inter alia* his "The 1980 Earthquake: Realignment, Reaction, or What?" in Thomas Ferguson and Joel Rogers, eds., *The Hidden Election* (New York: Pantheon, 1980), pp. 122–24.

40. This summary characterization of the traditional Michigan approach to partisan identification cannot hope to do full justice to all its nuances. All this essay has space for is a description of the basic tendency.

Key himself, of course, pioneered the more recent "issue oriented" approach to voting analysis. For references and more detailed analysis than is possible here, cf. Morris Fiorina, *Retrospective Voting in American National Election* (New Haven: Yale University Press, 1981), ch. 1.

41. For 1980, cf. the various essays in Ferguson and Rogers, eds. *The Hidden Election*. For 1984, cf. David Brady and Patricia A. Hurley, "The Prospects For Contemporary Partisan Realignment," *PS* 17, 1 (Winter 1985):63–68. If, as suggested in Ferguson, "Party Realignment and Industrial Structure," realignments are defined by reference to major changes in investor blocs, than the late 1970s and the rise of Reagan assuredly signaled a true realignment. For a detailed discussion, see Thomas Ferguson and Joel Rogers, *Right Turn: The 1984 Election and the Future of American Politics* (New York: Hill and Wang, forthcoming).

42. Cf. Kristi Andersen, *The Creation of a Democratic Majority 1928-36* (Chicago: University of Chicago Press, 1979).

43. Cf. Walter Dean Burnham "The Politics of Crisis," *Journal of Interdisciplinary History* 8, 4 (Spring 1978): 757–58, esp. n. 16, or Robert S. Erickson and Kent L. Tedin, "The 1928–36 Partisan Realignment: The Case for the Conversion Hypothesis," *American Political Science Review* 75, 4 (December 1981):951–62. A striking feature of this discussion is that no one even bothers to consider how the rise of unions might have affected the issues in this controversy.

44. Andersen, *Creation*, p. 124. Note that Andersen herself doubted that her hypothesis fitted well with the 1896 realignment.

45. Allan J. Lichtman, *Prejudice and the Old Politics* (Chapel Hill: University of North Carolina Press, 1979), p. 212.

46. See the various works of these authors, inventoried in Campbell and Trilling, *Realignment*.

47. See the discussion in my papers cited in note 6.

48. The data for "policy change" and "platform differences in the figures come from the corresponding tables in Ginsberg, *Consequences*, ch. 4. Note that because of the way the data are calculated, only elections in which the president's party lost control of the White House belong in the figures. Admirers of Ptolemy can always, of course, question the data, try another measure of "Margin of Victory," propose special rules for handling third parties, or perhaps experiment with specifications that include the strength of the president's party in Congress.

As note 33 suggested, non-Ptolemaic reservations about the data are also possible, of course, but I doubt that any but ad hoc corrections will fundamentally alter the results. (A regression using both platform differences and margin of victory was also tried out, but its corrected $R^2$ was less than for margin of victory alone. F tests, if one wishes to use them on this data, all show up as insignificant at the .05 level for regressions on either each variable alone or both together.)

Note also the discussion of candidates and issues in Benjamin Page, *Choices and Echoes in Presidential Elections* (Chicago: University of Chicago Press, 1978), especially ch. 10.

49. See the discussion in Ferguson, "Party Realignment and Industrial Structure," pp. 18, and the many cases cited in the sketches of individual party systems in section 4 of that paper.

50. See Robert Weber and J. Zvi Namenwirth, "Party Platforms, Economic Performance and Presidential Elections, 1892–1964," manuscript. Note especially their concluding comments on earlier work by Tufte, Kramer, Stigler, and others.

51. See especially his "Theory and Voting Research: Some Reflections on Converse's "Change in the American Electorate," *American Political Science Review*, 68 (September 1974).

52. Section 3 of Ferguson, "Party Realignment and Industrial Structure," develops several solutions to this problem and presents a method for graphically analyzing party coalitions within the business community.

# 4. DID THE 1984 ELECTION MATTER?

In the period between Ronald Reagan's 1980 victory and his inauguration, a position paper entitled "Avoiding a GOP Economic Dunkirk" circulated among Republican policymakers. Warning of a catastrophe that could ensue from some combination of high credit rates, recession, high budget deficits, and commodity (especially oil) shocks, the paper called for the rapid adoption of a radically new economic and social program, including governnment waste cutting, tax cuts, regulatory reform, reduction of social (or entitlement) programs, and decontrol of energy products. Further, the incoming president promised to disband the Energy and Education departments. Many commentators on the left anticipated that President Reagan would reintroduce suppression of civil liberties and deal a devastating blow to the feminist, environmental, consumer protection, and civil rights movements. Still others feared that Reagan would be reckless in foreign affairs and could even involve the United States in a nuclear confrontation with the Soviet Union.

In a word, then, both the zealous supporters and the bitter opponents of the new president anticipated that major changes in the role of government would occur as a result of the 1980 election. Some years later the picture is ambiguous, as it has been in the cases of prior presidents. Certainly the worst fears of Reagan's opponents have not been realized, yet there have been significant increases in defense expenditures (begun during the Carter Administration) and cutbacks in many social programs, some affecting the poor, but most affecting middle strata. At the same time, total government outlays increased from fiscal year 1980 to fiscal year 1984, but considerably less than half of this increase is attributable to increases in the national defense budget. In foreign affairs most of the President's actions have bordered on the timid rather than the rash. Neither the Energy nor the Education Department has been abolished, and although regulatory changes have taken place, the sweeping changes demanded by the authors of "Avoiding a GOP Dunkirk" have not been met.

Notwithstanding the Reagan Administration's problems in both recession and boom, the President clearly avoided a political Dunkirk. Indeed, his margin in the popular vote in the 1984 election was 59 percent to Mr. Mondale's 41 percent, carrying every state except Minnesota. At the same time, the Democratic party registered gains at every other level. Consider, for example, that in New Jersey and Tennessee the President won the popular vote overwhelmingly, yet Democratic senatorial candidates, whose views sharply differ from those of Reagan, decisively defeated Republicans sharing the President's beliefs. The election results, then, like Reagan's policies or performance, whether evaluated from the left or from the right, are ambiguous. Certainly, there are no immediately crystalline explanations for the election results or for Reagan's first-term performance. Like prior administrations, Ronald Reagan's does not seem informed by a grand plan. Rather, it seems to be subject to incremental, ad hoc decisionmaking.

What can be said, then, about the 1984 election in the context of whether elections matter? The three concluding essays show that the answers once again are not simple. The chapter by Martin Shefter and Benjamin Ginsberg argues that, indeed, the Reagan Administration has a strategy, albeit a mixed one, which blends attempts to reorient American politics and government, engage in sound economic management, and, at the same time, please important constituencies. Balancing these goals inevitably leads to ambiguity and inconsistency. Yet, considering the diversity of impulses, there is a higher consistency that one can see in the behavior of the administration. To some extent elections matter, but in some respects governance is independent of them.

One reason that candidates are often more interested in platitudes than in issues is illustrated by Robert Weissberg's essay. Taking a clear stand on an issue may be more costly than beneficial. It is possible that one may thereby lose more votes than one gains or assures. Virtually everyone in the United States favors equality of opportunity in the abstract. As soon as the general issue is translated into specific policy proposals, however, divisions begin to appear. If feelings over an issue are particularly intense, the fragile coalitions that constitute American political parties can be riven. But while this dynamic provides a very strong incentive to duck an issue, party activists will sometimes demand strong stands anyway—with deleterious electoral results, as Weissberg shows. Yet, as Jeremy Rabkin shows, in the case of regulatory policy, a general mood projected by a candidate can translate into some policy changes, although not changes as extensive as some would like.

To conclude, then, do elections matter? Yes and no.

# 4.1

# Institutionalizing the Reagan Regime

## Martin Shefter and Benjamin Ginsberg

Since the 1980 elections—and especially since Ronald Reagan's landslide victory in 1984—there has been much discussion of whether a critical realignment is underway in American politics; that is, whether the political coalition that elected and reelected President Reagan might endure and dominate American politics for another thirty years or more.[1] Most political scientists address this question simply by asking whether Reagan's *electoral* coalition is likely to survive, and whether its members are likely to support not simply Republican presidential candidates in the years ahead, but also Republican candidates in congressional, state, and local elections. However, the issue of realignment should be discussed in broader terms than this.

The half-dozen party systems that have governed the United States since the Jeffersonian era have been distinguished from one another by more than the composition of their electoral bases. There are at least five characteristics of a durable regime in American national politics. First, if a regime is to endure its leaders must succeed in defining the central issues of national politics—that is, the content of the nation's political agenda. Second, to be stable a regime must forge a support coalition that controls more in the way of politically relevant resources than the coalition supporting its opponents. A third characteristic of a stable regime is its ability to develop a legitimating ideology that plausibly presents the interests of its supporters as general or common interests. Fourth, a stable regime must inherit or construct governmental institutions and processes that enable it to enact policies beneficial to its supporters. Fifth and finally, to remain in power a regime must foster prosperity, and finance the flow of public benefits to its supporters without slowing the growth of the national economy.

Martin Shefter and Benjamin Ginsberg teach at Cornell University.

An analysis of recent developments in American politics that focuses on these dimensions suggests that the regime constructed by Ronald Reagan might well last long after Reagan himself leaves office.

## Defining the Political Agenda

With regard to the first of the conditions for regime stability, the Reagan Administration has been quite successful in defining the central issues of national politics, and there are reasonably good prospects that the political agenda Reagan has defined will endure to the advantage of Republican candidates in years to come. The central element of the Reagan strategy is to shift the focus of national political attention from the expenditure to the revenue side of the federal budget. If this strategy succeeds it would mark a major change from the pattern prevailing during the New Deal and postwar periods. From the 1930s through the 1960s the Democrats entrenched themselves as the nation's majority party by enacting expenditure programs channeling public funds to the party's constituent groups—crop subsidies for farmers, social security for the elderly, the social programs of the Great Society for blacks, and so forth. Throughout these decades, Democratic candidates campaigned for public office by warning each bloc of voters that the Republicans had plans to withhold or dilute their benefits.

In a parallel fashion, Ronald Reagan campaigned against Walter Mondale in 1984 by warning voters that "The Democrats want to take your tax cuts away." As for the future, the indexation provisions of the 1981 tax act in effect turn the Reagan tax cut into an entitlement program for the middle and upper classes, because every year these voters will be entitled to a further cut in nominal tax rates, and every other year Republican candidates can warn voters that the Democrats have a plan to omit or reduce the tax cut to which they are entitled.

At the same time that Reagan tax cuts provide the Republicans with an issue they should be able to use to advantage in years to come, they create a *structural* imbalance between public revenues and expenditures that makes it difficult for the Democrats to appeal to voters by promising to enact new expenditure programs, as they had done during the New Deal and postwar years. Rather, the Democrats have been compelled since 1981 to fight on terrain defined by Ronald Reagan—to propose budget cuts of their own. This is terrain on which it is difficult for the Democrats to win.

## Institutionalizing a Majority Coalition

This points to the second characteristic of a dominant regime—its capacity to establish stable linkages to a coalition of political forces that commands the votes and campaign contributions a president needs to gain power, and the talent and control over major private and quasi-public institutions he needs to govern the country.[2]

In 1984 Ronald Reagan won considerable support not only among tradition-al Republican voters, but also among the Southerners, Catholics, and blue-collar workers who had been part of the New Deal coalition but had shown tendencies in the 1960s and early 1970s to vote against Democratic presidential candidates because of the party's association with blacks and antiwar protesters. In addition, Reagan won solid support among young, colleged-educated professionals (the "yuppies")—the very social group that had participated in, or been sympathetic to, these protests.

Reaganites regard yuppies as a crucial swing group. The only contender for the Democratic presidential nomination in 1984 they feared was Gary Hart, because, unlike Mondale, he might win widespread support among upper-middle-class voters. And much of the Reagan Administration's behavior in office has been oriented toward attaching these voters to the Republican party in years to come. This explains why, for example, President Reagan has done almost nothing concrete on behalf of the so-called family issues of concern to the New Right but anathema to cosmopolitan professionals. Also, to meet the threat of the nuclear freeze movement—which must be seen as a calculated effort of the Administra-tion's opponents to mobilize the old antiwar constituency against Reagan—the President was determined to enter into arms control negotiations with the Soviet Union prior to the 1984 election. The most important way, however, in which Ronald Reagan is seeking to establish a durable linkage between middle-class professionals and the Republican party is by making tax reform the central goal of his second administration.[3] Upper-middle-class professionals are among the chief beneficiaries of the Administration's tax revision plan, for it will lower the maximum tax rate on earned income from 50 percent to 35 percent, while eliminating numerous deductions that business firms currently use to escape taxation.

This point is related to the discussion in the previous section of Reagan's seeking to make the revenue side of the budget the central focus of national politics and is sufficiently important to warrant further analysis here. The social group that today is called the "yuppies" was discovered, and was labelled the "New Class," by sociologists and political scientists in the 1960s.[4] It can best be defined as that segment of the nation's upper social strata whose chief asset is human capital—that is, high levels of education and training—rather than finan-cial capital. It has been argued that the New Class is inherently liberal, because its members have greater leverage in the public than in the private sector. In fact, however, this class has no inherent ideological tendencies. Ronald Reagan has undertaken to divide its members with his tax reductions and domestic budget cuts—expanding opportunities for middle-class professionals in the private sector while restricting opportunities in the public and nonprofit sectors. Those college-educated professionals who are in a position to take advantage of these opportuni-ties are being attracted into the Republican party. Those who are not in a position to take advantage of these opportunities—the quintessential occupational groups in this category are teachers, social workers, and college professors—remain attached to the Democratic party. The prospect that Reagan's strategy for winning support among middle-class professionals will succeed is suggested by what is perhaps the most striking finding of the New York Times/CBS 1984 exit poll. Of those respondents who use a computer on their job or at home, 62 percent voted for Ronald Reagan in 1984.[5]

If the tax and budget cuts of President Reagan's first and second terms have the potential for establishing durable linkages between the GOP and upper-middle-class professionals working in the private sector, they also are likely to drive ever more firmly into the Democratic camp the social forces with a stake in domestic spending or active governmental involvement in labor markets. This category includes low-level public employees and middle-class professionals who work in the public and nonprofit sectors. This can help explain both why teachers and other public-sector workers have come to play increasingly important roles in the Democratic party in recent years, and why the doctrine of "comparable worth"—which asserts that workers should be paid in proportion to their human capital—has become the preeminent goal of the women's movement.

It also can be noted that President Reagan's fiscal policies are doubly injurious to blacks, because the clients of federal social programs are disproportionately black, and because public-sector jobs are the most important channel of social mobility for blacks. This, in turn, can help explain the spectacular 90 percent black vote against Reagan in the 1984 general election, and the emergence of Jesse Jackson as the first nationally recognized leader of black America since Martin Luther King, Jr. Jackson's embracing of third world leaders such as Yasir Arafat, Fidel Castro, and Daniel Ortega expresses the profound alienation of middle-class blacks from the Reagan regime.[6] It may not be too farfetched to compare this to the alienation of intellectuals and professionals in third world countries, who also lack job opportunities commensurate with their skills and education.

Finally, the Reagan Administration has greatly weakened organized labor. Its fiscal and monetary policies, by driving up real interest rates and the value of the dollar, eroded the competitiveness of many sectors of American industry in domestic and world markets, increasing unemployment in these sectors and reducing labor's bargaining power. To protect themselves against this assault, in 1984 unions involved themselves in Democratic party politics more actively than ever before, and this level of involvement is likely to be maintained in future years. What is especially striking about labor's political role in 1984 was its joining forces with the National Organization of Women. Labor leaders and middle-class activists in groups such as NOW had been bitter opponents in Democratic party politics during the Vietnam War; they had been at odds with one another over the issues of affirmative action and environmentalism through much of the 1970s; and they had pursued different electoral strategies as recently as 1980. Moreover, the advocates of the doctrine of comparable worth seek to increase women's salaries by making invidious comparisons between the education required by many traditionally female occupations—such as teachers, social workers, and librarians—and that required of more highly paid unionized occupations, such as truck drivers or electricians. It is a mark of the desperation of organized labor in the face of Reaganite policies that union leaders are prepared to accept the elimination of these traditional pay differentials and ally with their former opponents. One of the terms of this accommodation is the displacement of market mechanisms of wage determination not only in blue-collar occupations—which is a major legacy of the New Deal—but also in white-collar and pink-collar occupations. Another facet of this accommodation between organized labor and middle-class professionals in the Democratic party is what has come to be called "industrial policy"—which promises jobs to blue-collar workers and influence over the allocation of capital to middle-class professionals.

If these trends continue into the future they may solidify a major development of recent years—a unification of most sectors of the business community in the Republican party. An explanation for this can be found by reading what the *Wall Street Journal* or *Barron's* has to say on the subjects of comparable worth, the damage inflicted on American business by regulatory policies the Democrats enacted in response to consumer and environmental activists, and the new era of free enterprise and prosperity that is dawning because of the decline of organized labor.[7] Businessmen value their autonomy above all else, and the protection Reaganism provides against government and union restrictions on managerial control evidently outweigh their unease over President Reagan's budget deficits.

## Developing a Legitimating Ideology

This leads to the third requisite of a stable regime—that it develop a legitimating ideology that plausibly presents the interests of its key supporters as "universal interests," in the words of Antonio Gramsci. It is quite unlikely that many supporters of Ronald Reagan in the business community have read Gramsci, but the more thoughtful among them have read Irving Kristol, who argued in the 1970s that it was important not to cede the realms of culture and ideology to the enemies of their class. In recent years businessmen have contributed a good deal of money to institutions such as the American Enterprise Institute, the Heritage Foundation, and the Hoover Institution, and these have financed an efflorescense of conservative thought.[8]

A mark of the success of this conservative ideological offensive is the substantial delegitimation of the public philosophy of the New Deal regime—"interest-group liberalism."[9] This is indicated by the widespread criticism of Walter Mondale during the 1984 campaign for caving in to the Democratic party's "special interest groups" when he made concessions to organized labor, the National Organization of Women, blacks, and homosexuals. This indicates the failure of the Democrats to present plausibly the interests of their supporters as universal interests—that is, their failure to present a plausible vision of the *common* good.

If one extrapolates from the experience of 1984, it is not inconceivable that the Democratic party might in future years find itself in the same position it was in between 1896 and 1932.[10] A party that repeatedly nominated William Jennings Bryan for the presidency, Pitchfork Ben Tillman for the U.S. Senate, and Tammany's Big Tim Sullivan for the House of Representatives was regarded by metropolitan elites as incompetent to govern an industrial society. In a parallel fashion, a party that must pay heed to Jesse Jackson's views on foreign policy, Lane Kirkland's on trade policy, and Bella Abzug's views on wage policy may come to be regarded in similar terms by metropolitan elites in the late twentieth century.

By contrast, the Republicans under Ronald Reagan have been remarkably successful in presenting the interests of *their* core supporters as universal interests. The 1981 tax cut was enacted on the premise that everyone would benefit if taxes on the wealthy and on business were cut. Similarly, the claims of equity embodied in the Administration's tax simplification plan are sufficiently persuasive that even Common Cause, the liberal public-interest lobbying organization, announced its support for the plan. And it is Ronald Reagan's political genius to have persuaded millions of Americans that there is a relationship between the performance of American athletes at the Olympics, on the one hand, and the administration's arms build-up, on the other—both are examples of America's new spirit, of America's coming back. Clearly, the Republicans have elaborated a vision of a nation that is prosperous at home and respected abroad—a vision that millions Americans, working class, middle class, and upper class alike, find compelling. It is not inconceivable that they will continue to find it compelling in years to come.

## Building Governing Institutions

A fourth characteristic of a stable regime is its ability to alter political processes and institutions that had worked to the advantage of its predecessors, and to establish new institutions that enable it to enact and implement policies benefitting its supporters.[11] It is crucial to note that neither of these tasks has to be accomplished through the mechanism of political parties. For example, from the 1940s into the 1960s a national security apparatus that was largely insulated from the vagaries of party competition coordinated executive and legislative activity in foreign and military affairs and generated a fairly consistent set of policies over a period of twenty years. And during the late 1960s the opponents of the foreign and domestic policies that the nation had pursued in the postwar era developed a new set of institutional alliances through which they attacked their opponents and secured enactment of the policies they favored. This involved an alliance among U.S. senators, the national news media, and the federal judiciary—an alliance in which political parties did not play a major role.

The most important example of this alliance occurred during the Watergate affair, when investigations by the *Washington Post* and the Ervin Committee in the Senate, along with the Supreme Court decision requiring release of the White House tapes, succeeded in driving a sitting president from office. More recent examples include the successful attacks upon Reagan's original national security adviser Richard Allen (for the crime of accepting two wrist watches from a Japanese corporation), and upon Environmental Protection Agency officials Ann Burford Gorsuch and Rita Lavelle. In 1985 the administration's opponents in the Congress and the national news media were able to block Reagan's effort to continue increasing defense expenditures by publicizing examples of fraud and excessive billing by major military contractors. This attack on military contractors is the equivalent of conservative crusades against welfare fraud. In both cases, abuses that are inevitable concomitants of large-scale spending programs are disclosed by the opposition in an effort to discredit the policy.

Since 1980 the Reagan regime and its supporters have systematically attacked the organizational and institutional power bases of their opponents. Reagan appointees in executive agencies have undertaken to "defund the left"—for example, halting the flow of federal funds to legal services agencies that file class-action suits on behalf of the poor. In addition, the Internal Revenue Service has threatened to withdraw the tax exemptions of nonprofit organizations that engage in political activism. These advocacy groups sought to defend themselves and their constituents by conducting a major voter registration drive among the poor in 1984, and President Reagan's appointees on the board of the Legal Services Corporation responded by initiating an investigation to determine whether this constituted a violation of the rights of poor people to make their own decisions concerning whether or not to register and vote.

The administration's tax reform proposal, by eliminating the deduction for state and local taxes, would have assaulted another institutional bastion of President Reagan's opponents—state and local bureaucracies in the Northeast. Had this proposal been enacted the predominantly Democratic state and local governments in the high-tax Northeast would have been placed in a bind. They would either have had to cut taxes and fire thousands of public employees (whose unions play an important role in the Democratic party) or see business firms and taxpayers flee to regions of the country where taxes are lower, thereby suffering a decline in wealth and population—and a loss of votes in the electoral college. It is little wonder, then, that Democratic politicians from high-tax states—most notably New York's Governor Mario Cuomo—fought so furiously against this proposal.

In addition to attacking these organizational bases of its opponents, over the past few years the Reagan regime and its supporters have sought to weaken or gain control of the public and quasi-public institutions through which their opponents had exercised influence in the 1970s. This is the political significance, for example, of the recent spate of libel suits against the national new media—most prominently the Westmoreland suit against CBS. These suits are encouraged and often financed by conservative organizations, such as the Capital Legal Foundation, the American Legal Foundation, and Accuracy in Media, Inc. When journalists and liberals charge that the threat of such suits could discourage the press from raising questions about the conduct of public officials, these conservative organizations are quite forthright in saying that this is precisely their intention.[12]

To counter the phenomenon of liberal political forces exercising influence through the federal judiciary, conservative public-interest law firms are now contesting suits filed by environmental and consumer groups. And, as Geraldine Ferarro discovered, they are beginning to make use of the ethics-in-government statutes that Common Cause drafted in the 1970s to create new categories of crimes that could be committed by public officials it opposed, and could be used to drive these public officials from office. On the affirmative side, the Reagan Administration has appointed a number of eminent conservative legal scholars to federal appeals courts—most notably, Robert Bork and Ralph K. Winter of Yale and Antonin Scalia and Richard Posner of the University of Chicago. By appointing these men, Reaganites clearly seek not simply to ensure that conservative judges will outnumber liberals on the federal bench, but also to stage an *intellectual* revolution, or rather counterrevolution. Liberalism has been the intellectually dominant force in American jurisprudence for the past fifty years, and the Reaganites seek to seize this terrain for conservatism.

Finally, conservatives coped with the Senate's serving as a liberal bastion by defeating a large number of liberal Democratic senators and gaining control of the chamber in 1980. Major contributors to this outcome were conservative political action committees that financed negative advertising campaigns. The fear of providing ammunition for such campaigns now makes liberal senators think twice before deciding how to vote on every roll call, and this may help to explain why the Senate Democrats have offered little effective resistance to President Reagan's initiatives.

With one major exception, the Reaganites have done more to attack the power bases of their opponents than they have to build new institutions or develop new governmental processes that would provide them with the capacity routinely and reliably to enact the policies they favor. That exception, however, is an important one. In recent years the Republicans have constructed a national party apparatus that raises enormous sums of money for distribution to GOP candidates in congressional elections.[13] This party apparatus also has played a leading role in recruiting attractive candidates to run for seats in the House and Senate. Finally, the Republicans in 1985 announced plans for what they euphemistically termed an "incumbent accountability program," which will conduct negative advertising campaigns against Democratic members of Congress who oppose President Reagan on key roll call votes.

These efforts contributed to the Republicans' achievement of a remarkably high level of party unity in the House and Senate on the issues of greatest importance to the White House during President Reagan's first term—most notably, votes on the administration's 1981 and 1982 budget and tax legislation and on the construction and deployment of the MX missile. Money raised and distributed by the Republican National Committee and the two Republican congressional campaign committees also enabled the Republicans to retain many more seats in the 1982 mid-term congressional elections—held at the trough of the deepest recession since the 1930s—than predicted by models linking economic conditions to election outcomes.[14]

On the other hand, the White House was unable to repeat its budget victories in 1983 and 1984, and despite Ronald Reagan's landslide triumph in his campaign for reelection the GOP lost two seats in the Senate and won only fourteen additional seats in the House in 1984. And during the President's second term, the administration's fiscal priorities faced further resistance in Congress. In particular, the Gramm-Rudman budget-balancing proposal was entirely a congressional inititative.

These last points have led a number of political scientists to argue that 1980 and 1984 were not critical elections, and that Ronald Reagan will not leave an enduring imprint on American politics.[15] This skepticism may, of course, ultimately prove to have been warranted, but it fails to pay heed to a central characteristic of Reaganism. Ronald Reagan is not Franklin Roosevelt or Lyndon Johnson. He does not want Congress to enact scores of new domestic programs. To the contrary, Reagan wants to reduce the scope of the federal government's involvement in domestic affairs, and the indexation provisions of the 1981 tax cut may well make it unnecessary for Reagan and his successors to wage major battles in Congress each year to accomplish this goal.

By creating a structural imbalance between federal revenues and expenditures, the 1981 tax act makes it politically difficult for Congress to enact new expenditure programs, because that would only add to the deficit and subject the proponents of such new programs in Congress to the charge of fiscal irresponsibility. And indeed this strategy thus far has been signally successful. During the first five years of Ronald Reagan's presidency, Congress did not enact a single new major domestic spending program.

In sum, the Reagan tax cuts may be as important for their impact on American politics as for their effects on the nation's economy. If the structural imbalance between federal revenues and expenditures continues on in future years, Congress may find it politically and fiscally impossible to reenact major domestic-spending programs regardless of its partisan composition. In this way, the 1981 tax cuts could prove to be the functional equivalents of an organic statute for a new Reagan regime. This statute may structure the conduct of government and politics in ways that would work to the advantage of the Reagan coalition even if the Democrats were to control one or both houses of Congress. In this situation, the President's heirs in the White House would not find it necessary to win more than a few key votes in each session of Congress in order to preserve the programmatic legacy of Ronald Reagan.

## Promoting Economic and Fiscal Viability

Finally, if a regime is to endure and dominate national politics over several decades, it must be economically and fiscally viable: It must foster prosperity and finance its expenditures in ways that do not gravely injure the national economy. If the Reagan regime has its Achilles heel, it is the enormous budget and trade deficits generated by the combination of major tax cuts and major increases in military spending. The budget deficit has kept real interest rates at historically high levels and contributed to the dollar's reaching record high levels as well. High interest rates, in turn, restrict business investment, and the high dollar reduces the competitiveness of American firms in both domestic and foreign markets. A Republican majority grounded on the promise of sustained prosperity is not likely to survive a sustained period of economic sluggishness produced by these deficits. In addition, the issue of how to cope with these problems can create serious strains between the Wall Street and Main Street wings of the GOP. Once Ronald Reagan leaves the scene these tensions could divide the party and weaken it in future presidential elections.

Two factors, however, have thus far mitigated this threat to the durability of the Reagan regime. The first is the emergence of an interesting pattern of tacit bargaining among the Federal Reserve, the Congress, and the White House. In his congressional testimony in 1982 and again in 1985, Paul Volcker indicated that if the administration and Congress took steps to control the deficit, the Fed would ease monetary policy so as to foster economic expansion. If these steps were not taken, he warned, the Fed would tighten the money supply, raise interest rates, and perhaps precipitate a recession. If this pattern of tacit bargaining between the Fed, the White House, and the Congress continues in the years ahead it could help control the deficit, thereby diminishing the fiscal and economic threats to the survival of the Reagan regime.[16]

The second mitigating factor is an insufficiently appreciated consequence of Ronald Reagan's fierce anti-Communism and massive defense build-up. During the Reagan presidency, foreign capital has flooded into the United States, helping finance both the federal deficit and American business investment. A major reason for this inflow of capital is that every time Ronald Reagan denounces the Soviet Union and announces his support for a major weapons system, it convinces foreign investors that the United States is the safest place in the world to invest their funds. In this way, Reaganism is a seamless web: Its politics help make it economically viable, and its economics help make it politically viable.

Moreover, the budget and trade deficits produced by the Reagan Administration's fiscal policies should not be seen simply as threats. These deficits also provide the Reaganites with important political benefits and opportunities. As noted previously, by making it difficult for politicians to appeal for votes by proposing new public-expenditure programs, the budget deficit impedes efforts by the Democrats to reconstruct their political base. In addition, the trade deficit functions as a novel revenue-collection apparatus that, at least in the short run, enables the Reaganites to fund their budget deficits without raising taxes and alienating their political constituency.

This apparatus works as follows. By increasing the value of the dollar, the Reagan Administration's fiscal policies encourage Americans to purchase foreign—most notably, Japanese—goods. At the same time, America's high interest rates and political stability encourage foreign bankers—again most notably, Japanese—to purchase U.S. Treasury securities with the profits their nation's manufacturers make selling goods in the United States. Thus during the 1980s what might be called ''Toyota dollars'' or ''autodollars'' are being recycled by Japanese banks, much as ''petrodollars'' were recycled by American banks in the 1970s. These Toyota dollars, invested in U.S. government securities, are being used to finance the Reagan deficits. In essence, Japanese industrialists and bankers are serving as the equivalent of tax collectors for the Reagan administration. While Americans, in their capacity as voters, demonstrated in 1984 that they oppose increased taxation as a means of financing the federal government's expenditures, as consumers they willingly—indeed, enthusiastically—hand over billions of dollars that will be used for this purpose whenever they purchase Japanese and other foreign-made goods.

To be sure, this process cannot continue indefinitely without totally destroying American industry (and consuming much of the world's capital). The expenditures that help produce these deficits, however, may contribute to the solution of the very economic problems that deficits create. The Reagan Administration's enormous military build-up is, of course, a major source of the deficit problem. Beyond its military functions, this build-up can be seen as a central component of the Reaganite version of industrial policy. Through military spending the Administration is seeking to promote the reconstruction of American industry. For example, research for the SDI or ''Star Wars'' program, as Robert Reich notes, ''could create whole new generations of telecommunications and computer-related products that could underpin information-processing systems in the next century.''[17] Combined with efforts to reduce the labor costs of American industry by weakening unions and curtailing social spending, and to reduce other production costs by loosening federal regulations, this industrial reconstruction may help restore the international competitiveness of leading sectors of the American economy. If this effort succeeds, the Reaganites will not only have devised a long-term solution to the deficit problem, but also could fulfill the final precondition for an enduring reconstitution of American politics.

## Conclusion

The success of Ronald Reagan's efforts to promote an enduring reorientation of politics and government in the United States is by no means assured. It has yet to be demonstrated that tax policy can be made as salient to voters on a continuing basis as New Deal expenditure programs proved to be. Moreover, the Reagan economic strategy is a high-risk venture, and the enormous budget deficits the Administration has thus far tolerated may indeed lead to the disasters so many economists have predicted. Finally, the Republicans would face more formidable opposition in future presidential elections than they did in 1984, if opponents of the political forces that supported Walter Mondale succeed in gaining control of the Democratic party and in getting the Democrats to shed their image as the party of society's losers. Uncertain as they may be, however, the prospects for an enduring realignment in American politics are stronger today than they have been for at least a generation.

## Notes

1. See the essays in Michael Nelson, ed., *The Elections of 1984* (Washington, D.C.: CQ Press, 1985), and Gerald Pomper, Ross K. Baker, Charles E. Jacob, Scott Keeter, Wilson Cary McWilliams, and Henry A. Plotkin, *The Election of 1984* (Chatham, N.J.: Chatham House, 1985).

2. Samuel P. Huntington, "The United States," in *The Crisis of Democracy*, ed. Michael Crozier, Samuel Huntington, and Joji Watanuki (New York: New York University Press, 1975), pp. 91–106.

3. *New York Times*, May 29, 1985, sec. A, p. 17.

4. See, e.g., B. Bruce-Briggs, ed., *The New Class?* (New York: McGraw-Hill, 1981); cf. Steven Brint, " 'New-Class' and Cumulative Trend Explanations of the Liberal Political Attitudes of Professionals," *American Journal of Sociology* 90 (July 1984):30–71.

5. *New York Times*, November 8, 1984, sec. A, p. 19.

6. Walter Dean Burnham, "The 1984 Election and the Future of American Politics," in *Election '84: Landslide Without a Mandate?*, ed. Ellis Sandoz and Cecil Crabb (New York: New American Library, 1985).

7. See, e.g., *Barron's*, November 5, 1984, p. 11; February 25, 1985, p. 9.

8. David Vogel, "The Power of Business in America: A Reappraisal," *British Journal of Political Science* 13 (January 1983):19–44.

9. Theodore Lowi, *The End of Liberalism*, 2d ed. (New York: Norton, 1979), ch. 3.

10. Walter Dean Burnham, "The System of 1896: An Analysis," in *The Evolution of American Electoral Systems*, ed. Paul Kleppner (Westport, Conn.: Greenwood Press, 1981).

11. Martin Shefter, "Party, Bureaucracy, and Political Change in the United States," in *Political Parties: Development and Decay*, ed. Louis Maisel and Joseph Cooper, Sage Electoral Studies Yearbook 4 (Beverly Hills: Sage, 1978), pp. 211–65.

12. *New York Times*, October 16, 1984; December 11, 1984.

13. Benjamin Ginsberg, "Money and Power: The New Political Economy of American Elections," in *The Political Economy*, ed. Thomas Ferguson and Joel Rogers (Armonk, N.Y.: M. E. Sharpe, 1984), pp. 163–79; David Price, "Parties in the Reagan Years," in *The Reagan Presidency and the Governing of America*, ed. Lester Salamon and Michael Lund (Washington, D.C.: Urban Institute Press, 1985), pp. 253–59.

14. Gary Jacobson and Samuel Kernell, *Strategy and Choice in Congressional Elections*, 2d ed. (New Haven: Yale University Press, 1983), pp. 94–109.

15. See, e.g., the essays by Lester Salamon and Michael Lund, Theodore Lowi, and Allen Shick, in *The Reagan Presidency and the Governing of America*, ed. Salamon and Lund. See also Lester Salamon and Alan Abramson, "Governance: The Politics of Retrenchment," in *The Reagan Record*, ed. John Palmer and Isabel Sawhill (Cambridge: Ballinger, 1984), pp. 31–68.

16. *New York Times*, May 20, 1985, sec. D, p. 7.

17. Robert Reich, "High Tech, a Subsidiary of Pentagon Inc.," *New York Times*, May 29, 1985, sec. A, p. 23.

## 4.2

# The Democratic Party and the Conflict over Racial Policy

## Robert Weissberg

> It's just a continuation of white flight. When black people
> move in, the whites move out.
> —Johnnie Wells, Jesse Jackson supporter in 1984, on the
> failure of Democratic coalition politics

In the 1950s and early 1960s it was customary to view the Democratic party as the dominant party in U.S. politics. Democrats far outnumbered Republicans and, despite their lower turnout, were routinely victorious at both the state and national levels. Indeed, following the disastrous 1964 performance of Barry Goldwater and many other Republicans, there was even a fear for the survival of the two-party system. Democratic hegemony seemed insured and virtually unchallengeable.

By the 1980s the situation had noticeably turned around. A sizeable "decline of parties" literature has emerged, and the decline of the Democratic party is now almost taken for granted. Democrats have won but one in five presidential contests since 1964, and in 1980, for the first time in twenty-four years, they lost control of a branch of Congress. In 1984 the Democratic candidate for president suffered one of the most serious electoral defeats in history. Though the proportion of Democratic party identifiers has remained roughly constant, the proportion of "strong Democrats" has dropped sharply and voting defection from party loyalty has increased at all levels. More important, however, the Democratic party's New Deal coalition seems to have come apart. Since 1964 Democratic candidates can no longer count on almost automatic majorities among urban workers, white Southerners, union members, and members of certain ethnic and religious groups. This erosion of traditional voting support cannot easily be explained by some momentary event or prominent personality.

Robert Weissberg teaches at the University of Illinois at Urbana-Champaign.

The war in Vietnam and inflation may have contributed to the defeat of some Democratic candidates, but it is difficult to imagine these issues having a long-term, two-decade cumulative impact.

Two major schools of thought have developed regarding the weakened position of the Democratic party. The first perspective emphasizes generational replacement.[1] The basic argument here is that the source of the Democratic party's strength lay in the policies of the New Deal. People directly exposed to the New Deal were the party's electoral backbone, but by the early 1970s these staunch supporters had begun to die off. Their younger "replacements" lacked the firsthand exposure to the New Deal era and were thus more likely, temporarily or permanently, to abandon the partisan attachments passed on to them by their Democratic parents. From the generational replacement perspective, the 1970s mark the start of the inevitable and irreversible decline of a stable partisan majority.

The second perspective sees the Democratic party as the victim of what can be called the "new politics." This "new politics" involves several breaks with the past. Higher levels of education have created an electorate more likely to rely on issues than on party loyalty in their voting.[2] Moreover, the power of parties as organizations has been weakened by such things as primaries, greater use of television, the further reduction of patronage, the advent of candidate-centered campaigns, and numerous antiparty reforms within the Democratic party itself.[3] Issues *per se* have not necessarily weakened the Democratic party; rather, changes in the political environment have allowed specific issues to overcome the inertia generated by partisan attachment. And since partisan inertia favored the Democratic party, a weakening of it has helped to loosen the party's grip on the electorate.

The analysis presented here offers a third perspective on the weakening of the Democratic party: Sharp disagreements on racial issues among Democrats have been responsible for at least a large portion of the party's declining electoral fortunes. Conflict over race within the Democratic party is not a new phenomenon (recall, for example, the Dixiecrat bolt in 1948). What is new is the changed racial composition of the Democratic party and the increased importance of racial policy at the mass level. Put bluntly, my contention is that beginning in the late 1960s the party's inability to be all things to all party members on the issue of race has resulted in sizable defections among whites, and this race-policy–caused defection is frequently the difference between defeat and victory.

Before undertaking the analysis, one further point must be made. A thorough analysis of changes in the Democratic party's strength is, obviously, an enormous undertaking. In choosing one aspect of this change—the impact of race-related issues—I am certainly not making any claims that this factor is the only important one. I am not attempting to disprove the two other perspectives described above. The decision to focus exclusively on one aspect of a complex phenomenon derives from both the importance of this one factor and the fact that it has received only passing attention in recent research. My goal is to make clear a set of relationships, not to reinterpret all recent political history from a racial conflict perspective.

## The Blackening of the Democratic Party

Beginning in the early 1950s the Democratic party's citizen base has undergone two important changes. As was previously noted, the attachment of Democrats in terms of strength and partisanship and willingness to vote a straight party ticket noticeably weakened. Less well known is the change in the party's racial composition. Table 1 depicts two aspects of this change. In the 1950s about one out of ten Democratic identifiers was black; by the 1980s this figure had changed to one out of five.[4] Also, between 1964 and 1968 the proportion of the white population identifying with the Democratic party noticeably declined (last line in Table 1). In 1960 and 1964 nearly half of the white population was Democratic. By 1984 only a third of all white people shared this identification.

The increasing role of black Democrats is made even more clear when we consider voting behavior. As black Democrats replaced white Democrats in the party, and as blacks both increased their turnout levels and more strongly than other groups supported Democratic presidential candidates, the votes of black Democrats became more prominent. The data in Table 2 show that in the 1950s and in 1960 black Democratic voters did not constitute a significant block among

Table 1

**Racial composition of Democratic Party, 1952–1984**

| | Year | | | | | | | | |
|---|---|---|---|---|---|---|---|---|---|
| | 1952 | 1956 | 1960 | 1964 | 1968 | 1972 | 1976 | 1980 | 1984 |
| Proportion of Democrats who are: | | | | | | | | | |
| White | 89.4 | 90.4 | 91.6 | 64.2 | 71.6 | 83.1 | 71.5 | 79.2 | 80.5 |
| Black | 10.6 | 9.6 | 8.4 | 35.8 | 28.4 | 16.9 | 18.5 | 19.8 | 19.5 |
| | 100.0 | 100.0 | 100.0 | 100.0 | 100.0 | 100.0 | 100.0 | 100.0 | 100.0 |
| N = | 838 | 762 | 545 | 906 | 790 | 1,066 | 854 | 650 | 806 |
| Proportion of all whites who are Democrats | 40.8 | 44.0 | 47.9 | 49.6 | 41.0 | 37.0 | 35.5 | 36.7 | 33.6 |

*Source*: SRC/CPS Elections Studies

Table 2

**Racial composition of Democratic loyalists, 1952–1984**

| | Year | | | | | | | | |
| --- | --- | --- | --- | --- | --- | --- | --- | --- | --- |
| | 1952 | 1956 | 1960 | 1964 | 1968 | 1972 | 1976 | 1980 | 1984 |
| Proportion of Democratic presidential vote coming from: | | | | | | | | | |
| White Democrats | 91.5 | 94.4 | 93.9 | 68.5 | 65.6 | 75.4 | 80.2 | 70.1 | 78.4 |
| Black Democrats | 8.5 | 5.6 | 6.1 | 31.5 | 34.4 | 24.6 | 19.8 | 29.9 | 21.6 |

*Source*: SRC/CPS Elections Studies

party loyalists. Twenty years later, when Democrats go off to the polls to support their party at the presidential level, one of five of these loyal Democrats is black. Put somewhat differently, blacks are significantly overrepresented among those who can be deemed "hard-core" Democratic supporters.[5] This overrepresentation is even greater in the South and large, electorally important states such as New York, Michigan, and Illinois. According to 1984 ABC exit polls, more than half of Walter Mondale's vote in the South came from blacks.[6]

## Continued Tensions over Racial Policy among Democratic Followers

While the racial character of the Democratic party was changing significantly between the 1950s and the 1980s, at the leadership level the party became the one most strongly advocating the rights of blacks. Every Democratic presidential nominee from Lyndon Johnson to Walter Mondale unambiguously supported the cause of black rights. In 1984 Mondale went out of his way to court black leaders and to maintain good relations with Jesse Jackson. The Democratic-controlled Congress passed several landmark civil rights bills and beat back numerous attempts to circumvent problack Supreme Court decisions.

Given these events, plus generational replacement of older, less educated Democrats by better educated, younger Democrats, one would expect a significant liberalization of racial attitudes among white Democrats. That is, whites opposed to black civil rights would leave the party (or die) so the mass base of the party would increasingly reflect a more liberal racial perspective. This more liberal orientation would then be consistent with the policies espoused by party leaders and embodied in party platforms. Let us examine this possibility by considering the views of white Democrats on school integration and government aid to minorities.

## School Integration: 1956–1976, 1984

As reflected in opinions on school integration, this expected liberalization of white Democrats onward from the 1950s did not occur. Table 3 presents the proportions of white Democrats opposing federal intervention in school integration from 1956 to 1976 (the question asked whether the federal government should impose integration or stay out of this issue). In each of six surveys, a majority of white Democrats oppose federal intervention, and, even more surprising, there is no downward trend between 1956 and 1976. Indeed, opposition was more common in 1976 than twenty years prior. Obviously, the strong public commitment of Democratic leaders to vigorous federal efforts to eliminate segregation was at odds with a majority of the party's white following.

The gap between how most white Democrats feel about school integration and the party's position on this issue is also clearly revealed by the data in Table 4. In both 1972 and 1976 respondents were asked to rate themselves and the Democratic party on a seven-point scale, where the end points were "bus to achieve integration" and "keep children in neighborhood schools." The discrepancy between a person's own stand and his or her perceptions of the party's position can easily be derived. These data strikingly show party followers believing themselves to be far less problack than their party. Even in 1976 with a southerner as the presidential nominee, an overwhelming proportion of white Democrats

Table 3

**Support for federal intervention in school integration among white Democrats, 1956–1976, in % (N in parentheses)**

|  | Year | | | | | |
| --- | --- | --- | --- | --- | --- | --- |
|  | 1956 | 1960 | 1964 | 1968 | 1972 | 1976 |
| Favor federal intervention | 40.4 | 43.2 | 50.0 | 44.9 | 43.1 | 35.4 |
| Leave to state and communities | 59.6 | 56.8 | 50.0 | 55.1 | 56.9 | 64.6 |
|  | 100.0 | 100.0 | 100.0 | 100.0 | 100.0 | 100.0 |
|  | (270) | (190) | (258) | (383) | (485) | (356) |

*Source*: SRC/CPS Election Studies

Table 4

**Perceptions of Democratic party's stand on busing vis-à-vis own busing stand, white Democrats, 1972, 1976, in % (N in parentheses)**

| White Democrats who perceive their party as | 1972 | 1976 |
|---|---|---|
| Much more antibusing than themselves | 1.1 (5) | .7 (3) |
| More antibusing than themselves | 5.1 (24) | 4.6 (19) |
| No difference | 25.3 (117) | 14.3 (59) |
| More probusing than themselves | 25.1 (116) | 23.9 (99) |
| Much more probusing than themselves | 43.4 (201) | 51.9 (215) |

*Source*: SRC/CPS Election Studies

viewed their party as much more probusing than themselves. Moreover, this ordering does not result from moderately probusing white Democrats seeing their party as more liberal than themselves. In both 1972 and 1976 the overwhelming majority of white Democrats endorsed the most extreme antibusing positions.[7]

One final piece of data on the racial attitudes of white Democrats in terms of schools is presented in Table 5 and concerns busing. Again, the message is clear—the overwhelming majority of white Democrats reject the use of busing to achieve racial integration. It might be added that these figures closely match the distribution for white Republicans and white Independents.

There are two possible simple explanations for these findings. In view of the Democratic party's strong southern roots, these data could conceivably be explained as part of the party's lingering heritage. That is, the views of white southern Democrats are disproportionately prominent. Or, the presence of numerous older and socially conservative "New Deal" Democrats may exaggerate the extent to which the party is perceived to be to the "left" of its followers on busing. To explore this possibility, the 1972 and 1976 data were analyzed in greater depth. Controlling for age and region separately shows that this perception of the Democratic party is not simply produced by the presence of numerous southern and older Democrats to the right of their party's busing stand.[8] In both 1972 and 1976, southern white Democrats were somewhat more likely to be more opposed to busing than their party. But, the patterns found in Table 4 were also strongly evident among nonsouthern white Democrats. In 1976, for example, 46.5 percent of these nonsoutherners saw the Democrats as *much more* probusing

Table 5

**White Democrat's views on busing, 1984, in % (N in parentheses)**

| | | |
|---|---|---|
| Bus to achieve integration | 1 | 2.0 |
| | 2 | 2.0 |
| | 3 | 2.4 |
| | 4 | 7.6 |
| | 5 | 10.8 |
| | 6 | 20.4 |
| Keep children in neighborhood schools | 7 | 54.8 |
| | | 100.0 |
| | | (250) |

*Source*: SRC/CPS Election Study of 1984

than themselves (the comparable figure for southerners was 53 percent). Moreover, since white southerners are a minority of the Democratic party, the majority of those well to the right of their party reside in nonsouthern states.

To examine the impact of age, respondents from both 1972 and 1976 were divided according to year of birth into pre–New Deal (born before 1921), New Deal (born between 1921 and 1935), and post–New Deal (born after 1936) Democrats. In both 1972 and 1976 there was a moderate curvilinear relationship between age and propensity to see the Democratic party to the left of oneself in busing—those born between 1921 and 1935 were most likely to hold this view. Both the youngest and oldest groups, however, likewise overwhelmingly shared the belief that their party was markedly more probusing than themselves. In 1976, for instance, 32.6 percent of the youngest groups believed that their party was more probusing than themselves (a gap of one to two scale scores), and 41.4 percent were three or more scale scores beyond the Democratic position.

It is clear that school integration is a troublesome issue for the Democratic party. Blacks have become a crucial element of the party, the national leadership is probably irrevocably committed to advocacy of strong problack government intervention, and yet an overwhelming majority of white Democrats diverge from their party on this issue.

## Government Aid to Minorities: 1980–1984

Though the issue of busing remained on the political agenda during the early 1980s, the busing questions were dropped in the 1980 Michigan surveys, and the 1984 survey used a limited version of the previous set of items. To examine further the views of white Democrats in the 1980s I have used questions dealing

Table 6

**Support for government aid to minorities among white Democrats, 1980 and 1984, in % (N in parentheses)**

|                        | 1980  | 1984  |
|------------------------|-------|-------|
| Favor government aid   | 34.6  | 52.3  |
| Oppose government aid  | 65.4  | 47.7  |
|                        | (269) | (369) |

Table 7

**Perception of Democratic Party's stand on aid to minorities vis-à-vis own position, white Democrats, 1980 and 1984, in % (N in parentheses)**

| White Democrats who perceive their party as: | 1980  | 1984  |
|----------------------------------------------|-------|-------|
| Much more pro-aid than themselves            | 33.4  | 41.5  |
| More pro-aid than themselves                 | 23.8  | 17.7  |
| No difference                                | 24.4  | 44.0  |
| Less pro-aid than themselves                 | 14.5  | 13.3  |
| Much less pro-aid than themselves            | 3.9   | 4.6   |
|                                              | 100.0 | 100.0 |
|                                              | (512) | (618) |

with government assistance to blacks and other minorities. These questions also likely tap a more general orientation to race relations policy. The basic format was a seven-point scale, with government aid at one extreme and letting minorities help themselves at the other end.

Table 6 shows that many white Democrats reject a government commitment to helping minorities. Indeed, in 1980 opponents of such aid outnumber supporters by about a two to one margin. In 1984, with Ronald Reagan as the incumbent, more white Democrats are sympathetic to minority aid, but nearly half (47.7 percent) continue to oppose such aid. Table 7 assesses how white Democrats see themselves *vis-à-vis* their party on this minority-aid issue. As was true with school integration, a clear majority in 1980 and 1984 believe themselves to be to the right of their party on this race issue. Less than 20 percent are more liberal than their party.

In sum, though the Democratic party may be the champion of blacks in Congress and in drafting presidential party platforms, this view is not mirrored strongly among white party identifiers.

## The Race Issue and Defections among Democrats

What happens to white Democrats who are at odds with the racial policies of their party and Democratic presidential candidates? Basically, assuming all other factors to be equal, such an individual faces two choices. The most extreme action would be to leave the party altogether. Less drastic would be to remain identified with the party but withhold one's support when a Democratic candidate strayed too far from one's more conservative policy preferences. Let us consider the second possibility first by examining voting in the presidential elections between 1968 and 1984.

To assess the possible impact of racial issues in voting I created measures that reflected the distance between an individual's own issue position and the perceived issue position of the Democratic presidential candidate. In 1968 I used the urban unrest issues; in both 1972 and 1976 the busing issue was employed. In 1980 and 1984 the government aid to minorities issue was used. If these issues do effect voting, it would be expected that as the perceived issue gap between the Democratic candidate and respondent increases, defections from the Democratic party will also increase. The data for the five elections are displayed in Figure 1.

Two conclusions can be drawn from these data. First, the percentages at the bottom of Figure 1 show that, consistent with the perception of the Democratic party presented above, most white Democratic voters see themselves to the right of their party's presidential candidates. Though this might be expected in 1972 since George McGovern made no effort to disguise his decidedly liberal views, the proportion of white Democratic voters three or more scale points to the right of Jimmy Carter in 1976 is only slightly lower—45.0 percent compared to 51.2 percent in 1972. In 1980 and 1984 most white Democratic voters are again to the right of their party's presidential nominee.

Second, with one slight exception (1976), the more to the right of a candidate a voter is on these race-related issues, the greater the likelihood of a defection from the party. In 1984, for example, Mondale received 88 percent of the vote of white Democrats who agreed with his position on aiding minorities. Among those well to the right of Mondale—a much larger group—only 65 percent supported him. In other words, there was a 23 percent fall-off in support among white Democrats in 1984 associated with this issue. When we figure that a party's identifiers have a strong predisposition to support their party, the magnitude of the defection rates in the extreme right side of Figure 1 is remarkable. Even in 1976, when the impact of the perceived gap between candidate and voter was comparatively modest, Carter won only 55 percent of the white Democrats who believed themselves much more conservative than Carter. In 1968 and 1972 fewer than half of these Democrats well to the right of their party's candidate remained loyal. Also, note that both Carter in 1976 and Hubert Humphrey in 1968 lost support among those who believed themselves to be more liberal than the candidates. Given the small number of these people, however, this loss was

213

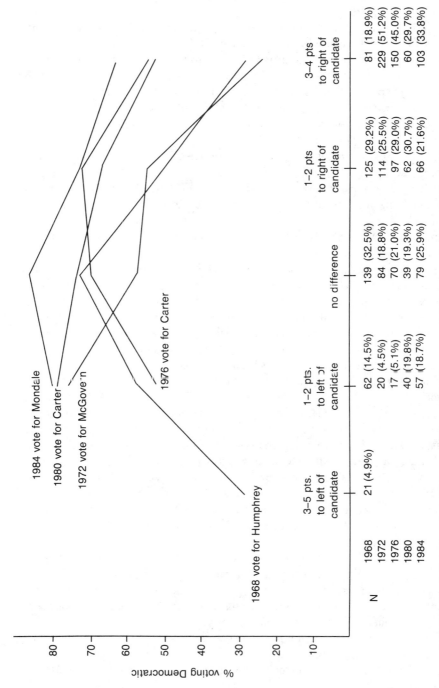

Figure 1  **Perceived distance from Democratic candidate on racial issue and vote, 1968–1984**

% voting Democratic

| N | | | | | | |
|---|---|---|---|---|---|---|
| | 3–5 pts. to left of candidate | 1–2 pts. to left of candidate | no difference | 1–2 pts to right of candidate | 3–4 pts to right of candidate | |
| 1968 | 21 (4.9%) | 62 (14.5%) | 139 (32.5%) | 125 (29.2%) | 81 (18.9%) | |
| 1972 | | 20 (4.5%) | 84 (18.8%) | 114 (25.5%) | 229 (51.2%) | |
| 1976 | | 17 (5.1%) | 70 (21.0%) | 97 (29.0%) | 150 (45.0%) | |
| 1980 | | 40 (19.8%) | 39 (19.3%) | 62 (30.7%) | 60 (29.7%) | |
| 1984 | | 57 (18.7%) | 79 (25.9%) | 66 (21.6%) | 103 (33.8%) | |

1984 vote for Mondale
1980 vote for Carter
1972 vote for McGovern
1976 vote for Carter
1968 vote for Humphrey

relatively minor compared to defections among more racially conservative Democratic voters.

Thus far we have seen that as the perceived gap between Democratic identifiers and Democratic presidential candidates increases, the greater the likelihood of voter defection. This refusal to follow one's party is not the only response to a perceived policy discrepancy. An individual greatly at odds with the Democratic party's racial policies could also leave the party, becoming a Republican, Independent, or completely apolitical. In many respects, party defection, as opposed to temporary voting defection, is far more important for a party's long-term electoral prospects.

To assess the possible impact of race-related issues on defection from the Democratic party, a further analysis of whites in the 1976 CPS survey was conducted. Respondents were divided into two groups: lifetime Democrats and former Democrats, regardless of present party identification or nonidentification. These groups were then compared on a variety of race-related issues. The expectation was that the party defectors would be more likely to take the antiblack position on a race-related issue.

This expectation was consistently borne out, especially in those issues that have been widely debated.[9] For example, on the seven-point school busing scale, ex-Democrats were even closer to unanimity than white Democrats (not one of sixty-seven ex-Democrats gave any type of probusing response). Comparable results were found on the handling of urban unrest and feeling thermometer ratings of blacks, black militants, and civil rights leaders.

The most striking differences between the Democratic defectors and those remaining with the party occur in their views of where the Democratic party and Jimmy Carter stood on the busing issue in 1976. Ex-Democrats were almost twice as likely to see Carter as being very probusing. And some 57.4 percent of these fallen away Democrats saw the Democratic party as strongly endorsing busing (the two most probusing alternatives of the seven-point scale), compared to less than a quarter of those remaining within the party. Finally, some 87 percent of these ex-Democrats were three or more busing scale score positions to the right of where they perceived their former party to be, compared to 50.3 percent of the loyalists. In short, as a group, fallen away Democrats were much more likely than loyalists to be well to the right of the Democratic party and its presidential candidate on the busing issue.

Obviously, all of these data on voting and party defection cannot prove beyond a doubt that dissatisfaction with the Democratic position on racial issues was the prime force in driving people away from the party and/or its presidential candidates. Even if the surveys did provide a battery of relevant questions on this topic, the inherent complexity of defection plus the sensitivity of racial matters makes it difficult to offer a definitive explanation. Our argument for the role of racial issues is suggestive. That support for Democratic candidates declines as party identifiers diverge from their party on the race issue only makes it plausible that this issue played a role in causing this defection. Likewise, that ex-Democrats are likely to hold more conservative positions on race than loyalists gives credence to the argument that race issues were involved in people's decisions to leave the party.

## Some Future Possibilities

The Democratic party clearly faces a dilemma. On the one hand, it has come to rely on the votes of blacks. The overwhelming support of black Democrats played a major role in Carter's 1976 victory, and few Democratic leaders would seriously consider antagonizing this key element in their electoral coalition. In 1984 every effort was made to accommodate blacks in the presidential convention delegate selection process, platform planks, and built-in representation at the national party level. On the other hand, vigorously reassuring black Democrats that the party is their protector appears to drive away numerous white Democrats who oppose many problack policies. Moreover, since neither white nor black partisans can deliver electoral victory on their own, both must somehow placated. If the results of presidential elections since 1964 are considered, such strategies have been less than successful.

What is likely to come of this difficult situation? One hope of the Democratic party is that generational replacement will eventually eliminate the antagonism between two-coalition members. That is, younger, less anti–civil-rights Democrats will replace older whites less attuned to the aspirations of blacks. Though age and position on racial issues are generally related, the figures are not comforting to the Democratic party. In 1976, for instance, only 11 percent of all white Democrats under forty placed themselves in the busing end of the seven-point busing/neighborhood school scale. Like their elders, they clustered almost entirely at the antibusing end of the scale. Equally important, most young white Democrats, like their elders, view the Democratic party as being to the left of their own position on busing. If these attitudes continue with aging, generational replacement will have only a limited impact on reducing tensions within the party.[10]

Another possibility is that this intraparty conflict will be resolved if the issues can be made to go away. This prospect is likewise unlikely. Though executive actions could remove the Vietnam war and the hostages in Iran from the public agenda, racial issues seem far less amenable to such solutions. Short of numerous constitutional amendments on busing, the use of racial quotas, and the like, these controversies are likely to surface even if political leaders would like to avoid them. This is especially true since so many policy questions, such as crime, welfare, and mass transit, can so easily become racially related issues. A "benign neglect" strategy is too easily upset. Race-related issues are likely to endure for decades.

A more complex resolution might be a reshuffling of partisans so that differences on race would exist between the two parties rather than within one or both parties. That is, white Democrats unhappy with their party's racial stand would migrate to the GOP, while racial liberals in the GOP would become Democrats. Until the 1980s and the policies of the Reagan Administration this possibility—a white exodus from the Democratic party to the GOP—did not seem likely. Basically, data prior to the 1980s showed that many white Democrats disenchanted with their party's race-related policies did not see the Republican party as a hospitable alternative.[11] There was not, as they say, "a dime's worth of difference." For example, in 1976 nearly 45 percent of white Democrats perceived the GOP as a party that supported the use of busing. This view was especially pronounced among those white Democrats most vehemently opposed to busing—80 percent of this group did not see the GOP as an ally.

The policies and public statements of the Reagan Administration may be altering this image. In the 1984 study there were 394 white Democrats to the right of their party's stand on government aid to minorities (61 percent of all white Democrats). Of this group, 71 percent perceived the GOP as endorsing their own or a more conservative position on this issue. Perhaps most important, perceptions of where the GOP stands on this race issue were strongly related to voting defection. Nearly 35 percent of white Democrats who saw the Republican party as identical or to the right of their own view on helping minorities voted for Reagan. This compares with a defection rate of 13 percent of those who saw the GOP to their left on this issue. In other words, taking the conservative ground on this issue pays off electorally for the Republican party (and analysis of Republicans shows that this "right" image on race has no negative consequences for holding their own supporters).

What would happen if a migration of partisans occurred based on race-related issues? It would be a disaster for the Democrats. On such issues as busing and helping minorities there are very few racially liberal Republicans (in 1984, for example, a mere 3 percent of Republican identifiers favored busing). A swap of these liberal Republicans for racially conservative Democrats would create a dominant GOP and a much smaller, largely black Democratic party. This situation would be dealignment, not realignment. Party politics might resemble the 1896–1928 era at the presidential level, when the real battle was within the GOP.

Such a wholesale migration based on race does not, however, seem a strong possibility at this moment. Change will probably be gradual. As has been well documented, partisan loyalties tend to change slowly. It would probably take several Reagan-like Republican administrations plus years of racial divisiveness among Democrats to produce such shifts. There is also the possibility that particular Democratic presidential nominees can finesse the issue. Southern, relatively conservative Jimmy Carter was able to win a majority among white Democrats, even among those to the right of his perceived stand on busing. There is certainly no shortage within the Democratic party of Carter-like candidates who will stress patriotism, self-reliance, and other virtues that contrast with the social-change position of a Humphrey or McGovern.

Even if Democratic nominees can finesse the intraparty tension on race and the choice among presidential contenders is not clear-cut on racial policies, the prospects for the continued supremacy of Democratic party affiliation are not bright. Recall that the Democratic party since the 1960s has been losing its appeal among whites. These losses, to some extent, have been made up by the addition of black Democrats. Obviously, simple demographic factors place major limits on this trend. Moreover, attempts to compensate for the smaller number of blacks by higher levels of voter mobilization have had only limited success. Even in the 1984 race whites continued to vote at higher rates than blacks.[12] Even if those numerous white Democrats opposed to problack policies do not leave the party en masse, the steady trickle of temporary and permanent defections can have a major electoral consequence in a system where many outcomes are decided by 5 percent or less of the vote. This problem will be compounded by the traditionally lower turnout rates among Democrats—under normal conditions Democrats must out-number Republicans to be equal on election day. As a party with a strong attachment among, say, 30 percent of the electorate as opposed to, say, 45 percent of the electorate, the Democrats will be less successful in congressional and state races. Like the Republicans since the New Deal, the Democrats will have to depend on very high mobilization rates among supporters and heavy support among independents to achieve victory. This will be a far cry from the days when merely getting Democrats to the polls in reasonable numbers would usually insure victory.

## Conclusion

What this analysis has shown should come as no surprise to anyone familiar with the turmoil within the Democratic party since the 1960s. It has merely provided some empirical support for the contention that the Democratic party is caught in a dilemma on race. The only possible surprise among the findings is the size of white estrangement from the race policies believed to be advocated by the Demo-cratic party and its presidential candidates. Moreover, this estrangement is not limited to elderly southerners, and it is not some sort of abstract feeling of unease. Dissatisfaction is strongly translated into voting behavior.

The existence of this dilemma within the Democratic party (as opposed to, say, within the GOP or as a conflict between the two parties) is an important datum in U.S. politics. For one, it greatly hinders the emergence of a clear set of electoral choices on racial policy. Given the conflicts within its ranks, it is foolish for the Democratic party to offer much more than generalities or ambiguous specifics regarding black demands. Conflicts are resolved by semantic devices such as opposing quotas while endorsing affirmative action. Prominent blacks are given enough power to scare some whites while frustrating many more militant blacks.

Given this state of affairs within the Democratic party and white opinion on race-related issues, it would seem to make sense for the GOP to take a strong, clear stand on issues such as busing and reverse discrimination. Obviously, some Republican candidates have done this, but the party as a whole has avoided this strategy.[13] No doubt there are powerful social norms operating that prohibit any respected public figure from appearing to be antiblack or racist. To argue vehemently against programs designed to help blacks—even where the benefits are unclear—is to acquire a reputation as antiblack. This is unacceptable in contemporary politics. Except in a few localities, such a person would be publicly ostracized regardless of people's private sentiments. Few public figures want to be known as the George Wallace of the 1980s.

The GOP's unwillingness to capitalize fully on the Democrats' dilemma is also rooted in more practical considerations. There remain many moderate and liberal Republicans who refuse to concede the black vote to the Democrats. Especially at the state level, Republican appeals to blacks, if successful, can spell the difference. To take a clear stand against policies such as affirmative action and to appeal to antiblack Democrats may thus be an unwise choice where blacks are a sizable part of the electorate. GOP success may be achievable by simply avoiding these emotional issues and stressing an "improved business climate to better the lives of everyone."

The upshot of this situation is a lack of clear party choice. A citizen who opposes government policies designed to achieve racial equality rarely has the opportunity to express this view when voting. Without the existence of such a verdict, these issues remain on the public agenda half-resolved. Perhaps for this reason the federal courts—the unelected branch of government—have often played the strongest role in deciding policy on race-related issues.

The Democratic party's policy dilemma can also be viewed from a second perspective. To the extent that accommodation of divergent preferences occurs *within* a party, the impact of a highly divisive issue on society is moderated. Imagine, for a moment, what political life would be like if national elections provided clear choices on racial policy. Levels of violence and separatist demands would undoubtedly increase, especially among blacks, since they would be frequent losers. Obviously, what constitutes a muddled set of policy alternatives can also be viewed as a beneficial reduction of conflict.

In sum, to the question of why the Democratic party cannot translate its overwhelming advantage in partisan loyalty into electoral victories, my answer is that internal division over race prevents a full mobilization of supporters. To maintain strong black support means alienating numerous white Democrats. Moreover, this dilemma is not easily resolved by either changes in party policy or demographic changes in party composition.

## Notes

1. See, e.g., Paul R. Abramson, "Generational Change and the Decline of Party Identification in America: 1952–1974," *American Political Science Review* 70 (1976):469–78; Norman H. Nie, Sidney Verba, and John R. Petrocik, *The Changing*

American Voter (Cambridge: Harvard University Press, 1976); and Paul Allen Beck, "A Socialization Theory of Partisan Realignment," in *The Politics of Future Citizens*, ed. Richard G. Niemi et al. (San Francisco: Jossey-Bass, 1974).

2. Gerald Pomper, *Voters' Choice: Varieties of American Electoral Behavior* (New York: Dodd, Mead, 1975).

3. William J. Crotty and Gary C. Jacobson, *American Parties in Decline* (Boston: Little, Brown, 1980); David B. Hill and Norman R. Luttberg, *Trends in American Electoral Behavior* (Itasca, Ill.: F. E. Peacock, 1980).

4. This "blackening" of the Democratic party has its roots, of course, in the New Deal era. This transformation is more fully described in Everett C. Ladd, Jr., and Charles D. Hadley, *Transformation of the American Party System* (New York: Norton, 1975), pp. 57-60, 111-14. Using Gallup Poll data, Ladd and Hadley find that only 44 percent of blacks identified with the Democratic party in 1937; by 1960 this figure had risen to 58 percent.

5. For a somewhat different approach to calculating the importance of blacks to the Democratic electoral coalition, see Robert Axelrod, "Where the Vote Comes From: An Analysis of Electoral Coalitions, 1952-1972," *American Political Science Review* 68 (1974):11-20, and "Communications," *American Political Science Review* 68 (1974):717-20. Axelrod finds that while the black contribution in the 1950s was 5 to 7 percent of the total Democratic vote, by 1972 this contribution had risen to 22 percent.

6. Cited in Bill Peterson and Dale Russakoff, "Southern Democrats' Race Fears," *The Washington Post National Weekly Edition*, November 26, 1984.

7. To insure that the use of just one issue did not generate atypical findings, several other issues—urban unrest and government aid to minorities in particular—were also analyzed. The results were consistent with the relationships found with the busing scale.

8. The South was defined in terms of the so-called solid South plus the border states.

9. Previous research on the question of what is responsible for whites leaving the Democratic party has generated several diverse findings. Beck, using data from 1960, 1964, 1968, and 1972, shows that white, prosegregation, native southerners who saw the Republican party as closer to their own position still largely maintained their Democratic affiliation. Nevertheless, Beck does suggest that "a significant share of the partisan change within the native white electorate may be attributed to racial conservatives' desertions of the Democratic party because of its racial policies." Paul A. Beck, "Partisan Dealignment in the Post-War South," *American Political Science Review* 7 (1977):494. Campbell finds that the civil rights movement does not seem to be associated with change in partisanship among white southerners. However, the issues of federal power and guarantees of jobs do seem to be associated with the movement of Democrats toward the Republican party. Bruce A. Campbell, "Patterns of Change in the Partisan Loyalties of Native Southerners: 1952-1972," *Journal of Politics* 39 (1977):730-61. It should be kept in mind that both Beck and Campbell use different data points and measures than those in this analysis.

10. This assessment may initially seem somewhat at odds with the conclusion reached by Edward G. Carmines and James A. Stimson, "Issue Evolution, Population Replacement and Normal Partisan Change," *American Political Science Review* 75 (1981):107-08. These authors find that more recent Democratic identifiers (most of whom are young) are more liberal on racial desegregation than older Democrats. However, this shift was modest in size. More important in terms of a comparison between the present analysis and

that of Carmines and Stimson, this analysis focuses on the absolute value of a response, that is, whether a respondent favors or opposes a policy. Carmines and Stimson focus on relative orderings, in other words, whether new identifiers are more or less liberal than long-time partisans. It is entirely possible that both analyses are correct—new identifiers are more liberal on race but still hold conservative positions on a particular scale. My argument is that even if shifts in a liberal direction do occur, it will be a long time before young white Democrats transform the basic policy orientation of the white Democratic group.

11. Further evidence on the attractiveness of the Republican party for dissatisfied Democrats is offered by Cassel. Carol A. Cassel, "Cohort Analysis of Party Identification among Southern Whites," *Public Opinion Quarterly* 41 (1977), pp. 28–33. Employing a cohort analysis of white native Southerners, Cassel finds that ex-Democrats become Independents, not Republicans. The increase in southern Republications, she finds, is due to interregional migration. On the other hand, Campbell (1977) does seem to suggest a shift toward Republicanism among ex-Democrats, but he does not make it clear whether ex-Democrats have become Republicans or merely moved in that direction (i.e., gone from Democratic to Independent).

12. U.S. Department of Commerce, "Voting and Registration in the Election of 1984 (Advance Report), Population Characteristics," series P.20, no. 397.

13. Writing in the early 1970s, James Sundquist argued that racist appeals are not likely to find too much sympathy among many national Republican leaders. For one, many large contributors to the GOP and traditional Republican allies in the media would strongly resist a dramatic rightward shift. Overall, Sundquist concluded that the race issue by itself will not generate a party realignment. Whether this is true in the 1980s is open to question. James L. Sundquist, "Whither the American Party System," *Political Science Quarterly* 88 (1973):559–81.

# 4.3

# The Reagan Revolution Meets the Regulatory Labyrinth

## Jeremy Rabkin

Americans have long been haunted by two different nightmares in relation to regulatory policy. One is that a new president, despite a sweeping electoral mandate, will be unable to impose his policies on an entrenched federal bureaucracy. The other is that he will.

In its first term in office, the Reagan Administration managed to stir both fears in almost equal proportion. Liberals protested that the new administration was "gutting" or "subverting" established programs; conservatives complained that it was not sufficiently committed to systematic change. The truth is that the 1980 elections did bring about substantial changes in regulatory administration. But the early experience of the Reagan Administration also suggests the difficulty of imposing lasting change in the substance of policy at the level of mere administration. For better or worse, decisive changes in regulatory policy are hard to achieve without major political battles—and winning a presidential election gives no assurance that the new administration will even join forces in all the necessary subsequent battles.

## New Patterns in Regulatory Politics

One should hardly expect a presidential election to bring dramatic changes in regulatory policy. The American system is designed to frustrate centralized policymaking, and authority is particularly fragmented and dispersed in relation to regulatory policy. The pattern is most vividly illustrated by the so-called independent regulatory commissions. These multiheaded agencies are,

Jeremy Rabkin teaches at Cornell University.

in most cases, required by law to contain a rough balance of commissioners from the two major parties. All the commissioners are guaranteed a fixed term of service, protected by law from presidential removal. But in truth, the "independent" commissions simply present a more formalized version of a far more pervasive pattern.

The Constitution accords some decisive administrative powers to Congress. The absence of strong party discipline in Congress—itself largely a consequence of the constitutional separation of powers—means that the president cannot always deliver legislative support for "administration" policy. In contrast to parliamentary systems, the American system thus forces administrators to pay close heed to powerful or protective factions in Congress and the particular constituencies they represent. This, in turn, has engendered alternating moods of possessiveness and suspicion toward the bureaucracy in Congress and largely explains why the United States has never developed the cadre of nonpartisan, senior civil servants—or the broad trust in their expertise—that is so characteristic of the parliamentary systems in Western Europe. On the other hand, the American system has come to rely on judges to check administrative decisions, through the mechanism of ordinary litigation, to an extent that is unimaginable in Western Europe.

This fragmentation of authority has not shielded regulatory policymaking from political pressures. If anything, it has rendered regulatory activity more thoroughly politicized than in Western Europe. But it certainly has made it difficult to hold presidents accountable for the whole range of regulatory operations encompassed in "their" administrations. A succession of blue ribbon panels and administrative reformers, beginning with Franklin Roosevelt's Committee on Administrative Management, have urged that steps be taken to strengthen presidential control of administration, sometimes in the name of increased accountability, sometimes in the name of improved coordination or enhanced efficiency. One response was that, in the 1950s, presidents were given the power to name new commission chairmen at will from among the roster of incumbent commissioners. But on the whole Congress has resisted such pleas, and the Watergate scandals seemed to place the imprimatur of experience on the traditional warnings against presidential Caesarism.

Yet, paradoxically, the dramatic expansion of regulatory activity in the course of the 1970s—which was no doubt much facilitated by the continuing fragmentation of policymaking authority—served in the end to strengthen the demand for presidential control. President Reagan proved perfectly situated to capitalize on this trend, allowing him to effect rapid changes in regulatory policy to a greater degree than any president since Roosevelt. But the conditions that made this possible also suggest the sharp limitations in the emerging new pattern of presidential oversight.

Prior to the 1970s, peacetime federal regulation was largely a matter of localized economic controls. Whether the regulation was focused on a single industry (as with the Federal Communications Commission) or a particular industrial flashpoint (as with the National Labor Relations Board), regulatory activity tended to engage a limited number of interest groups and encouraged fairly consistent patterns of compromise and accommodation among them. The wave of regulatory expansion that began in the mid-60s, however, shifted the focus of federal regulation from particular commercial sectors to broad social concerns, from discrete questions of economic stabilization to encompassing isues of safety, equity, and "quality of life." New agencies like the Occupational Safety and Health Administration and the Environmental Protection Administration (neither of which was organized as an "independent" commission) were given sweeping mandates that covered the entire economy, extending even to nonprofit and municipal institutions. An array of antidiscrimination agencies were given equally sweeping mandates with equally encompassing jurisdictions.

Where the old regulatory commissions generally spoke for an abstract "public interest" on behalf of an unorganized (and largely indifferent) general public, the new agencies were egged on by an array of well-organized, publicity-conscious, and highly ideological "public interest" groups that sprang up in the late 1960s and early 1970s: civil rights groups, environmental and conservationist groups, and consumer groups were only too ready to speak for the "public" and denounce the selfish influence of "special interests." Quickly falling in step with the new political climate, the federal courts allowed such groups to litigate on behalf of the general public as well (a prerogative traditionally reserved in federal administrative law for federal agencies—which were now often as not the defendants in "public interest" suits). And if the new "public interest" groups had originally mobilized around new regulatory concerns, they were not slow in turning their attention to older regulatory agencies, whose decisions were now recognized to have significant implications for racial or sexual equality, the environment, or the "consumer" interest.

Three related consequences of the new regulatory environment proved to be of long-term political importance. First, it raised the temperature of regulatory politics, engaging broad public attention—and fierce partisan passions—to a degree unknown since the 1930s. Second, it greatly increased the direct costs of regulatory compliance—by some estimates to as much as 4 percent of GNP by 1979—and, in a period of mounting concern about inflation, propelled regulatory costs into the mainstream of macroeconomic policy debates. Third, it galvanized small businesses and the business community in general into a shared sense of alarm at regulatory excesses. Notwithstanding prevalent Marxist myths to the contrary, "business" had displayed very little political cohesion through most of the postwar era, since different firms and different industries were so differently affected by the piecemeal pattern of the economic regulation emerging from the New Deal. The increasingly vocal and unified expression of "business" concerns by the late 1970s, however, was in many ways a natural counterpart to the clamor of the "public interest movement," as previously discrete interests on both sides were mobilized into broad ideological coalitions.[1]

All of this made regulatory politics a good deal less fun for Congress. By the late 1970s, Congress was awash in proposals for "regulatory reform," most of which sought to straddle particular regulatory controversies with abstract restraining devices: varying provisions for "legislative veto" of new administrative rules, an annual "regulatory budget" to fix allowable compliance burdens, periodic "sunset" review of regulatory charters, and so on.[2] Even such abstract procedural devices aroused too many conflicting passions for Congress to agree on an acceptable set of "reform" measures, however. Movement came instead from the White House.

President Ford had issued an executive order in 1975 requiring regulatory agencies (apart from the independent commissions) to consider the "inflation impact" of new rules before their promulgation. President Carter issued an expanded order of this kind in 1978, requiring agencies to assess the relative costs and benefits of new regulatory proposals. To encourage agencies to take these requirements seriously, Carter's order also established a Regulatory Analysis Review Group, headed by representatives of all the executive departments and agencies with regulatory responsibilities but actually staffed by economists from the Council on Wage and Price Stability in the White House. President Carter also established a central "regulatory calendar," requiring agencies to announce a formal, advance agenda of major rule considerations—presumably to facilitate coordination among different agencies—and subsequently issued an executive order aimed at reducing regulatory paperwork requirements. None of these White House initiatives seemed to have a significant impact on the momentum of regulatory expansion, and none was pressed very vigorously. But they did encourage expectations of greater central control on regulatory activity.[3]

It was symptomatic of the changing political climate that President Carter took some pains to stress his administration's commitment to cutting "overregulation" and needless "red tape" during the 1980 campaign. And Senator Edward Kennedy, his challenger from the left in the Democratic primaries, was equally concerned to advertise his legislative contributions to deregulation of the airline and trucking industries. Ronald Reagan, who had railed against the stifling effects of "big government" for almost two decades, was obviously the candidate best positioned to exploit public and business concerns about regulatory excesses, however. Reagan made the most of it, and regulation thus emerged as a major campaign theme for the first time in decades.[4] Whatever the inevitable ambiguities of Carter's position, Reagan was unambiguously for less regulation. And his sweeping November victory gave him an unusual opportunity to make good on this unusually simple commitment for a new president.

## Ready Levers and Ready Changes

Whatever else it may be, all regulation is a form of law enforcement. Every regulatory agency starts with a congressional enactment (or in rare cases, an executive order from the president); most promulgate formal regulations or administrative standards to implement and clarify the law; agency staff then investigate indications of noncompliance on a case-by-case basis and apply sanctions to some portion of obdurate offenders. Roughly speaking, then, there are three routes to changing regulatory policy in any particular field: by changing the law, by changing the formal regulations, or by changing priorities and operating procedures at the level of actual enforcement. The catch for a new administration is that the quickest routes to change may be the least far-reaching and reliable— because changes that are easily accomplished may be as easily reversed.

Changing laws is a difficult and cumbersome process. As a general matter, Congress has many incentives to avoid committing itself to particular new proposals. And Congress tends to be especially averse to revising an existing law, because this requires it to renegotiate the compromises arranged—and reopen the wounds incurred—when the original law was enacted. The resulting delays give opponents of change the chance to mobilize and so reinforce the tendency to prevarication and delay. To induce legislative changes, therefore, a new administration must generally exercise a good deal of political leadership and build up broad public support for its proposals.

Changing rules and standards at the agency level is easier, but even this is not so easy. The Administrative Procedure Act requires that all new regulations first be published in the *Federal Register* as proposals and that the public be given at least thirty days to comment on the proposals before they go into effect. Beyond this, many agencies are required to hold hearings and follow elaborate procedures before adopting new rules or standards. Often in such cases, the agency's operating statute also provides for court challenges to new regulations before they have even been implemented—thus occasioning further delay and uncertainty. But even where rulemaking procedures are less cumbersome, the agency is required to publish reasons for its proposal, and the mere act of committing its policy proposals and rationales to public record provides opponents a clear target for organized protest.

Blocking new proposals before they are ever published is much easier than changing existing regulations, because it can be done with less visibility. Changes in ground-level enforcement practices are also much easier to achieve, because, again, they are less clear and visible. And by no coincidence, the Reagan Administration devoted most of its efforts to these two areas. It made no major proposals for revisions in regulatory statutes and made relatively few changes in established standards. But it moved very quickly to strengthen mechanisms for centralized oversight of new regulatory proposals. It also moved quickly to put its stamp on informal agency operations by the pattern of its appointments and budget recommendations.

The changes in orientation were soon noticeable in the pattern of new rules that did emerge in the *Federal Register*. Table 1 compares announcements of

Table 1

## Major rule notices in the Federal Register

| | | Final rules | | Proposed rules | | |
|---|---|---|---|---|---|---|
| | | New controls | Decontrols | New controls | Decontrols | Total |
| 1977 | May | 17 | 1 | 22 | 5 | 45 |
| | June | 22 | 5 | 22 | 5 | 53 |
| | July | 34 | 3 | 22 | 4 | 63 |
| | | 73 | 9 | 66 | 14 | 161 |
| 1980 | March | 12 | 3 | 17 | 2 | 34 |
| | April | 15 | 2 | 22 | 7 | 46 |
| | May | 12 | 2 | 21 | 5 | 40 |
| | | 39 | 7 | 60 | 14 | 120 |
| 1981 | May | 0 | 15 | 5 | 11 | 31 |
| | June | 4 | 18 | 3 | 13 | 38 |
| | July | 4 | 11 | 3 | 8 | 26 |
| | | 8 | 44 | 11 | 32 | 95 |
| 1984 | July | 10 | 5 | 3 | 4 | 22 |
| | August | 7 | 9 | 6 | 5 | 27 |
| | September | 4 | 9 | 4 | 4 | 21 |
| | | 21 | 23 | 13 | 13 | 70 |

nontrivial rule changes during three-month intervals at the beginning and near the end of the Carter Administration, then at the beginning and near the end of the first Reagan Administration. The notices have been divided into those imposing (or proposing) additional regulatory requirements and those primarily concerned with lifting or cutting the scope of existing controls.[5]

Though such simple aggregations obviously cannot account for the enormous variation in the scope and impact of all the particular rules involved, the three-month samples do reflect a broad cross-section of regulatory initiatives from different agencies. The dramatic increase in decontrol initiatives at the outset of the Reagan Administration—from four to five times the number in the Carter-era samples—is striking. But still more revealing is the dramatic *decrease* in proposals for new controls, even compared with the 1980 sample, reflecting an election-year period in which agencies are generally more cautious about publishing new rules and new proposals. Compared with the first year of the Carter Administration, the sample from the outset of the Reagan Administration shows only 11 percent of the volume of new (or proposed) controls and still only 20 percent of the volume of new (or proposed) controls in the 1980 sample. This pattern remained relatively consistent through the end of the first Reagan term, as well: Even in the 1984 sample, Reagan-led agencies issued only one-third as many new (or proposed) controls as in the 1980 sample and only one-fourth as many as in the 1977 sample. Combining the two samples from each administration suggests that overall the Reagan Administration may have reduced the rate at which new controls appeared to barely one-fifth of what it was in the Carter years.

By whatever measure, there is no doubt that the Reagan Administration succeeded in imposing a very sharp slowdown—screeching brakes, one might even say—in the pace of regulatory expansion. As the last line of the table suggests, however, the burst of decontrol initiatives at the outset of the new administration did not continue. Conservatives and market enthusiasts who expected a revolution in regulatory policy were certainly disappointed.[6] Liberal Democrats, on the other hand, charged that the changes at the level of official rulemaking concealed far greater and more destructive changes at the level of informal enforcement practices.

And changes in enforcement activity there certainly were. Both the Antitrust Division of the Justice Department and the Federal Trade Commission, for example, dropped or settled some long-pending cases in 1981 and showed far greater caution and selectivity in taking up new cases.[7] Businessmen reported that the Securities and Exchange Commission was also assuming a less aggressive enforcement posture than in the recent past.[8] The Occupational Safety and Health Administration announced a policy of concentrating investigations on plants with poor safety records, rather than dispersing investigations to check technical compliance at all sites.[9] The examples could readily be multiplied.

One striking indication that the relaxation of enforcement pressures was a fairly prevalent phenomenon was the response from private law firms in Washington. These firms, whose business derived heavily from clients fighting federal regulatory sanctions, expanded rapidly in size and number throughout the 1970s, through good times and bad for the nation's economy as a whole. But 1981 saw an end to the boom for Washington lawyers: Most firms cut back in hiring for the first time in years.[10]

This hardly proves that enforcement was being "gutted" or subverted throughout the government. It is always open to question whether the deterrent value of a punitive enforcement action is worth the commitment of the extensive agency resources required to see it through: More might be achieved by compromising with particular offenders in order to free up resources for other investigations or other enforcement actions. This is the rationale commonly offered by criminal prosecutors for their extensive reliance on plea bargaining. In the regulatory context, moreover, it is often argued that a less confrontational approach by the government can encourage greater cooperation from regulated interests and hence secure greater net benefits to the public.[11]

The extraordinary dispersion and inherent complexity of regulating enforcement activities makes it extremely difficult to evaluate such claims on a generalized basis, however. And even where one focuses on the performance of a single, discrete program, claims about the effectiveness or efficiency of a particular enforcement strategy often founder on underlying disagreements about the proper goals or concerns of the program. The safest generalization is simply that regulatory officials inevitably retain a large amount of discretion in setting or shifting enforcement priorities. And because the implications of these scattered, informal decisions are hard to pin down, it is hard to call them to account. But if this allows new appointees to divert agency resources to less "productive" concerns—as critics may see it—it is still hard to leave enforcement personnel and investigators standing entirely idle. Accordingly, the fastest way to cut an agency's enforcement activities is simply to cut its budget. But that is at best a crude means of redirecting long-term policy.

## The Budget Ax Is a Crude Lever

Critics of the Reagan Administration were indeed quick to fasten on its budget proposals as a sign of malevolent intentions toward regulatory enforcement. And there is no doubt that the Administration did try to use budget proposals as a quick handle on regulatory operations. Of course, the new administration was under great pressure to cut agency budgets in any case, given its commitment to curb federal spending while simultaneously pursuing a military build-up. And in overall terms the results might not have appeared that drastic. The budget for fiscal year 1982, which went into effect in October 1981, was the first to reflect the spending policies of the new administration. A survey of appropriations for fifty-seven regulatory agencies showed that the Reagan budget for FY 1982 involved an overall cut in regulatory funding of only 4 percent (adjusted for inflation), compared with actual FY 1981 expenditures and compared with the spending proposals of the Carter Administration for FY 1982. In the aggregate, the first Reagan budget simply rolled back regulatory appropriation totals (in constant dollars) to what they had been in 1979—which was still nearly three times the total for regulatory operations in 1970.[12]

Yet these aggregate figures conceal some very sharp bites from particular agencies compared with 1980 totals. The 1982 Reagan budget actually cut full-time staff positions by a massive 27 percent at the Consumer Products Safety Commission and the National Highway Traffic Safety Administration. Staff cutbacks of over 15 percent were imposed on the Occupational Safety and Health Administration, the Federal Trade Commission, and the Commodity Futures Trading Commission. The targets appear to have been strategically chosen: Every one of these agencies had encountered heavy criticism in Congress long before the 1980 election (CPSC and CFTC for confusion and ineffectualness more than heavy-handedness). Amidst its larger victories in early budget battles, then, the new administration had little trouble getting Congress to accept these cuts.

By the end of its first year, however, the Reagan Administration had begun to encounter strong resistance to proposals for still further cuts in regulatory budgets. In particular, there were loud, bipartisan protests in Congress against plans for reducing manpower and operating budgets at the Environmental Protection Agency by as much as one-third below 1980 levels.[13] The Administration was forced to content itself with more modest cutbacks at EPA in its first two years—representing about 15 percent in overall staffing levels—and thereafter felt compelled to seek annual funding and staffing increases. By the spring of 1984, the Reagan Administration itself was urging Congress to restore EPA staffing to 1980 levels.

Most regulatory agencies did not, in fact, make up initial budget cuts during the Reagan first term. Some continued to be trimmed back a little more each year.[14] Agencies that relied on ambitious, individual prosecutions, like the Federal Trade Commission, were thus obliged to curtail their initiatives. But the effect of these staff reductions did not always mean less pressure on business. Many regulatory operations maintain their controls through license or permit requirements, and understaffing in such programs may simply have exacerbated delays in approval of new permits. On the other hand, many agencies, like OSHA and EPA, promulgate elaborate engineering standards, and given the momentum of sunk investments, businesses could not often regard a cutback in enforcement activity as significant relief from compliance obligations.[15] Sharp personnel reductions may also have made some regulatory officials reluctant to experiment with alternatives to existing mechanical requirments, since more flexible standards often require more effort to devise and more investigators to check compliance. In the extreme case, the Consumer Products Safety Commission abandoned a proposal to lift certain safety standards in 1981 on the grounds that the necessary formal hearings (and subsequent legal battles in the event of a court challenge to its decision) would cost more than it could afford with its reduced budget.[16]

Cutting budgets, then, is at best a crude and short-term means of inducing change in regulatory patterns. The problem for a new administration is that the more appropriate means are hard to direct from the center.

## Personnel and Procedure

Apart from budget reductions, the Reagan Administration relied on two other means to control regulatory expansion: a rather single-minded pattern of appointments and a new system for prescreening agency rules at the Office of Management and Budget. Neither required as much cooperation from Congress and in this sense facilitated more central control. But both of these approaches present problems of their own for any long-term reorientation of regulatory policy.

Staffing a new administration is always a challenge. In a few fevered months after the election, before the new administration has really gotten its bearings, it must fill some 2,600 scattered posts, about 500 of which require direct presidential appointment.[17] Selection decisions cannot turn entirely on personal competence and loyalty to the president's concerns, moreover, because appointments must also accommodate congressional and party patronage demands, reassure important constituencies, and see to the administration's overall public image.

The Reagan Administration nonetheless seemed unusually alert to the policy implications of its appointments, at least in top regulatory posts. Or perhaps it simply had an unusually clear sense of what it wanted from regulatory appointees: responsiveness to business concerns and a dedication to lessening regulatory burdens on the economy. In contrast to the relatively lax approach of the early Carter Administration, the Reagan White House developed a very active personnel office, which sought to keep a close watch on the ideological tone of appointments, even second-level appointments by the new department secretaries and agency heads. Where Carter's regulatory appointments drew heavily from established issue networks in Washington, moreover, the Reagan Administration brought in a large number of outsiders. The Reagan White House seems to have calculated that lack of experience in government service or in relevant policy fields would render new appointees more receptive to White House concerns—or at least more resistant to "capture" by permanent agency staffs.

The overall staffing pattern certainly offered a remarkable contrast with the Carter Administration. *The National Journal* described the Reagan regulatory appointees as "a reverse image of their predecessors."[18] The top post at the National Highway Traffic Safety Administration, for example, passed from Joan Claybrook, a close associate of Ralph Nader, to Raymond Peck, a regulatory spokesman for the National Coal Association. At the Occupational Safety and Health Administration, the reins were transferred from Eula Bingham, a medical toxicologist, to Thorne Auchter, a Florida building contractor who was quoted as saying that OSHA "symbolizes government overregulation." At the Environmental Protection Agency, Douglas Costle, a former environmental research director for the Congressional Budget Office, was replaced by Anne Gorsuch (later Burford), a Colorado state legislator who had frequently expressed opposition to environmental "extremism." And where Costle had recruited many of his chief assistants from leading environmentalist groups, Burford replaced them with corporate lawyers and business lobbyists.

That the new appointees all shared President Reagan's concern to reduce regulatory burdens was quite plain. That they had the capacity to reorient policy within their own agencies in effective ways was much less clear in many cases, however. Blocking new regulations and accommodating sizable budget cuts require no great skill. But appointees with no prior experience in their agency's policy field may fail to recognize the most promising—and politically viable—opportunities for reforming existing rules and procedures. Appointees with a hostile or suspicious attitude toward their own agency's programs may fail to develop the trust and cooperation of their civil service staffs, thus forfeiting the expertise and experience they might offer to reform initiatives. And appointees who seem too sensitive to immediate industry pressures may fail to build public trust and confidence, thus strengthing the hand of their critics in Congress.

The unhappy experience of Anne Gorsuch Burford at EPA vividly illustrates the dangers in placing an inexperienced regulatory critic in a top regulatory post. She was finally forced to resign at the beginning of 1983, amidst a tangle of charges concerning improper dealings with and irregular concessions to particular business firms. Twenty top officials of the agency resigned—or were fired—along with Burford, and one was subsequently convicted of perjury for concealing evidence from a congressional investigation of malfeasance at EPA. The extent of actual wrongdoing by Burford herself remains a matter of dispute. But it is quite clear that her overall conduct of EPA alarmed and antagonized even many Republicans in Congress who were in general sympathy with the Administration's outlook.

From the outset Burford showed herself unusually receptive to pleas from business executives while remaining aloof and suspicious toward EPA staff and openly contemptuous of environmental groups. This led to strings of much-publicized resignations by senior civil servants at EPA—and leaks to the press from frustrated bureaucrats remaining behind—which greatly undermined Burford's credibility in Congress. Without a firm base of support in Congress, the prospect of major reform initiatives within the agency was greatly diminished. In fact, though, Burford's extreme distrust of EPA staff made her quite reluctant even to explore such possibilities. In 1982, for example, the director of EPA's planning and policy staff, one of Burford's own political appointees, abruptly resigned: He was reportedly disgusted with Burford's dismissal of economic incentives for pollution reduction, a very promising cost-cutting approach whose main taint for Burford seemed to be its backing from career analysts in the agency. By the time Burford herself was forced to resign, the EPA had a large backlog of standard-setting obligations and very few changes in substantive policy or long-term orientation.[19]

Whatever its value in other respects, the system for preclearing new rules with OMB—in a sense the Reagan Administration's backstop for its regulatory appointees—can hardly cope with problems of this kind. OMB's reviewing authority derives from an executive order issued by President Reagan in his first month in office. Like Carter's order, it does not apply to "independent" commissions. But it goes considerably beyond Carter's executive order in several respects. Where the Carter order merely directed agencies to consider the relative costs and benefits of "major" new regulations, the Reagan order explicitly forbids agencies to adopt *any* new rule whose benefits do not outweigh its costs (except where required by express statutory directive). The Reagan order directs agencies to set regulatory priorities in such a way as to maximize *net* benefits to society—taking into account such offsetting factors as the condition of the national economy, the condition of the immediately affected industries, and the impact on those industries of projected new requirements by other agencies. Regulations that might push too many firms into contraction and layoffs are plainly to be given a hard look.

In themselves, these standards may not be as constraining as they seem. Estimates of social benefits and projections of regulatory "costs" (even direct cost of compliance to industry, let alone the social costs and incidental economic effects) are notoriously uncertain and manipulable; widely differing approaches might all be justified under the same "cost-benefit" standards. The real teeth in the Reagan order derive from its provision for OMB enforcement of the new standards. Where Carter's order simply authorized White House economists to comment on agency proposals after their publication in the *Federal Register*, the Reagan scheme requires OMB to approve any proposal before it can even be published. Where the Carter system left the final decision to each agency itself, the new system allows OMB to hold up promulgation of final rules until its cost-benefit objections have been satisfied—or OMB is overruled by the President himself.

Public interest groups were quick to denounce the new system as a conduit for "special interest" pressures:[20] unlike the Carter system, where the advice and comments of White House economists remained part of the public record, the new system allows OMB to hold up a regulatory proposal without any public disclosure of its particular objections or its motives. But a more fundamental problem with the new system may be that OMB is simply not equipped to undertake searching cost-benefit reviews.[21] The Office of Information and Regulatory Affairs, the unit in OMB charged with enforcing the Reagan executive order, has other responsibilities as well, and only about seventy-five staffers to get through all this work. By the end of 1981 this relatively small staff had reviewed over 27,000 new rules and quickly approved about 90 percent of them—in most cases after little more than a brief telephone check with the agencies involved and a once-over glance at their cost-benefit documentation.[22]

OMB officials have insisted that they do not really aspire to undertake extensive analysis or investigation of regulatory proposals, but simply to prod the responsible agencies to greater self-scrutiny. And perhaps the chief effect of OMB's role will be to discourage impulsive or ill-digested regulatory proposals. Veterans of the Carter Administration's Regulatory Analysis Review Group have expressed concern, however, that such a highly centralized, closed-door review system may actually be less effective than the Carter system in ventilating fresh thought and disseminating new analytical techniques throughout the bureaucracy. One critic also warned against OMB's announced policy of waiving through ostensibly cost-cutting initiatives while giving the "full treatment" to cost-inducing proposals: "It undermines agency incentives to do serious analysis" and "returns regulatory analysis to the primitive stage of justifying predetermined outcomes."[23]

It is plain, at all events, that OMB review is best suited to blocking or delaying new regulations, not to guiding or inspiring overall new approaches. In particular, though President Reagan's executive order authorizes OMB to designate existing rules for reconsideration by the responsible agencies, OMB plainly lacks the resources and the detailed expertise to comb through the *Code of Federal Regulations* on its own, to locate the most needlessly burdensome requirements and develop priorities for reform. OMB did very little of this, in fact, during Reagan's first term.

Some efforts to prod reconsideration of existing rules were indeed made by a much touted Presidential Task Force on Regulatory Relief, a high-level committee of cabinet secretaries and top presidential advisers, chaired by Vice President Bush. Assembled in the first days of the new administration, the group was given no formal powers, but its visibility and prestige allowed it to focus attention on regulatory requirements that business leaders condemned as unusually burdensome. In all, the task force took aim at over ninety regulations in 1981—many of them affecting the auto industry, which was singled out for special solicitude in view of Detroit's continuing economic troubles. The task force boasted that it had jawboned federal agencies into revising or eliminating thirty-seven of these rules by the end of 1981 (almost a third of them at the National Highway Traffic Safety Administration).[24]

The task force may have helped to publicize the Reagan Administration's overall concern about regulatory burdens. Such an ad hoc group could not, however, cut deeply into the substance of policy at particular agencies. And certainly no group of this kind can ensure that new appointees will exercise imagination and sound judgment in directing their agencies. Nor that they will retain enough public confidence to make lasting changes.

In the long run, decisive changes usually require changes in regulatory stautes by Congress. And neither the Presidential Task Force nor the new system of OMB oversight—nor even the pattern of regulatory appointees—contributed much at all to this.

## The Missing Pieces: Legislative Challenges, Political Opportunities

There are three reasons why serious and lasting regulatory reform requires statutory revision. First, many laws, particularly those dealing with environmental and safety regulation, leave little or no scope for administrative discretion on important policy questions: Given certain factual findings by the administering agency, particular prohibitions or requirements are supposed to be automatically triggered by such statutory provisions.

To be sure, agencies somtimes find ways of evading or delaying these mandated responses. But in this era of continuing judicial activism, too great a disregard of statutory requirements is likely to provoke legal challenges by "public interest" groups—and constraining interventions from the courts. Thus, for example, the first year of the Reagan Administration witnessed a dramatic upsurge in environmental suits against EPA.[25] More generally, an apparent disregard of statutory mandates adds to the political strength of opponents, since it is often much easier to rally opposition in the name of "legality" than in the name of particular discarded policies. Thus the Labor Department was denounced by labor organizations for allowing exceptions to minimum wage laws for piece-rate home workers—though the merits of the old approach were certainly debatable.[26]

A second factor underscoring the importance of statutory revisions is the danger that mere administrative changes will be reversed by a new administration. The awareness of this possibility may encourage administrators to focus on changes with immediate payoffs to particular constituencies, rather than working toward fundamental, long-term reforms that may take years to implement and years to prove their full value. This is precisely what many critics warned the Reagan Administration was doing, for example, in its eagerness to make piecemeal changes in regulatory burdens on the auto industry. Statutory changes encourage more systematic thinking and more long-term approaches.

Third, and perhaps most important, legislative changes can alter the political climate or the framework of expectations in which ongoing policy is conducted. Nothing in a democracy is quite so decisive or confers so much legitimacy on the winning side as a legislative head-count. It is for just this reason that Congress is usually quite reluctant to commit itself to a clear legislative verdict in a controversial policy dispute. But when it does so, the losing side is morally or politically disarmed to a degree that rarely obtains in administrative or judicial battles—where policy initiatives can be challenged and rechallenged through a wearing and distracting series of separable decisions. Legislative pronouncements can also be whittled down in this way in the course of implementation, but for an administration that knows what it wants they can provide an indispensable degree of political momentum and legal protection. Thus the Reagan Administration's most dramatic deregulation inititative in its first year—an accelerated lifting of price controls on domestic oil—was achieved with remarkably little controversy: the northeastern liberals who fought for permanent price controls through most of the 1970s had already been decisively defeated in the legislative battles over energy policy during the Carter years.

To be sure, few regulatory fields will admit of such clear-cut decisions, for or against the principle of continuing controls. No one seriously expects an end to pollution controls, safety standards, or nondiscrimination requirements. But there is much dispute about approaches and priorities. In particular, many regulatory statutes contain unduly rigid or hyperbolic standards which—as President

Reagan's executive order acknowledges—seem to preclude any cost-benefit analysis or administrative balancing of competing considerations.[27] For example, the 1970 Clean Air Act Amendments (extended in 1977) prohibit *any* deterioration of air quality standards in large sections of the country—regardless of how imperceptible to human senses, how insignificant for human health, and how obstructive to local economic development. The Occupational Safety and Health Act (1970), to cite a still more revealing example, directs OSHA to set standards to reduce workplace hazards to "the maximum extent feasible"—a legislative "standard" which is essentially meaningless, but a no less powerful invitation to regulatory extremism. It is absurd for regulatory enthusiasts to claim that concern for human life and safety must transcend all consideration of costs—no one, in fact, would tolerate devoting half of our GNP to safety measures—but such emotional rhetoric is much harder to face down without the moral ballast of a realistic legislative standard.

Yet in its first term in office the Reagan Administration actually gave remarkably little attention to bolstering its regulatory reform efforts with an appropriate legislative agenda. No major statutory revisions were proposed by the Administration, and none was enacted. Partly this may be explained by the Administration's reluctance to take on an ambitious legislative agenda while embroiled in massive congressional battles on taxes and budgets. Yet the Administration's congressional leverage was probably at its height when its sweeping election victory was still fresh in mind and the momentum for regulatory reform was sharpened by the nation's continuing economic difficulties.

The extent of the Administration's legislative abdication is well illustrated by the fate of the procedural reform bills that had been percolating in Congress since the late 1970s. The Administration's reform effort tried to force the regulatory agencies themselves to weigh cost-benefit considerations through a system of centralized controls within the executive branch. But the bill enacted by the Republican-controlled Senate in the spring of 1982 actually threatened administrative autonomy with its provisions for expanded judicial review of regulatory activity and legislative veto of new agency rules. The Administration was left, incongruously, to give (silent) thanks for the bill's demise in the Democratic-controlled House of Representatives.[28]

Still more revealing—and more consequential—was the Administration's failure to exert strong leadership in the struggle to revise the Clean Air Act. It is the most far-reaching and the costliest regulatory measure ever enacted by the federal government: The Business Roundtable estimated that by 1987 accumulated compliance costs from its enactment in 1970 could exceed $400 billion (in 1980 dollars). Enacted in hasty response to the sudden public clamor against air pollution, the original measure was filled with unrealistic standards and deadlines, rigid, even draconian requirements, and perverse incentives for new construction.[29] Though most observers acknowledge numerous defects in the resulting program, environmentalist groups have bitterly opposed significant changes in the law, for fear this would open the way to an overall weakening of the federal commitment to clean air.

The Clean Air Act was due to expire in 1981. But when the EPA circulated draft proposals for revising the law in the summer of 1981, it provoked indignant denunciations from House Democrats. Instead of rising to the challenge, the Administration backed off. Congress itself put off consideration of the Clean Air Act's extension, and the Reagan Administration seemed disposed to let congressional factions wrangle over the appropriate revisions on their own.[30] The Administration seemed unwilling to fight for its own version of regulatory reform in a head-to-head battle with militant environmentalists. Perhaps its leadership capacity was already too weakened in this field by its efforts to slash EPA's budget and by the initial performance of its EPA appointees. But by failing to stake out a strong, public position in the legislative battles, the Administration effectively conceded moral ground to its environmentalist critics, suggesting that it lacked full confidence in its own regulatory philosophy of cost-benefit balancing.

A curiously simliar pattern emerged in the Administration's approach to nondiscrimination requirements. The 1980 Republican platform expressed strong opposition to the twisting of civil rights measures into racial quota schemes. President Reagan's attorney general, William French Smith, echoed this theme in several publicized speeches in 1981, and his assistant attorney general for civil rights announced that the Justice Department would no longer seek racial hiring quotas in settling employment discrimination cases. Yet the Administration took no initiative to promote statutory restrictions on quotas or other race-conscious remedies, despite some indications of congressional receptiveness (a bill to this effect actually passed the House in 1980).

The Administration did not even attempt to make substantial changes in this direction in an entirely executive-based program—the system of racial hiring "goals" imposed on all government contractors under an executive order dating back to President Johnson. The Reagan Labor Department did propose to modify the implementing regulations for this program at the beginning of 1981. The revisions focused on reducing paperwork and compliance costs for business, however, rather than limiting the program's disturbingly broad reliance on racial and ethnic classifications. What could have been a powerful inspiration to broader congressional action seemed instead a tacit endorsement of congressional passivity.[31]

Here too the Reagan Administration evidently feared to enter a highly charged confrontation, in this case with civil rights groups and their congressional champions. Perhaps it calculated that its credibility with minorities had already been too strained by its proposed cuts in social spending, or by the altered enforcement posture of the Justice Department. But as in the struggle with enviromentalists, the Administration's lack of legislative leadership in this area seemed to cede the moral high ground to its opponents—suggesting that it was eager to please business, but reluctant to submit its avowed principles to the test of congressional debate.

In one regulatory field after another, a similar pattern might be observed. The Reagan Administration seemed to regard legislative initiatives as an awkard, perhaps even a dangerous distraction from its efforts to redirect policy by administrative means. And in some ways, it may have been justified in this view. Legislative debate focuses public attention and can provide critics of administrative performance with a very prominent platform for their attacks. At the same time, legislative coalition-building requires a calculated strategy of stroking and fence-mending with key congressional factions. That may be particularly difficult for inexperienced ragulators, kept on a short leash by OMB.

Still, the Reagan Administration's failure to advance a serious legislative agenda left many questions about its capacity—or even its determination—to put its own lasting stamp on major regulatory programs. The momentum of its smashing election victory, culminating an apparent shift in public attitudes toward regulation, allowed the new administration to apply sharp brakes to the regulatory patterns of the 1970s. But in the process, the Reagan Administration also seemed to revitalize the "public interest" constituencies that had so much to do with the previous regulatory expansion. The Administration's reluctance either to consider these critics in its initial regulatory decisions or to face them down in debate over precise legislative proposals may have undermined support for its regulatory orientation in Congress. And its initial eagerness to accommodate business concerns may actually have dissipated the momentum for more systematic regulatory reform. If so, the short-term impact of budget cuts, partisan appointments, and OMB oversight may have jeopardized the Administration's potential for long-term influence on the substance of regulatory policy. In the long run, the President's greatest leverage on regulatory policy must derive from his role as legislative and political leader, not as chief administrator. All the changes wrought by the 1980 elections could not change the American system in that respect.

## Notes

1. Revealing of this trend was the emergence of the Business Roundtable and the U.S. Chamber of Commerce as significant actors in Washington regulatory disputes by the mid-70s. Both had previously taken a back seat to particular trade asociations. Also revealing was the emergence of such market-oriented research institutes as the Center for the Study of American Business at Washington University, St. Louis (whose director, Murray Weidenbaum, was appointed chairman of the Council of Economic Advisers at the outset of the Reagan Administration) and the Center for the Study of Government Regulation at the American Enterprise Institute (whose director, James C. Miller, was appointed by President Reagan to organize the new system of OMB oversight and subsequently appointed chairman of the Federal Trade Commission).

2. For discussion of these proposals see the series of articles by Senator Abraham

Ribicoff, Representative Clarence Brown, and Professor Ernest Gellhorn in *Regulation* (May/June 1979):17–26.

3. An extended description of President Carter's regulatory control arrangements is provided by Susan Tolchin, "Presidential Power and RARG," *Regulation* (July/August 1979):44–49; and Christopher DeMuth, "Constraining Regulatory Costs—The White House Programs," *Regulation* (January/February 1980):13–26.

4. This assessment is placed in broader context in Alan Stone, *Regulation and Its Alternatives* (Washington: Congressional Quarterly Press, 1982) pp. 237–242.

5. The classification of "rules" as "nontrivial" necessarily involves some subjective judgments. In general, published notices involving individual firms, individual substances, or individual sites or land tracts have been omitted from this compilation, along with notices clarifying the language of existing regulations or simplifying existing forms. In fact, by these standards the vast majority of new "rules" were judged too "trivial" to be counted. Thus the Reagan Administration greatly understated the extent of the change when it announced that the total number of proposed and final regulations declined from 12,171 in 1980 to 8,965 in 1981. (*New York Times*, April 25, 1982, p. 27.) A much more revealing indication was the 50 percent decline in the number of court challenges to regulatory changes in 1981, compared with 1980 (ibid.), but even this figure doubtless understates the full scale of the change. I would like to thank Stephen Wirls and Michael S. Greve, graduate students in the department of government at Cornell, for assistance in preparing Table 1.

6. "Reagan Administration Rates Itself High on Cutting Regulations; Analysts Differ," *Wall Street Journal*, December 31, 1981, p. 4. Also, "Reagan's Reforms Are Full of Sound and Fury, but What Do They Signify?" *National Journal*, January 16, 1982, pp. 92–98.

7. "FTC, with a Finger to the Wind, Shortens Its Regulatory Reach," *National Journal*, July 4, 1981, pp. 1206–10.

8. "Flabbier Cop? SEC May Be Losing Its Former Toughness, Some Observers Think," *Wall Street Journal*, March 22, 1982, p. 1.

9. "They're Still Telling OSHA Horror Stories, but the 'Victims' Are New," *National Journal*, November 7, 1981, pp. 1985–89. And "Auchter's Record at OSHA Leaves Labor Outraged, Business Satisfied," *National Journal*, October 1, 1983, pp. 2008–13.

10. "Washington Lawyers Seeing Signs that the Boom Times Have Passed," *Wall Street Journal*, March 18, 1982, p. 29.

11. For example, Michael Levin, "Politics and Polarity, The Limits of OSHA Reform," *Regulation* (November/December 1979):33–39.

12. "Regulation and the 1982 Budget," *Regulation* (July/August 1981):9–11.

13. "EPA Budget, Staff Cut Plans Stir Concern on Capitol Hill," *Congressional Quarterly*, October 10, 1981, pp. 1957–58.

14. "Regulation and the 1985 Budget," *Regulation* (March/April 1984):9–11.

15. The Reagan Administration explicitly acknowledged the "cost" of exacerbating delays with staff cuts when it proposed staff and budget increases for the Nuclear Regulatory Commission in order to speed up license approvals. But the effects of budget cuts on other permit programs have not been closely studied. Surveys by the Urban Institute found that investment in pollution abatement equipment by major industries did not notably decline during the early 1980s and in some cases actually increased—supporting the notion

that sunk investments were continued in spite of the apparent relaxation of EPA enforcement efforts. See Perry D. Quick, "Reagan's Industrial Policy," in *The Reagan Record*, ed John L. Palmer and Isabel V. Sawhill (Cambridge: Ballinger, 1984), pp. 308–10.

16. "Taking a Dive at the CPSC," *Regulation* (July/August 1981):7.

17. A useful review of changing personnel policies is provided in John W. Macy, Bruce Adams, and J. Jackson Walter, eds., *America's Unelected Government, Appointing the President's Team* (Cambridge: Ballinger, 1983).

18. "OMB to Keep Its Regulatory Powers in Reserve In Case Agencies Lag," *National Journal*, March 14, 1981, p. 424.

19. A useful review of the early signs of trouble (before a 1982 marriage gave Anne Gorsuch a new last name) is "Move Over Jim Watt, Anne Gorsuch is the Latest Target of Environmentalists," *National Journal*, October 24, 1981, pp. 1899–1902. A more thoughtful retrospective assessment is offered by Paul R. Portney, "Natural Resources and the Environment: More Controversy than Change," in *The Reagan Record*, ed. Palmer and Sawhill, pp. 142–51.

20. A very thoughtful account of the new system is offered by George Eads, "Harnessing Regulation: The Evolving Role of White House Oversight," *Regulation* (May/June 1981):19–26.

21. "More Power, Yet More Criticism for OMB," *National Journal*, January 16, 1982, p. 93.

22. "The Reagan Regulatory Ax," *National Journal*, January 16, 1982, p. 96.

23. Eads, "Harnessing Regulation," p. 25.

24. "The Reagan Regulatory Ax," p. 96.

25. "Environmentalists Sue to Put an End to 'Regulatory Massive Resistance,'" *National Journal*, December 19, 1981, pp. 2233–34.

26. "Anatomy of a Regulatory Proposal—The Battle over Industrial Homework," *National Journal*, June 6, 1981, pp. 1013–16.

27. Further examples are provided in Murray L. Weidenbaum, "Reforming Government Regulation," *Regulation* (November/December 1980):15–18.

28. The progress of the legislation can be followed in successive reports in *Congressional Quarterly*, especially "Administration Backs Regulatory Reform Bill," April 11, 1981, pp. 627–29; "Senate Panel Approves Reform Bill With Review Compromise," July 18, 1981, pp. 1291–92; "Senate Unanimously Passes Broad Regulatory Reform," March 27, 1982, pp. 701–702.

29. A review of such provisions with sensible proposals for statutory reform is David Harrison, Jr. and Paul R. Portney, "Making Ready for the Clean Air Act," *Regulation* (March/April 1981):24–31. Other critiques are reviewed in "The Clean Air that You're Breathing May Cost Hundreds of Billions of Dollars," *National Journal*, October 10, 1981, pp. 1811–20.

30. Cf. "Senate Committee Begins Clean Air Revision," *Congressional Quarterly*, November 7, 1981, pp. 2191–92, and "Environmentalists Hold Edge as Laws Come Up for Renewal," *Congressional Quarterly*, January 12, 1985, pp. 81–83.

31. Cf. "Affirmative Action May Fall Victim to Reagan's Regulatory Reform Drive," *National Journal*, July 11, 1981, pp. 1248–52, and "Affirmative Action Is Here to Stay," *Fortune*, April 19, 1982, pp. 143–62.

# ABOUT THE
# EDITORS

BENJAMIN GINSBERG is Professor of Government at Cornell University. He is the author of *The Consequences of Consent: Elections, Citizen Control, and Popular Acquiescence*; *The Captive Public: How Mass Opinion Promotes State Power* (forthcoming); and (with Theodore J. Lowi) *Poliscide*.

ALAN STONE is Professor of Political Science at the University of Houston. His previous books include *Economic Regulation and the Public Interest*; *Regulation and its Alternatives*; (with Richard P. Barke) *Governing the American Republic*; and (with Kenneth Prewitt) *The Ruling Elites: Elite Theory, Power, and American Democracy*.